Books by Henry F. Howe

Massachusetts: *There She Is—Behold Her*
Salt Rivers of the Massachusetts Shore
Prologue to New England

REGIONS OF AMERICA

*A series of books that depict our natural regions,
their history, development and character.*

Edited by Carl Carmer

Massachusetts: *There She Is—Behold Her* by Henry F. Howe
Already published

South Carolina: *Annals of Pride and Protest* by William Francis Guess
Yankee Kingdom: *Vermont and New Hampshire* by Ralph Nading Hill
Virginia: *A New Look at the Old Dominion* by Marshall W. Fishwick

MASSACHUSETTS

There She Is—Behold Her

by Henry F. Howe

A Regions of America Book

Illustrations and Maps by John O'Hara Cosgrave II

Harper & Brothers, New York

MASSACHUSETTS: *There She Is—Behold Her*

Copyright © 1960 by Henry F. Howe

Printed in the United States of America

FIRST EDITION

I-K

Library of Congress catalog card number: 60-13447

To My Sons,
Walter B. Howe
and
Oliver Hunt Howe

CONTENTS

CONTENTS

ACKNOWLEDGMENTS

I wish to express my appreciation to Carl Carmer for his patient encouragement and wise editorial support. I am particularly indebted also to Stephen A. Riley, Director of the Massachusetts Historical Society, who found time in his busy schedule to read and criticize almost the entire manuscript. Correction of some historical misrepresentations has been made possible by his friendly help. For permission to quote from their works I wish to thank Claude M. Fuess, Oscar Handlin, Samuel Eliot Morison, Cleveland Amory, and the heirs of James Truslow Adams. To Rinehart & Co. I am grateful for their willingness that I use some material adapted from my previous book, *Salt Rivers of the Massachusetts Shore*, which they published. For assistance in locating information that was at times difficult to find, I am indebted to Edward Pierce Hamilton, Clifford K. Shipton, G. Prescott Low, Walter Muir Whitehill, Dr. William A. R. Chapin, and Dr. Lawrence R. Dame.

To Miss Ethel M. Hodgdon and to Mrs. George A. Kelley I am especially grateful for patient efforts in transcribing my penciled first drafts into excellent typescript.

The staffs of the Boston Public Library and its Kirstein Business Library Branch, of the Massachusetts Historical Society, of the Boston Athenaeum, of Sturbridge Village and Plimoth Plantation, and numerous other libraries and historical societies have been always co-operative and helpful in hunting down otherwise inaccessible material that appears in these pages. Many other indebtednesses are expressed all too impersonally in the Bibliography.

To all the above-mentioned workers in the vineyard, as well as to many others for which there is not space here to mention, I offer grateful thanks.

HENRY F. HOWE

PREFACE

A one-volume history of a state like Massachusetts may turn out to be just a mirror to the author's prejudices. So awesome are the choices as to what is significant among the hero-studded procession that marches out of the Bay State's past that one ends such a manuscript humbled by a sensation of one's treason of omission. A whole army of heroes completely ignored in this book cry out for recognition, and no one knows better than this author that they have been badly treated.

As a physician, my prejudices lean obviously to the social and economic aspects of history. Any lawyer among my readers will recognize that many political matters have been neglected. My chief hope is that I may arouse in some readers an understanding of what it felt like to participate in a few of the episodes that built Massachusetts. I know that my pride in my native soil shines through this book—if this seems too aggressive, please indulge this patriot's enthusiasm by taking it with a grin. In this world of nuclear physics my prejudice is to err on the sentimental side. I prefer keeping some idols unsmashed. Yet I have tried not to ignore the more obvious failings in Yankee character.

I have been concerned to allot the available space in so brief a book in reasonable proportion to the three and a half centuries of history described. In so doing, a progressive biographical injustice is done, since one proceeds from no population at all to one of five million. Inevitably, this process also slights certain geographical areas, particularly those whose population is relatively thin and whose history is short in comparison with that of older communities. The limitations of space cruelly restrict discussion of specific towns in peripheral and rural areas since 1800. I have tried to compensate for this by resorting to typical instances and general discussion of characteristic problems in each period, in the hope that each regional reader will apply such material to the particular area in which he is especially interested. I have deliberately emphasized life in the towns rather than in Boston, since I believe the inherent strength of Massachusetts has always been in its towns, and the Boston story has forever been told. If the reader will overlook my omission of his particular village, or his own justly famous ancestor, and attempt with me to understand the issues that bothered Massachusetts as a whole, I hope he will feel rewarded. The only conceivable value of capsule history is the over-all look. This is the way Massachusetts history looks to this country doctor.

Cohasset, Mass.
February, 1960

                                    HENRY F. HOWE

I shall enter on no encomium upon Massachusetts; she needs none. There she is. Behold her, and judge for yourselves. There is her history; the world knows it by heart. The past, at least, is secure. There is Boston, and Concord, and Lexington, and Bunker Hill; and there they will remain forever. The bones of her sons, falling in the great struggle for Independence, now lie mingled with the soil of every State from New England to Georgia; and there they will lie for ever. And Sir, where American Liberty raised its first voice, and where its youth was nurtured and sustained, there it still lives, in the strength of its manhood and full of its original spirit.

DANIEL WEBSTER, *January 26, 1830, from his Second Speech on Foot's Resolution, usually known as his "Reply to Hayne"*

CHAPTER ONE

Medieval Massachusetts

First came the Norsemen. The year was A.D. 1003. From
Greenland Leif Eriksson and a crew of thirty-five men
brought their high-prowed Viking ship to three successive
landfalls, usually identified as Labrador or Newfoundland,
then Nova Scotia, and finally an island called Vinland, somewhere in the Cape Cod area of Massachusetts. They built a
house at Vinland, and spent the winter, before sailing back
to Greenland with a cargo of dried grapes and ship timber.
In 1005 Leif's brother Thorvald Eriksson came again to Vinland. Although Thorvald was killed in an encounter with the
native "skraellings," perhaps on Cape Cod, his party stayed
three years in the island settlement, pasturing cows on the
islands and trading with the natives. And again in the years
1010-1013 the wealthy Icelandic merchant Thorfinn Karl-
sefne, a friend of Leif's, lived three years in Vinland with an
expedition of eighty people, building additional houses in the
colony and exploring the mainland to the southwest. He
encountered increasing resistance by skraellings in large flotil-
las of canoes, and while he returned to Greenland and eventually to Norway with profitable cargoes of furs, he believed
that further settlement in Vinland was impracticable. In 1013
and 1014 Leif Eriksson's half sister Freydis organized a fourth
brief voyage to Vinland. After a winter of bickering, during

1

which Freydis is believed to have murdered two of her associates in Vinland, she returned to Greenland with a load of timber. This was the end of the Vinland enterprise.

This, in brief summary, is what we know of the twelve-year occupation of Massachusetts by the Norsemen. The story was handed down through generations of professional Viking storytellers, and only reduced to writing by Icelandic monks more than three centuries after the events it describes. There are numerous fragmentary references to the same events, however, written within a century of the Vinland voyages, and these lead us to believe that the main outline of the story in the written sagas rings true. Furthermore, the coincidences of undisputed detail in the Greenland and Icelandic versions of the sagas so generally fulfill the requirements of a Massachusetts background for Vinland that most authorities have come to regard the Cape Cod-Martha's Vineyard region as the site of the settlement. If so, then Massachusetts enjoys the distinction of participating not only in the first discovery of America but also in its first attempted European colony.

Recent zealous efforts to pin down a precise site for the Vinland settlement have thus far proved fruitless. So alluring are the puzzles involved in the entire Viking episode that men spend whole lifetimes following thin clues that might seem to link the legendary lore of the sagas with some archaeological proof as yet undemonstrated. Their failure is partly due to our ignorance of the fate of the Greenland colony from which the Vinland voyages sailed. There are no sure records of the western settlements of Erik the Red and his associates in Greenland after the twelfth century. Minnesotans who claim the migration of the Norsemen into the heart of the continent as yet can offer no very good proof. Perhaps better archaeological investigation in Greenland itself will eventually turn up clues. Perhaps in Massachusetts the earth will yet unfold more evidence. Until then we must be content to speculate about the fate of our first Norse families.

No amount of speculation, however, can connect the Vinland events with the chain of rediscovery that was necessary to the final permanent colonization of Massachusetts and North America. Those were the work of other nations than the Norse. No one can find even a shred of evidence that sixteenth-century Massachusetts Indians remembered Vinland or were in any way influenced in their attitudes toward Europeans by the brief sojourn of the Vikings in Massachusetts. The unique Norse discovery remains only a bright isolated incident in the exploration of Massachusetts, and no more.

Yet archaeologists are increasingly successful in assembling patterns of the Indian cultures in Massachusetts. The ground has yielded up testimony of at least three successive occupations of the state by aborigines over a period of four thousand years. The earliest datable evidence is associated with an ancient fishweir in the Back Bay of Boston constructed more than thirty-five hundred years ago in estuaries of the Charles River then existing sixteen feet below the present low-tide mark. Near Ipswich there have been found stone projectile points of a type associated elsewhere in the United States with preglacial man. Unfortunately no dating of these fragmentary discoveries is possible. But in Andover, at Titicut in West Bridgewater, and along the shores of Assowampset Pond in Lakeville, extensive excavations of stratified levels in Indian village sites have turned up abundant proof of repeated occupations by Indian cultures so distinctively different in pottery and stone implement characteristics as to leave no doubt of successive waves of migration of aboriginal peoples over the woodlands of the state. Carbon-14 datings of the earliest of these peoples already are supporting the notion that some of them lived in these Massachusetts villages three thousand or more years ago. Where the Norsemen's "skraellings" fit in with these changing patterns of aboriginal occupation no one as yet knows. Indeed such poor evidence as there is in the sagas suggests that the skraellings may have been a coastal extension southward of an Eskimo-like people, perhaps related to the Beothuk tribes of Newfoundland. We must be content to admit that we know too little, as yet, to describe with accuracy the civilizations of any native peoples prior to those found in Massachusetts by the French and English explorers after the year 1500. All we know is that the earlier peoples existed, and that their imperishable stone tools, earthenware and weapons differed significantly from those of the Algonkian Indians our ancestors knew.

About these Algonkians we can write with some assurance. From both archaeological and historical testimony we know that they were an agricultural people. They lived in oblong or beehive-shaped houses of bark and straw mats in the midst of corn fields and kitchen gardens which they cleared by burning the forest and planting around the burned tree stumps. Corn and beans, pumpkins, tobacco and squashes were their crops, and they had learned to rotate crops on the land, leaving each field fallow in certain years to allow recovery of fertility. They cooked in fired-clay pots. Their artisans made not only wooden bowls and ladles, but birchbark boxes, willow and rush baskets, bark fiber mats and blankets, and fish lines and nets from Indian hemp. Their clothing included many varieties of dressed deer and moose skins, and mantles of lynx and beaver. From snake-skin girdles around their waists they hung little bags containing tobacco, soapstone and copper tobacco pipes and iron pyrites fire-striking sets. We still cannot improve on their moccasins and rawhide boots, their birchbark canoes, their pack baskets, and their bows and arrows. Even their dugout canoes still persist in the pirogues of Louisiana bayous. Snowshoes, fishing through the ice, snares and box traps, and the New England ritual of the spring herring run are all direct survivals of Algonkian culture. Their colored beadwork, porcupine quill designs, and pottery decoration have all crept into our artistic heritage, as have their use of copper and seashells in necklaces and bracelets. Succotash, the New England clambake, Indian pudding, elderberry wine, and baked beans we owe to the Indian. When these were supplemented by such Massachusetts delicacies as venison, lobster, green corn, partridge, roast turkey, broiled mackerel, blueberry cakes, wild strawberries and pumpkin pie, one need not feel that the wretched Indian necessarily lived a miserable life.

CHAPTER TWO

The Sixteenth Century

Into this somewhat idyllic forest setting there began to intrude, after 1500, increasing numbers of European seafarers bent on exploration and various kinds of commercial profit. The earliest of these expeditions that touched Massachusetts were the immediate result of the English voyages of John and Sebastian Cabot to Newfoundland in 1497 and 1498, following hard on Christopher Columbus' rediscovery of the New World in 1492.

In presenting the whole period of the New England explorers, it will be well to consider that the years from 1500 to 1620, during which all the preliminary work was done that made it possible for the Pilgrims to establish Massachusetts' first permanent plantation, divide themselves naturally into three phases. The first of these, extending from 1500 to 1600, was a century of spasmodic investigation by all the great European maritime nations, largely with the purpose of sampling the products of these northern coasts to see if any such loot could be obtained from them as the Spaniards were beginning to find around the Caribbean Sea. Tentative attempts, by the French and English, to found colonies in North America to the north and south of New England during this century came to grief for lack of adequate resources to maintain them. During the second phase of the period, from 1600 through

1614, concerted campaigns for colonization were made by both France and England in New England, and both failed, though permanent beachheads were established by France on the St. Lawrence and by England in Virginia. By the end of this phase France, England, and the Netherlands all laid claim to Massachusetts. The third phase, 1615–1620, brought about changes within Massachusetts itself which turned a somewhat inadvertent landing of the Pilgrims at Plymouth into a successful culmination for which many of the previous failures and disasters seem in retrospect to have prepared the way.

The sixteenth century, which is our first segment in the grand architecture of Massachusetts' exploration, began with a fishermen's enterprise. The wondrous tidings that off Newfoundland John Cabot had been able to catch codfish in baskets in 1497 created great excitement in all the fishing ports of Western Europe. Literally hundreds of fishing vessels promptly transferred their codfishing from Iceland to the Nova Scotia and Newfoundland banks. Inevitably many of these enthusiastic fishermen, faced with a limitless market for fish in Catholic Europe, especially in the season of Lent, looked farther afield for fishing banks and therefore coasted New England. Even John Cabot's second voyage had done so in 1498. Coincident with the formation of a Portuguese fishing company in the Azores a nobleman named Gaspar Cortereal had explored Greenland and Labrador in the year 1500, and in 1501 he again set sail to search for new lands. Separating from his accompanying vessels at Newfoundland, he sailed southward, and was never heard of again. The next year his brother Miguel set out in search of him, with three vessels. Separating at Newfoundland to pursue their search, Miguel's ship likewise failed to meet a rendezvous and similarly disappeared. The only clue to Miguel's fate appears in an inscription on Dighton Rock in the mouth of the Taunton River in

Massachusetts. It reads "M. Cortereal 1511 V. Dei Dux Ind."
and is followed by an emblem which might be a simplified rendering of the seal of Portugal. Freely translated, the Latin
abbreviations say "by the grace of God, Leader of the Indians."
In view of the continuous activities of Portuguese fishermen
during the subsequent four and a half centuries in the New
England fisheries, it is of especial importance that the first,
even though doubtful, record of a modern European landing
in Massachusetts is that of the Portuguese Miguel Cortereal.

Little more than a dozen years after the date of the
Cortereal inscription, Giovanni da Verrazano visited the same
region, but brought back no report of Miguel Cortereal. Sent
out on a voyage of exploration, hopeful of finding a Northwest Passage through North America, Verrazano sailed under
orders from the French king François I. During 1524 he explored the coast from Florida to Newfoundland, stopping in
New York harbor, and for a period of two weeks in Narragansett Bay into which Massachusetts' Taunton River flows. He
was met by about twenty Indian dugout canoes filled with
people eager to trade. His eloquent report of the voyage described their embroidered deerskins, their copper ornaments,
their circular straw houses, and a funeral ceremony which he
attended. Many of these Indians were probably ancestors of
the Wampanoags with whom the Pilgrims contracted the
peace of Massassoit only a hundred years later.

In 1525 a Spaniard, Estevan Gomez, repeated Verrazano's
voyage in the reverse direction, spending apparently three
winter months on the New England coast. On the Spanish
Ribeiro map of 1529 the results of the Gomez voyage are recorded, including St. Christopher's Bay for Boston harbor,
Cape St. James for Cape Cod, and the Cape of Shoals for the
island of Nantucket. An unnamed indentation on the west
side of Cape Cod Bay suggests Plymouth harbor, indicating

that Gomez was probably the first recorded discoverer of that hallowed spot. Five other navigators are known to have entered it before the landing of the Pilgrims. How blandly we forget our truly early discoverers!

The year 1527 was marked by a similar English voyage. The *Mary Guildford*, commissioned by King Henry VIII, after vainly searching for a passage to India by way of icebound Davis Strait, turned southward to Newfoundland. In the harbor of St. Johns they saw eleven Norman, one Breton and two Portuguese ships, "all a fishing." During the late summer and fall they coasted southward, reaching Puerto Rico and Santo Domingo in November. Somewhere along the coast their Italian pilot, who may have been Giovanni da Verrazano, was killed in a skirmish with Indians. This expedition likewise probably visited Massachusetts' shores. "From this time forth," writes Francis Parkman, "the Newfoundland fishery was never abandoned. French, English, Spanish and Portuguese made resort of the Banks, always jealous, often quarrelling, but still drawing up treasure from those exhaustless mines, and bearing home bountiful provision against the season of Lent."

The Portuguese attempted a colony on Cape Breton in 1527. Jacques Cartier led a French expedition up the St. Lawrence in 1536 and spent the winter near Quebec. In 1541 he returned to Canada and built a fort on the St. Lawrence above Quebec, in which the Sieur de Roberval and two hundred settlers wintered in wretched suffering before giving up the project. One of Roberval's pilots, Jehan Allefonsce of Saintonge, reported sailing southward in 1542 to a great bay in the latitude of 42 degrees, unquestionably Massachusetts Bay. A corrupt version of Allefonsce' description of these more southern coasts was rendered into French verse by Jehan Maillard, poet royal, about 1547, the first appearance of New England in literature. In that same year of 1542 French fur traders are believed to have found their way up the Hudson River as far as Albany, where they established a trading post. During the same year the Spaniard Diego Maldonado coasted New England, extending his search for the missing explorer Hernando de Soto as far north as "Baccalaos," the Portuguese name for codfish, often applied to Newfoundland.

In 1556 the French cosmographer André Thevet visited the "Fort of Norumbega," on the Penobscot River in Maine, staying five days and writing an amusing account of his reception by the Indians. Aside from his somewhat grotesque attempts to transliterate Indian language into the French alphabet, he did leave a recognizable contribution in describing sailing directions for entering Penobscot Bay, and he probably examined the shore of Massachusetts on his way up the coast to Maine. The name Norumbega was applied to the New England coast by most French seafarers from this time on for half a century.

The English freebooter Sir John Hawkins explored the North American coast from Florida to Newfoundland on the way home from a slave-trading voyage in 1565. Three years later, accompanied by Sir Francis Drake, his ship was dismasted on the coast of Mexico in a battle with the Spaniards, and a castaway member of his crew, David Ingram, perpetrated one of the most astounding improbabilities in history when with two companions he *walked* from a point near Tampico, Mexico, to New Brunswick, Canada, where he was rescued by a French trading vessel in the Bay of Fundy eleven months later. A confused story of his wanderings, dictated before witnesses to a secretary after fourteen years, adds little to our knowledge of Massachusetts or New England, but his exploit was well attested as a fact by Hawkins himself. The appearance of a French trading vessel in the neighborhood of eastern Maine by that period was not unusual. Sir Richard Whitbourne reported in 1578 that there were a hundred Spanish, fifty English, one hundred fifty French, and fifty Portuguese ships on the Newfoundland banks during that single season.

In 1583 Sir Walter Raleigh and his half brother, Humphrey Gilbert, met only disaster in an attempt to colonize Newfoundland. Two years later Raleigh sent seven ships and a hundred men under command of his cousin Richard Grenville to found a colony on Roanoke Island in the Carolinas. Most of them were rescued and brought back to England by Sir Francis Drake. Still other colonists were sent out to Roanoke, and these were either massacred by Indians or died when the Armada crisis in England stopped the supply convoys necessary to support the colony.

So passed the sixteenth century, which we have called the first phase of New England's exploration. None of its voyages were aimed specifically at Massachusetts, but we can be reasonably certain that in turn Miguel Cortereal, Giovanni da Verrazano, Estevan Gomez, Jehan Allefonsce, and David Ingram, and their shipmates, all had visited Massachusetts. Dozens, perhaps hundreds, of other vessels had certainly coasted Cape Cod and the adjacent shores in their searches for codfish, furs, and a Northwest Passage. In both the counting-houses of the great merchants of Europe and the geographers' libraries in the palaces of Europe's sovereigns there now existed maps, ships' logs, sailing directions and descriptions of the coast available to sea captains who might contemplate new voyages for trade or colonization.

Coastal Massachusetts was certainly known to hundreds of individual European sailors and pilots twenty years before the Pilgrims came. Their familiarity with available beaver skins, codfish, and other products of trade was by now well enough advanced to make further commercial investigations of these shores not only desirable but inevitable. Projects for the pursuit of profitable trade by ambitious Elizabethan merchants must surely be the next move.

CHAPTER THREE

Skirmish and Rebuff

The second phase of the exploration of Massachusetts now began with just that kind of project. A little company of merchant adventurers in the western ports of England sent out Bartholomew Gosnold in 1602 with thirty-two men in the bark *Concord*, bent on securing a cargo of sassafras, which had been described in Verrazano's report of his voyage seventy-eight years earlier. Sassafras root was at that period considered a valuable medicine for several diseases. Especially, it was thought to be "of sovereign virtue for the French poxe." The adventurers also hoped to found a small trading station or colony in the area. Sir Humphrey Gilbert's son Bartholomew was a member of the party. The *Concord* sailed from Falmouth, England, to the Azores, and thence directly to the coast of Maine. Finding no sassafras there, the vessel coasted southward. Off Cape Neddick Gosnold encountered a Biscay shallop under oars and sail manned entirely by Indians in European clothing, who came aboard the *Concord* and drew a map of the coast, seeming to be acquainted even with places in Newfoundland. So far had New England Indians become familiar with European techniques and activities by 1602!

Gosnold entered Provincetown harbor on May 18 and, while an exploring party landed, the crew caught more codfish than they could use, and had to throw some of them overboard. They found the fishing there better than at New-foundland, and therefore gave the place the name Cape Cod, the first Massachusetts landmark to receive its modern name. They also noted two easterly prolongations of Cape Cod, which have washed away in succeeding years, and bartered there with the Nauset Indians, whom they found "very thiev-ish," and quite numerous. A week of reconnoitering south of Cape Cod brought Gosnold to Martha's Vineyard and the Elizabeth Islands, to both of which he gave their modern names. On Cuttyhunk island the expedition built a sedge-thatched house and fort big enough "to harbor twenty per-sons," on the island in the Cuttyhunk pond. At Martha's Vineyard they planted wheat, barley, oats and peas "which in fourteen daies were sprung up nine inches and more." During three and a half weeks the *Concord*'s company gath-ered a cargo of sassafras and traded actively with Indians who came to them both from the islands and from the mainland. The two journals of the expedition, written by John Brereton and Gabriel Archer, present a wealth of information about the Indians and the experiences of the bark's personnel. Hostile attitudes of the natives soon cooled the enthusiasm of the twenty men of the company who had planned to stay and found a colony. Possibly Gosnold's theft of an Indian canoe contributed to this hostility. All thoughts of remaining in the country were abandoned, and on June 17 the *Concord* and its entire party sailed for England. where its sassafras was sold for a good profit.

The Gosnold voyage set in motion a chain of circum-stances that led to more ambitious English efforts to colonize New England. Only eight months later Richard Hakluyt, the famous collector of voyages, organized a second sassafras expedition under a Devon skipper, Martin Pring, with Robert Salterne, Gosnold's pilot, as Pring's assistant. Instead of pro-

ceeding south of Cape Cod, Pring's *Speedwell* and *Discoverer*
put in to Massachusetts Bay and found around Plymouth harbor an abundance of the sassafras they wanted. There they
built "a small baricado to keep diligent watch and ward in,"
because upward of two hundred Indians began to gather in the
vicinity of the woods in which the men worked. These Indians
at first were friendly and eager to trade. They even danced
in a circle around one of the sailors who accompanied them on
a guitar. Pring took pains to describe their clothes and equipment, and was particularly impressed with their bows and
arrows, their birch canoes (of which, again, he took one back
to England), and their gardens. He also listed the trees, plants,
animals, birds, and potential products of the country. But after
the smaller bark *Discoverer* had been loaded with cargo and
sent off to England, the reinforced Indians, who had been
coming in by canoes from all the surrounding country, began
to be menacing, and just before the loaded *Speedwell* put to
sea the natives set fire to the woods where the Englishmen had
cut their sassafras. Plymouth in 1603 was obviously no safer
than Cuttyhunk as a site for English settlement.

One can read between the lines that Massachusetts was
considered too hot to handle. For the next English voyage, in
1605, went to the Monhegan region of Maine, where George
Weymouth's experiences exploring the St. Georges and Kennebec Rivers seemed less provocative of Indian enmity than
Gosnold and Pring's skirmishes into Massachusetts. Indeed
Martin Pring himself was sent to the same Maine area in 1606,
and was followed that year by Thomas Hanham in what
appears to have been a concerted search for a better site for
an English colony than had been found in Massachusetts.

It was plain that English merchant adventurers were by
now determined to establish colonies in the New World. The
five exploratory voyages we have just mentioned, while ini-

tiated by different groups of merchants, were part of a uniform scheme in which such promoters as the Gilbert and Popham families, Richard Hakluyt and Sir Ferdinando Gorges were all interested. In 1606 two great companies were set up in England under charters from King James dividing between them all the North American coast from Nova Scotia to the Carolinas. Each company organized for the year 1607 an ambitious expedition to found a plantation in its half of that long coastline, then collectively known as Virginia. The fact that the London Company's colony at Jamestown, despite many vicissitudes, succeeded in maintaining its beachhead and producing a permanent settlement has obscured what happened in northern Virginia, which was New England. The equally ambitious expedition of the Plymouth Company, following the preliminary researches of Gosnold, Pring, Weymouth and Hanham, established in 1607 the Sagadahoc Colony of 120 men at Popham Beach beside the mouth of the Kennebec River in Maine. Through a typically severe Maine winter, during which a storehouse burned, a minor Indian massacre killed eleven men, and the planters suffered privations for which they were probably ill prepared, the colony hung on. But with the death, in the colony, of George Popham, its president, and in England of the brother of Raleigh Gilbert, second in command, requiring his return home, the planters lost heart, gave up, and all returned to England in the summer of 1608. Thereafter the energies of the Plymouth Company promoters were largely transferred to support the faltering Jamestown Colony, and no further effort was made to colonize northern Virginia. New England as a whole came to be considered in England as a subarctic region, not suitable for colonization. Anyone who had spent a winter among the bleak ledges of Popham Beach might be excused for forming such an opinion, even in modern days. But to place Massachusetts in the same category was unfortunate. It seems unlikely that a 1607 colony in Boston Bay would have failed. Yet the fact remains that Sagadahoc did fail and that New England was abandoned by the English for another dozen years.

Meanwhile the French had simultaneously been making New England exploration with a view toward settlement. After preliminary investigation in the Gulf of St. Lawrence in 1603, de Monts and Pontgravé, with Samuel de Champlain as geographer, extended their explorations in 1604 to the Bay of Fundy, and founded a colony on Dochet Island in the St. Croix River mouth, at the head of Passamaquoddy Bay. Half the colonists died during the winter, hemmed in on the little island by river ice floes that prevented their reaching the mainland, and in 1605 the survivors were moved across to a much better site, Port Royal, in Nova Scotia, now known as Annapolis. In the meantime Champlain made, in 1605 and 1606, two voyages of exploration southward, thoroughly investigating and mapping all the New England shores south to Cape Cod and around it to Woods Hole. His account of these voyages is entertaining reading, and he illustrated it with detail maps of such harbors as Gloucester, Plymouth, Eastham and Chatham. The Frenchmen washed their clothes in the little stream that enters Gloucester Harbor inside Rocky Neck and avoided a skirmish with the Indians only by a show of force with muskets. They presented pater-nosters to the Indians of Boston harbor, and watched them build a dugout canoe. After going aground on one of Cohasset's ledges, but getting off again at high tide, the French went into Plymouth harbor overnight, even making an attempt to enter Jones River there. At Eastham Indians killed a French sailor who tried to recover a stolen kettle. At Chatham a real ambush occurred, in which six Frenchmen lost their lives. After taking vengeance on six Indians, Champlain returned to Nova Scotia, convinced that he had found no site for settlement as good as the one they already had at Port Royal. Again, Massachusetts' Indians seem to have been successful, through their warlike demeanor, in preventing a European nation from choosing it as a site of projected colonization.

The French were not quite through with New England, however. After Champlain's 1608 transfer to Quebec, where he did his real empire building in the founding of French Canada, the Port Royal trading post continued to collect furs from eastern Maine. In 1611 French Jesuits became interested in establishing a Penobscot mission, and two years later sent an expedition which inadvertently landed instead on Mount Desert Island. After two weeks this colony was destroyed by an armed vessel from Jamestown under Sir Samuel Argall, sent by Governor Dale for the purpose. English sea power thus put an end to French efforts at colonizing New England, even though the English themselves had failed in similar efforts.

In the closing years of our second phase of Massachusetts' explorations a third nation made brief appearances along our shores and began to lay claim to southern New England. Henry Hudson was an English navigator who had made futile attempts to reach the Far East by sailing in 1607 across the Arctic Ocean north of Spitsbergen, and in 1608 around the northern coasts of Russia. These unsuccessful voyages were made for the English Muscovy Company. But in 1609 he was hired by the Dutch East India Company to try again to find a Northeast Passage around Russia. Again he failed, but rather than turn back to the Netherlands he resolved on a search for a Northwest Passage through North America, an idea which Captain John Smith had laid before him in a letter sent from Jamestown. After spending a week in Maine's Penobscot Bay in July, his *Half Moon* touched briefly at Cape Cod in August, explored Delaware Bay, and in October sailed up the Hudson

River to Albany, staying a full month fur trading on that river. His reports of this profitable Hudson River fur trading led the Dutch to pursue further activities in that region.

As a consequence, Adrian Block and Henrik Christiansen lay off Manhattan Island in the fall of 1613 in two vessels loaded with furs. One of the vessels caught fire and burned to the water's edge. Rather than leave one crew as castaways, the Dutch built houses on Manhattan and spent the winter, constructing there a small "yacht," the *Onrust*, to transport the marooned crew back home. In the early spring of 1614 the *Onrust* made a shakedown cruise through Long Island Sound, exploring the Connecticut River, Narragansett Bay, and Massachusetts Bay before setting sail back across the Atlantic. Block's map, published in 1616, gave the name Crane's Bay to Plymouth harbor, and included Massachusetts in the territory designated "New Netherland." On the basis of this voyage the Dutch subsequently established trading posts on the Connecticut River, and were only finally eased out of their claims on the fur trade of both the Massachusetts and Connecticut portions of that great valley by a treaty imposed on them in 1650 by the Massachusetts Bay Colony.

Thus by early 1614 the second phase of Massachusetts' explorations was over. Major investigations of Massachusetts and major attempts at settlement in Maine had been made by both France and England, and these had all failed. The Dutch had laid the basis for fur trading in Connecticut and New York. England had a permanent colony in Virginia, France at Quebec. Active fur trading and fishing was still carried on in the Bay of Fundy and the Penobscot by French vessels and around Monhegan and the Kennebec by the British. But the Massachusetts coast was held by the Indians; only occasional vessels penetrated Massachusetts Bay. Massachusetts Indians had repelled all explorers who entertained thoughts of planting a colony there. No one had even temporarily established a trading post in Massachusetts.

The third, or precolonial, phase of Massachusetts' explorers' history began in 1614 with the arrival of Captain John Smith, a man whose single-minded enthusiasm for Massachusetts was to influence powerfully the English colonial movement. He had already been governor of the Jamestown Colony. Though stormy in temperament, he had learned in a hard school how to get co-operation from lazy colonists and hostile Indians alike. He knew that it took resourcefulness and discipline to survive in the wilderness.

Arriving in April, 1614, at Monhegan on an ordinary trading and fishing voyage, he left Thomas Hunt with his larger vessel to get a cargo of codfish. Smith himself took the smaller vessel southward for fur trading for six weeks, and devoted himself to geography. He thus drafted the best and most detailed map of the coast from Penobscot Bay to Cape Cod ever produced up to that time. The names New England, Massachusetts, Plymouth, Charles River, and Cape Ann first appeared in connection with this map, and some of the Indian place names he recorded could never have survived otherwise, as events developed. He also demonstrated that the Massachusetts Indians, at Plymouth, could be successfully fought, and afterward bargained with, a fact that few besides himself had had sufficient experience to prove. He seized the Indians' canoes during the Plymouth fight and then returned them to the natives in exchange for beaver skins when the fighting was over. It was this kind of resourcefulness, used repeatedly by Myles Standish and William Bradford ten years later, which accounted for the survival of the Pilgrims.

Smith returned to England with a profitable cargo of furs, and spent the remaining seventeen years of his life promoting Massachusetts as the proper site for an English colony. In

book after book he described Massachusetts as "the Paradise of
all those parts." He clearly drew the distinction for the first
time between the barren coast of Maine and the more fertile
shores around Massachusetts Bay. Of Massachusetts he wrote
"could I have but meanes to transport a Colonie, I would
rather live here than anywhere." He tried to pull every wire he
could find to get the leadership of such an expedition, but no
one would hire him. Yet his writings, which were voluminous,
seem to have made a strong impression on English merchants,
and probably determined the destination of the Massachusetts
Bay Colony migrations from 1628 on. He was also consulted
by the adventurers who financed the *Mayflower*. For Massachusetts he performed a function similar to that of Sir Walter
Raleigh in the English colonization of North America. He
was also New England's Hakluyt, for his collected works are
the best single history of the English voyages to New England. For all these services John Smith received no greater reward than the vague title "Admiral of New England." He
died in obscurity in 1631, never having seen again the country
he did so much to acclaim after his brief six weeks' sojourn in
1614.

There was a strange sequel to Smith's historic Massachusetts cruise. Thomas Hunt, whom Smith had left fishing at
Monhegan, got his cargo of codfish aboard, and then himself
made a foray into Massachusetts Bay. At Plymouth he coolly
kidnaped twenty Indians, and at Eastham on Cape Cod seven
more, stowed them below decks in irons, and sailed away for
Málaga in Spain. There he sold them into slavery "for 20 £ to a
Man" in a typical seaman's side bet added to the profits of his
codfish cargo. For this he was universally condemned and
never allowed to be employed again in such voyages. And in
Massachusetts itself the immediate effects were apparent.
When Nicholas Hobson, later in 1614, tried to trade at Nan-

tucket, his vessel was attacked by Indians in a full-scale battle. He returned to England empty handed, with the news that "there was a War broke out between the English and the Indians." Massachusetts was now forbidden territory.

The quirks of history are sometimes more fantastic than fiction. Among the twenty wretched natives whom the rascal Thomas Hunt sold in Spain was an Indian named Squanto. Released from slavery through the good offices of a Spanish friar, Squanto found his way to England. There he lived for several years in the English household of John Slany, treasurer of the Newfoundland Company. Transported out to Newfoundland, he was picked up by Captain Thomas Dermer, who used him as a pilot for a New England voyage. Squanto was released in 1619, and was back at his native Plymouth, with his European education, to welcome the Pilgrims and act as their interpreter in 1621.

But in the meantime fate, or Providence, had intervened in Massachusetts in behalf of Englishmen. With British expeditions returning empty handed and a "war broke out," a European disease to which white men had complete immunity, and Indians none, began to rage among the natives in precisely the area where the Indians were most hostile to the English. The aborigines died in thousands, so fast that the living "would runne away and let them dy and let there Carkases ly above the ground without buriall," as Thomas Morton wrote from Quincy a few years later. Frank G. Speck estimates that the coastal Indians from Boston Bay to Narragansett Bay fell in population from a hundred thousand to five thousand during the years 1615–1617 when the plague was raging. Whether it was measles or scarlet fever or some other children's disease remains unknown. But the effect was immediate. In all the region that Smith had called "paradise," suddenly the land lay wide open to colonization. The Indian war was over. The only major obstacle to the settlement of Massachusetts just melted away.

Captain Thomas Dermer, with Squanto, cruised the coast in 1619, "searching every harbor and compassing every capeland." At Plymouth Squanto found "all dead" and had to travel west to Middleboro to find any living natives. Dermer met Massasoit and some of the Wampanoags and, thanks to Squanto's return, established friendly relations with Indians who a few years before would have greeted him with showers of arrows. Along the coast Dermer "found some ancient Plantations, not long since populous, now utterly void, in other places a remnant remaines but not free of sickenesse."

This was the Massachusetts to which, the next year, the Pilgrims came, wiped almost clean of the Indian obstacles which had in succession turned back Gosnold, Pring, and Champlain. Here were cleared fallow cornfields, ready again to be cultivated. This was the "paradise" of New England, foretold by Captain John Smith. The country was mapped, thoroughly explored, its furs and fisheries sampled and known to be profitable. On Monhegan and Damariscove islands in Maine, two sailing days away, there were friendly English traders who often spent the winter and could be called on for emergency supplies. Thomas Dermer had even found French castaways living among the natives at Pokanoket and near Boston. And thanks to rascally Thomas Hunt, a Spanish friar, the merchant John Slany, and Dermer, there was Squanto ready to interpret curious English behavior, or speech, to Massasoit and all his Wampanoags. This was the "stern and rock-bound coast" on which the Pilgrims landed.

CHAPTER FOUR

The First Settlements

It is not a worke for every one, to manage such an affaire as makes a discoverie and plants a Colony. It requires all the best parts of Art, Judgement, Courage, Honesty and Constancy, Diligence, and Industrie to doe but neere well." These words of Captain John Smith, written in 1615 for his *Description of New England*, well summarize what was now needed to found a New England colony. The English mercantile impulse by itself had succeeded in founding a permanent colony in warm Virginia but had failed in bleak New England. Massachusetts now lay wide open for settlement. Who was available with the "Constancy, Diligence and Industrie" to seize the opportunity?

In view of the extensive mercantile preparations that had been made, it seems curious that Massachusetts was eventually colonized by a religious group that had not shared at all in the preliminary studies of the coast. Yet in another sense it seems entirely appropriate that the rugged hazards of New England winters should be finally surmounted by an expedition supremely possessed of just those qualities that Smith considered necessary. The Pilgrims had already exiled themselves for twelve years for an act of faith and now were prepared to do so again, in the wilderness of North America. Of all Englishmen, who stood a better chance of success in an enterprise demanding character than they?

The English Reformation began as a political device of Henry VIII to set England's national policy free of domination by the Church of Rome. Neither Henry nor Elizabeth was interested in reform within the Church. But at Cambridge University a group of Puritans began to clamor against the sale of benefices, the sensual life of the clergy, and the many parasites among the clergy who performed no religious duties. These Puritans usually had no idea of separating from the church, but rather worked for reform within the church structure. A minority sect of Separatists grew restless, however, under the failure of the reform movement and set up their own congregations. For this their leaders were thrown into prison or took flight to avoid imprisonment, usually to the Netherlands.

The Pilgrims were such a Separatist parish, organized at Scrooby in 1606, from which in 1608 they fled to Amsterdam, and from there to Leyden, under leadership of their pastor John Robinson and their teacher William Brewster. William Bradford was an orphan in Brewster's household. Edward Winslow joined the group in Holland as an apprentice printer in Brewster's printing shop, where religious propaganda pamphlets were turned out for smuggling back into England. The congregation were desperately poor, maintaining themselves by learning trades in the Dutch leather and textile industries. The winds of hardship winnowed their numbers down to a most determined residue.

After ten years in the Netherlands, their leaders began to realize that the integrity of the parish would soon be dissipated among the Dutch around them. Their children were growing up uneducated and tempted by the easygoing life of their Dutch friends. If the congregation were to maintain its identity, it would be better to move again, probably to America. Negotiations were attempted at first with both Dutch and English governments, through intermediaries, but the results were not encouraging. Finally through Thomas Weston, a brisk English businessman known to some of them, it was found possible to organize a joint-stock company of English adventurers, mostly merchants, who put up sufficient capital to finance two vessels to carry the expedition across the Atlantic. Differences of opinion arose over whether New England was a proper destination for the colony. Some of the investors withdrew. There were other disagreements. Finally it was necessary, in order to prevent collapse of the project, to promise that for seven years all the work of the colonists must be applied to a common pool to pay back the indebtedness. At this point many of the Leyden congregation dropped out of the project.

Eventually only 41 Separatists sailed, 14 of them children, constituting only about one sixth of the parish. The merchant adventurers recruited 61 other good Church of England people to fill out the passenger list. Two months were lost in attempts to correct the deficiencies of the *Speedwell*, which the Leyden men had mistakenly fitted with masts too large for her hull. She had to be abandoned after two futile attempts to set sail. Finally, crowded aboard the *Mayflower*, the sturdy ship outfitted by the adventurers, the Pilgrims sailed in September instead of July. This delay of two months, deferring their arrival in Massachusetts until the onset of winter, proved to be a major disaster. Many of the deaths and unreasonable hardships of the Pilgrims during their wretched first winter could have been avoided by a July sailing.

The crossing of the *Mayflower* was marked by the ordinary maritime hardships of the day. Crowd 102 passengers on a ship of 180 tons, with a crew of thirty, and tack her back and forth monotonously against the North Atlantic's prevailing westerlies for two months and you have a prescription hard to equal for human misery. This voyage was unusual in that it included many women and children among the passengers. Previous New England expeditions had been limited to men. But now the primitive sanitary conveniences, principally buckets, and the absence of ventilation, heat or running water were shared by a community of families. The 'tween-decks area in which the passengers traveled was only about five feet high.

Yet these people carried with them two of the greatest advantages any colonial expedition ever brought to the New World: an obstinate religious conviction and the integrity of family loyalties. This was no escapist adventure; it was the building of a new society. They had cut loose completely from their home base in the Netherlands and considered that they had nothing to return to there that was better than the difficult life they were enduring. They brought with them their families, their church, and their community leadership, the factors best calculated to ensure self-respect and survival under conditions of hardship.

Against these advantages they had prodigious faults in their training and equipment. Aside from John Smith's map they had no knowledge of the New England coast. Among the entire ship's company only Robert Coppin, the third mate, had ever visited the coast before and his knowledge was fragmentary. They knew nothing of the fishing fleet that visited the Maine coast every year. Standard equipment like fishing gear and trinkets for trading with the Indians was missing. So inadequate was their geographical information that they spent five weeks exploring Cape Cod before finally deciding, in late December, that Plymouth was the best place to settle. Later, they wished they had found Boston Bay.

Faced with stirrings of discontent among some of the London "strangers," yet possessing no legal patent for the government of the colony, the Pilgrim leaders improvised a "Compact" to establish and preserve their authority. In church covenant phraseology, this document set up a "civill body politick" who agreed to frame "just and equall lawes" and "offices" for the "general good of ye Colonie," unto which the heads of families and most of the unattached men promised "all due submission and obedience." The elective system thus set up provided a basis for choice of officials by certain masters and goodmen who alone could vote. John Carver was elected governor or magistrate, a position from which he could legislate, judge and administer laws with the advice of his church leaders and the Bible. Hardly democratic, this basis of government prevented the numerous indentured servants from going ashore and doing as they pleased, yet did set a striking precedent in establishing even a limited consent of the governed as the source of authority. This was in strong contrast to the theocracy later established in Massachusetts Bay.

The *Mayflower* was brought over to Plymouth from Provincetown on December 26. Compassionate Captain Jones kept her there at anchor all winter, and he and his crew shared with the Pilgrims all the horrors of those first four awful months. He thus provided a barracks for the colony until houses could be built. Half his crew died during the winter. Such a contribution was one of those minimum essentials to the success of the Pilgrims, like the saga of Squanto, the plague among the Indians, and the work of merchant adventurers and previous explorers, that sometimes fail to be appreciated in our reverence for Pilgrim fortitude.

We need not be astonished that the Pilgrims, faced with so many tribulations of their own, failed to emphasize in their chronicles the contributions that other men, like the *Mayflower*'s crew, made to their undertaking. William Bradford's consummate record of the Pilgrim story quite naturally devotes

itself to the heroic sufferings and triumphs of the Separatists themselves. But in assessing the whole exploit we would be less than fair if we failed to recognize that common sailors, the ship's officers, English merchants, and about seventy unidentified investors in the joint-stock company all participated to varying degrees in the risks inherent in the expedition. Some of the investors and merchants no doubt were just speculators, hoping for a quick profit. There were others, however, who invested, and lost, fortunes in repeated similar projects because they were staking their lives, like Sir Walter Raleigh, Ferdinando Gorges and John Smith, on that stubborn, single-minded purpose to "make of America an English nation." We should not forget that even Plymouth Plantation was one episode in the obstinate struggle of the English nation to build for itself an overseas empire.

Building of the Common House was begun on January 4, the timber and plank being sawed out of the Plymouth woods in snow and sleet and bitter cold. Captain Standish kept constant guard from among his cannon mounted on a platform on Fort Hill. Sickness and death felled so many workers that at times only a half dozen men were well enough to work. When the nearly completed thatched roof of the new Common House caught fire on January 24, the sick, bedded side by side on the floor, had to jump out of bed to carry open barrels of gunpowder outside before the fire could reach them. Fishing and hunting were singularly unsuccessful among these inexperienced planters, and only rationing of the waning stores of the *Mayflower* sufficed to keep the remaining colonists alive. Respiratory infections wiped out whole families. Of eighteen wives, only four survived; of twenty-nine servants and unattached men, only ten; of the total, six died in December, eight in January, seventeen in February, and thirteen in March. Bradford wrote in his journal: "of a hundred persons, scarce fifty remain, the living scarce able to bury the dead."

This was the testing time, the stubbornly endured martyr-dom of the Pilgrims, through which every northern colony must pass to produce a lasting foothold. This had turned back Cartier in 1541 and the Sagadahoc Englishmen in 1608. Champlain's colony in Passamaquoddy Bay survived it in 1606, but had to move to do so. The Jamestown settlers had given up the ghost and embarked, for similar cause, only to resume the attempt after the lucky arrival of a supply convoy. Nowhere in the Pilgrim chronicles is there any indication that they even considered abandoning the enterprise. This is their chief glory.

Spring brought certain solid gains. One day in late March a tall, assured Indian named Samoset stalked into the little settlement, smiling and asking for beer. He was a Pemaquid from Maine, on a visit to his friend Massasoit, sachem of the local Wampanoag tribe. In the broken English he had learned from English fur traders he explained that most of the Wampanoags lived in their principal village of Sowams, or Pokanoket, forty miles away at the mouth of the Taunton River. He brought a few of them in to Plymouth with furs to trade, and several days later announced that Massasoit himself, with sixty warriors, was waiting on a nearby hill to meet the Pilgrim leaders. In this dangerous moment young Edward Winslow volunteered to go as a hostage, bearing an invitation to them from venerable Governor Carver to come and visit the plantation. A quickly improvised musket salute by Standish's guard of honor, with flourish of brass and drums, made a strong impression on Massasoit as he and twenty strapping braves strode down the little street and were ceremoniously received in a newly completed house by Carver and his assistants. Drinks were exchanged, and there followed a series of consultations, through interpreters, which resulted in a treaty of mutual assistance destined to endure for forty years. Indian offenders were to be tried by the English, and English offenders by the Indians. Each would come unarmed to visits upon the other. Subsidiary clans of Indians throughout southeastern Massachusetts, including Cape Cod and the islands, were to fall under this agreement. As a by-product of the agreement Squanto, that invaluable interpreter, guide and go-between, took up residence at Plymouth and soon taught the Pilgrims how to fish, hunt, and establish trade relations with all their neighbors around the bay.

At one blow, Plymouth Plantation had solved its Indian problem. No more brilliant example of sound leadership by a little group of half-starved refugees exists in American history than the adroit show of force, the ceremonial welcome and presentation of gifts, and the hardheaded bargaining which Governor Carver displayed on this occasion. A week later the *Mayflower* departed for England, and in still another week Governor Carver himself died, leaving as his monument the peace of Massassoit. It detracts not a bit from this achievement to note that the Wampanoags, themselves seriously weakened by plague and attacks by their Narragansett enemies, wanted the treaty quite as much as did the Pilgrims. The alliance probably saved both the Wampanoags and the Pilgrims from massacre. It did not prevent minor revolts from developing, at Weymouth and at Middleboro, nor did it remove completely the threat of attack by Canonicus, the powerful sachem of the Rhode Island Narragansetts. But it set a precedent for the fruitfulness of a bold Indian policy which was successfully repeated again and again by the new 32-year-old governor William Bradford and his doughty military adviser, Captain Myles Standish. It also demonstrated the agile diplomatic talents of the young printer's apprentice, Edward Winslow, who continued to carry on useful negotiating services to Massasoit's headquarters at Pokanoket, and eventually even to

London. This team of young leaders, tried in the fire, again and again proved their capacity for wise and effective guidance of the colony in crisis after crisis.

Bradford was a man of outstanding energy, wit and courage and less subject to the domination of church leadership than had been the devout graybeards of the older generation. He chose for his assistant Isaac Allerton, who shrewdly handled the business dealings of the plantation for the next ten years. Suave Edward Winslow and vehement Myles Standish took even greater part in the councils than before. Winslow visited Massasoit in June at Sowams and laid foundations for a long-standing fur-trading agreement which remained profitable for years. He arranged for the surrounding tribes to send to Plymouth their surplus corn, for both seed and food. During the first summer twenty acres of corn at Plymouth produced a good crop, enabling the plantation to entertain Massasoit and ninety of his people at a three-day Thanksgiving feast of venison in October. Eleven plank and timber buildings now stood along the little sloping street above the brook. Squanto had taught the Pilgrims to catch an abundance of lobsters, herring, eels and shellfish and had so improved their hunting techniques that their larder was supplemented by turkey, partridge, duck and venison. The little colony was healthy again after an active summer.

In November the *Fortune* added thirty-five new colonists to the village, but brought no supplies. Letters she brought from the adventurers criticized the Pilgrims for not sending a cargo home on the *Mayflower*. Seven of the newcomers were from Leyden; the rest were "Strangers." Bradford sent back the *Fortune* loaded with clapboards and beaver skins, worth in modern currency perhaps $20,000, but that cargo was captured by French pirates and did nothing to reduce Plymouth's indebtedness to the merchant adventurers. Trade in corn and

furs was well established, however, by repeated voyages of
Standish and Squanto to Barnstable and Eastham on Cape Cod
and to Squantum and Medford in Boston Bay. The Pilgrims
placed the names of Squantum, Point Allerton and the Brew-
sters on the maps of Boston harbor long before Salem and
Boston were even thought of. The squaws of Medford sold
them their beaver coats for cheap trinkets without the slight-
est hesitation. Thus the foundation for eventual lucrative
commerce was assured.

That this profitable economic base was so well established
was in large measure due to Bradford's bold Indian policies.
When Hobamock, a jealous rival of Squanto's, started a rumor
in August that the Middleboro sachem Corbitant had killed
Squanto and begun a revolt, Standish was immediately sent
with an armed party to intervene. Squanto was found alive,
and a stern warning was issued to the conspirators. The following winter when the Narragansett sachem Canonicus sent
Governor Bradford a snakeskin filled with arrows, the savage
equivalent of a declaration of hostility, the canny Governor
sent it back filled with powder and shot. This so frightened
the Indians that they returned it unopened. Winslow could
write home in December, 1621: "We walk as peacefully and
safely in the wood as in the highways in England."

The increase in population caused by the *Fortune*'s arrival
soon again depleted Plymouth's food supplies. A serious period
of hunger was narrowly averted in May of 1622 by the lucky
arrival of one of Thomas Weston's trading boats with the
news that thirty ships were then fishing around Monhegan
Island on the Maine coast. Winslow promptly sailed there
and obtained enough stores from these vessels to tide the Pilgrims over until harvest. Again a "starving time" threatened
in July with the unexpected arrival of two more of Weston's
vessels, the *Charity* and *Swan*, bringing fifty men, who ate up

Plymouth food while their advance party built a stockade and buildings for a new plantation at Wessagusset on the shores of the modern Weymouth. The *Swan* was used by both colonies for transporting corn from Cape Cod. This was facilitated by the lucky acquisition from a Jamestown vessel, which called at Plymouth in August, of a new supply of beads, knives and other trinkets for the Indian trade.

Sixteen-twenty-two was a nip-and-tuck year. We have to read between the lines how unremitting was the toil, how stern the leadership. Every increase in population meant sweating in the saw pits to make new planks for added houses and stockades. It meant clearing and planting new corn fields, hauling in firewood, digging postholes, splitting clapboards and shingles, repairing nets for fishing, hunting and skinning and cooking game, drying the pelts and the fish. We have to imagine the injuries and the illnesses, the near disasters at sea or while hunting, by men soaked in rain, half starved and fighting for survival. Such inevitable episodes, mostly ignored in the optimistic Pilgrim records, were always the price of maintaining a new foothold in the wilderness. Only backbreaking physical work under complete discipline could possibly have brought to success the Plymouth saga. Only their survival of this ordeal made possible the Puritan empire building in Massachusetts that soon followed.

Two years of struggle had firmly established Plymouth. The industrious chronicles of its success penned by Bradford and Winslow produced in some English adventurers a desire to participate in the profits. John Peirce, in whose name "and associates" a new Plymouth Company patent for the colony had been issued, succeeded in getting the patent rewritten in his own name exclusively. Only when he was already aboard ship and about to sail for his new dominion was his fraud discovered and the voyage canceled. Sir Ferdinando Gorges, who already held, on paper, a monopoly of the Cape Cod fisheries, began to lay plans to send his son Robert out to New England on a voyage to enforce his monopoly. Thomas Weston's men were already getting in on the act, with their Wessagusset plantation. Something like a gold rush was developing. William Bradford was faced with all the problems of English mercantile competition.

Although first in the field, Thomas Weston's men did not have what it took. Those who remained at Plymouth were a shiftless lot, stealing more green corn than they raised. Plymouth was heartily glad to be rid of them when they moved to Wessagusset in the fall. There they continued to get into trouble, abusing their Massachuset Indian neighbors, who reacted by hatching a conspiracy to exterminate them. In March of 1623 Massasoit, grateful to Edward Winslow for ministering to him in an illness, revealed to him the details of the Massachuset plot and advised the Pilgrims to kill the Indian ringleaders. By that time the improvident Wessagusset settlers were in the extremity of starvation. Their leaders were away in Maine trying to buy corn from Ferdinando Gorges' trading vessels. Many of those left in Wessagusset went native, building dugouts for the Indians in return for food, foraging for ground nuts and leaving the fort unguarded. The Massachusets were obviously merely waiting until emaciation and exhaustion should remove all resistance to the final stroke. When Phinehas Prat, a refugee from Wessagusset, managed to elude Indian pursuers and described this state of affairs to Bradford at Plymouth, a public court was called and the Pilgrims promptly empowered Bradford and Standish to adopt and execute whatever plan seemed best. Under the ruse of trading, Standish took eight men to Wessagusset, awaited his chance, and killed seven of the most insulting of the Indian conspirators. Three of Weston's men were killed by the Indians through negligence of Standish's orders, but the Pilgrims suffered no known casualties. Most of the Weston survivors took ship to Maine; a few accepted sanctuary in Plymouth. The Weymouth stockade was abandoned, though later used by various planters as an initial refuge before building their own establishments. Thomas Weston himself soon died, after various misadventures in shipwreck and embezzlement. In William Bradford, Weston had always found a compassionate friend in need. However often Weston sponged on Bradford, the Governor could never quite forget Weston's earlier services in finding investors to finance the voyage of the *Mayflower*. But his hastily conceived project to set up his own competitive fur-trading plantation under Plymouth's protection came to utter disaster. The episode affords a sharp-etched illustration of the difference between the scatterbrained opportunism of a colonial speculator and the shrewd vigor of the determined zealots who built Plymouth Plantation.

The gold rush continued in other forms. The summer of 1623 brought to Plymouth the *Anne* and the *Little James*, with sixty new planters. Some were wives and children of men already there, some new families, some so bad they had to be sent home the next year, and about a dozen "Particulars." These last came on their own account, not required to work for the common burden of repayment to the adventurers but otherwise subject to Plymouth's administration. Being "on their particular," they could work for themselves, sharing only in defense and the ordinary duties of the plantation. They could settle on land assigned to them by Governor Bradford. Here was the beginning of that response to the "land of opportunity" argument about which Captain John Smith had been writing for ten years: "Here every man may be master and owner of his owne labour and land—If he have nothing but his hands, hee may set up his trade; and by industrie quickly grow rich." To the unemployed and debt-ridden in Stuart England this was as potent a goal as that of religious freedom. Massacre of more than three hundred people in Virginia the previous year only increased the desire to seek one's fortune in safer Massachusetts. The summer of 1623 brought not only the Particulars at Plymouth, but also fourteen men at Gloucester sent by the Rev. John White's Dorchester Company to found a fishing colony. A few planters left by Robert Gorges during his desultory visit of inspection for his father reoccupied the abandoned Wessagusset stockade. Other independents settled around Boston: William Blaxton at Beacon Hill, Samuel Maverick at Mystick, Thomas Walford at Charlestown, and Thomas Gray, Walter Knight and John Balch at Nantasket. To this Nantasket group were soon added Roger Conant and John Lyford from Plymouth. The environment was gradually being developed into which the more massive Puritan migration would be poured a few years later.

Plymouth's response to these competitors was necessarily an attempt to strengthen its hold on fur trading and fishing. Standish was unsuccessful in driving out the Dorchester Company's fishermen from Gloucester in 1624, but soon established lucrative trading posts at Aptuxcet in Bourne, and at Augusta, Maine, on the Kennebec River. To Aptuxcet furs flowed in from Rhode Island and Connecticut Indians, and to Augusta, an active trade from inland Maine that eventually enabled Plymouth to pay off all its indebtedness to the *Mayflower* adventurers.

Boston Bay, however, was rapidly slipping out of Pilgrim hands. In 1625 a Captain Wollaston, sent probably by Ferdinando Gorges, settled temporarily at Wessagusset and then moved over to Passonagessit in Quincy, renamed Mount Wollaston, or Merrymount. After Wollaston in 1627 sailed off to sell some of his indentured servants to Jamestown for the re-

maining years of their service, a nimble-witted lawyer named
Thomas Morton usurped the command of the colony and proceeded to conduct a highly successful fur trade with the
Massachuset Indians through such devices as lavish entertain-
ment and selling firearms to the natives. While Bradford's
Historie harps on Morton's activities in connection with dances
with Indian squaws around a Maypole, the context of the
situation suggests that the Pilgrims were most irked by
Morton's effective competition in the fur trade and his arming
of the natives. In any case, with co-operation from other
groups around Boston Bay, Myles Standish and his little army
took Morton prisoner, tried him in Plymouth, and sent him
back to England.

Yet Plymouth's competitors still grew. The Gloucester
fishing post, despite a reinforcement of thirty-two additional
planters in 1624, was unprofitable. In the next year Roger
Conant, a Plymouth Particular then living in Nantasket, was
placed in charge of it, but the men were too shiftless to make
it a commercial success. In 1626 the Dorchester Adventurers
went bankrupt and the colony was withdrawn, but Conant
and his Nantasket associates, along with half a dozen of the
most persistent Gloucester families, decided to stay. Realizing
that the tip of Cape Ann had too little agricultural land to
feed the colony, this group of a dozen families moved to
Naumkeag, soon renamed Salem, and built new houses near
the present Beverly Bridge. There they pastured cattle and
worked hard to re-establish themselves. By 1627 it was evident
that this group, winnowed from the previous failures of the
Gorges and Gloucester enterprises, possessed the character and
leadership to build a firm plantation.

Momentous events in England meanwhile were turning
the attention of English investors to the little Salem colony
as a nucleus for a potential refuge for Puritans caught in eco-

nomic depression at home. The Tudor inflation had been followed in the early Stuart years by deflation, with falling prices and a breakdown in the system of poor relief. Great sections of the English middle class faced ruin as the economic pattern squeezed them between a small corrupt wealthy class and a miserable peasantry. Many businessmen and tradesmen joined the Puritan party for self-preservation against economic disaster. In Parliament they forced through the Petition of Right, requiring Charles I to obey the laws of the realm. The King responded by dissolving Parliament. In this situation a whole new group of merchants backed the Rev. John White with money for supplies to reinforce Conant's plantation at Naumkeag. Cattle arrived in 1627, clothes, salt, grain, and food supplies in the summer of 1628, and in September of that year the *Abigail* brought a new group of colonists under a new superintendent, John Endecott, who forthwith supplanted Roger Conant in command and rapidly developed the facilities of the settlement in anticipation of new arrivals. The "great house" built by the old fishing colony at Gloucester was moved over to Salem, new buildings were constructed, and restrictions were instituted to control trade and prices. Despite a winter producing much sickness, for which Plymouth's Dr. Fuller administered his services, feverish preparations went forward. In England the adventurers formed the Massachusetts Bay Company, hired ships, employed engineers, drew contracts for supplies, and put in motion a colonizing effort designed to dwarf all its predecessors.

In 1629 six ships brought three hundred new planters, sixty head of cattle and horses, and other supplies. In one summer Salem, and its new subsidiary at Charlestown, had grown in population more than Plymouth had been able to do in nine years. And when in 1630 the new Governor Winthrop arrived in the *Arbella*, in the advance guard of ships bringing five hundred more colonists into Salem and Boston harbors that year, it was evident what the future was about to unfold. The process was now well established by which during the next sixty years Massachusetts Bay was to engulf completely, and swallow up, the courageous Old Colony of Plymouth. The gold rush was over. The Massachusetts Bay Company now held the undisputed initiative. Not Pilgrims, but Puritans, were to frame the ultimate destiny of Massachusetts.

CHAPTER FIVE

The Arrogant Years of Massachusetts Bay

In the *Arbella* Governor Winthrop brought with him the actual charter of the Massachusetts Bay Company. This was something new. All previous English colonial enterprises had worked out of a London main office, from which, at long range, administrators operated the business affairs of the corporation. Plymouth had never had a legal charter and was still trying to buy its freedom from its English owners. But, save only to the crown, Massachusetts Bay started off with a clear title to its political and economic independence. This transfer of the charter changed a mere trading company into the self-governing commonwealth of Massachusetts Bay. Its leaders did not need to clear policies with London or bow to the decisions of a nonresident board of directors. Governor Winthrop and his assistants were their own board, their own parliament, even their own ministry, so long as their laws be not repugnant to the laws of England. For fifty-four years this fact set the character of the Massachusetts Bay government in its internal affairs and in its relationship to its neighbors and even to the mother country itself.

The dozen Puritan zealots who were thus legally exalted into ownership and control of the colony believed that all policies should be decided by appeal to Holy Scripture. Winthrop, Dudley, the Rev. John Cotton, and the other dominating leaders of the colony came to Massachusetts filled with a sincere conviction that they were chosen leaders, chosen of God to form a refuge for others of their own beliefs. They considered that the revealed word of God in the Bible was a sufficient basis to determine all human policies, administrative, legislative and judicial. They also believed that as the elect of God they themselves were uniquely endowed with infallible ability to interpret Scripture in the correct meaning. Their followers were expected to accept this superiority of theirs and be governed by their decisions. Any dissent, or even toleration of dissenters, was to be punished. They loathed democracy. Only the eighteen "freemen," or hand-picked members of the company, should be allowed to vote for governor, and from their number should also be chosen a smaller group of assistants to help the Governor administer all the plantation's affairs. This fundamental concept of a theocracy, or Bible Commonwealth, seemed to them a perfect and sublime plan for the new colony. They were totally unaware of the fact that the plan, combined with their own single-mindedness in its execution, would inevitably produce an arrogance of administration that must foredoom its downfall.

The two or three thousand colonists who by 1633 flocked into the dozen thriving little towns from Hingham to Saugus were by no means all of the same persuasion as their leaders. At the core of each town there was undoubtedly a group representative of the strong religious protest of the Puritan movement. But many of them were university trained, comparatively wealthy middle-class Englishmen, who could afford retinues of servants and fine houses. Some had been well connected with the Puritan Parliament or had been active in London's great mercantile establishments. In 1633 at Somerville Master Craddock had a palisaded corral for his cattle and was operating a shipyard which had turned out a 100-ton vessel. A windmill had been built at Boston, and Roxbury and Saugus already had water-powered gristmills running. A growing fishing industry was being conducted out of Dorchester, Marblehead, Salem and Ipswich. Boston people not only cut firewood and hay and pastured cattle on the harbor islands but were developing "Farms in the Countrey" in Brookline. Charlestown had a "Ferry-boate, to conveigh passengers over Charles River." Cambridge was "paled in with one generall fence, which is about a mile and a halfe long." The peninsula of Nahant was fenced off for pasturage of goats, cattle and swine.

So striking is the contrast between this ambitious economic picture and the poverty-stricken scene in all the previous Massachusetts plantations that one inevitably questions its religious nature. A first clue to such questions appears in the suggestion by John Palfrey and James Truslow Adams that only one in five of these new planters ever qualified for membership in the Puritan churches, despite a claim that such membership was made requisite for voting in the town elections. While this contention has been attacked by Samuel Eliot Morison, it seems likely that some of these householders deliberately chose to live disenfranchised in Massachusetts Bay rather than remain in England. Why did they uproot themselves and migrate to the wilderness of the New World if they were already so comparatively wealthy as to be capable of building substantial homes and business enterprises, and afford servants? If they were not church members, and therefore not accepted by the theocratic leaders of the colony, then surely religious protest was not their primary motive for coming. What did bring them to Massachusetts?

We have already noted in the preceding chapter the numbers of businessmen and tradesmen in England who had joined the Puritan party because of the economic squeeze which deflation and the despotic policies of Charles I had forced upon them. Particularly in the eastern and southeastern counties of England, from which most of the Massachusetts Puritans came, an economic disaster was impending. Already flooded with Dutch and Huguenot exiles from the wars in the Netherlands, these areas were further depressed when Charles I billeted homecoming troops among them and levied forced loans upon the middle class to pay his debts, the penalty for nonpayment being imprisonment. When Charles met the Puritan parliamentary protest by dissolving Parliament, many Puritans chose escape into exile overseas as their only alternative to complete financial ruin. Massachusetts Bay, with all the disadvantages of its Bible Commonwealth character, yet offered one surpassing bait to planters. The Bay Colony gave away land, in unlimited quantities, governed only by one's capacity to make it productive. Freely given to the planter, with no quitrents or strings attached, this offer of free land was the dominant advantage of the Puritan colonies. It produced a flood of immigration, particularly of just that group of industrious middle-class Englishmen who were most hard pressed by the policies of Charles I. By the same token, it introduced into Massachusetts a type of colonist whose skills in business, trade and industry were soon to set Massachusetts apart as an economic society of unusually high caliber. Puritan religious matters were probably secondary with most of them; these could wait for correction. But they promptly grasped with avidity the opportunity for subsistence, free land, and new means of livelihood.

The whole scene during the first ten years in Massachusetts Bay therefore grew into a series of boom towns. New shiploads of emigrants arrived every few weeks, numbering eighteen thousand in ten years. The market for corn, lumber, fish and farm animals grew steadily. In this expanding economy

everyone was busy; everybody prospered. Whoever was industrious might be sure of selling his surplus at a fat profit. It
was a paradise for just such capable merchants, building tradesmen and skilled artisans as already abounded in the colony and
as continued to arrive. Governor Winthrop's own son, John
Winthrop, Jr., a scientist who became a fellow of the Royal
Society, brought his fine library to Massachusetts Bay in 1631
and by 1643 had set up successful salt works in Beverly and
productive ironworks in Quincy and Saugus. Even when the
great Massachusetts migration came to a halt in 1640, because
the Long Parliament of the Puritans seized control of the
English government, the Massachusetts Bay merchants succeeded in reviving their economic boom by finding markets
for their goods in the West Indies, and later in the islands of
the Azores, Madeiras and Canaries. There good Yankee fish,
textiles, barrel staves and lumber could be exchanged for wine,
sugar, molasses and Spanish dollars. Thus was founded the
basis of Massachusetts' thriving maritime trade, by which she
continued to grow rich, prosperous, and even more arrogant
to her neighbors, and to the mother country, with which she
now successfully competed in commerce.

The growth of new towns was phenomenal. The Old
Colony of Plymouth could grow only very slowly, having
reached a total population of only 3,000 by the middle 1640's,
distributed in the new towns of Duxbury, Marshfield, Scituate,
Sandwich, Barnstable, Yarmouth, Eastham, and Taunton. But
Massachusetts Bay by the same period had 20,000 inhabitants,
and had founded Hingham, Hull, Concord, Ipswich, Rowley,
Andover, Reading, Danvers, Wenham, Manchester, Topsfield, Newbury, Woburn, Lynn, Chelsea, Dedham, Sudbury,
Springfield, and Longmeadow. These were in addition to the
original towns of Weymouth, Dorchester, Roxbury, Boston,

Watertown, Cambridge, Charlestown, Medford, Salem and Saugus.

The arrogance of the theocratic government at times contributed to the westward migration of men who disagreed with the rigid religious control of the older towns by the Puritan oligarchy. Many of the frontier towns within the Bay Colony's boundaries conducted their churches and community affairs on a far more liberal and democratic basis than prevailed in the original settlements. This gave rise to liberal movements along the frontiers which subsequently forced liberal changes in the religious and governmental structure of the commonwealth. In addition, certain even more liberal groups either were banished from Massachusetts Bay by edict of the theocracy or chose to leave Massachusetts of their own volition because of impending persecution for their democratic beliefs. Some of these found refuge, either permanently or temporarily, in the far more tolerant Plymouth Colony, or moved on to found new colonies in Rhode Island, Connecticut, or New Hampshire. Rhode Island was thus established by the exiled Roger Williams, who had been the liberal minister of the Salem church. Anne Hutchinson's Antinomians soon followed him there. Many persecuted Quakers subsequently took refuge in Rhode Island after their brutal punishment at the hands of Boston's oligarchy. The Saybrook and Hartford settlements which became the nucleus of Connecticut were founded by dissenters from Massachusetts Bay. Thus, as time went on, the Bay Colony became surrounded, both within and without, by communities of independents who had revolted against the strictures of the Bible Commonwealth leaders.

The year 1650 found Massachusetts Bay far out in front of the other colonies in material prosperity, commerce and political power. She treated her fellow colonies with an overbearing sense of dominance that aroused inevitable jealousy. She acted like an independent state during the era when the indulgent Puritan party of Cromwell in England was little inclined to interfere with its own offspring in colonial New England. Massachusetts set up her own mint in 1652 and converted Spanish dollars into pine-tree shillings. She ran her own foreign affairs with the French settlements in Acadia and Quebec, even taking sides in supporting La Tour in his private war against d'Aunay's trading post at Port Royal. She sent a punitive expedition under John Endecott in 1636 to destroy the villages of the Pequot Indians in eastern Connecticut, leaving matters there in so much worse a state of anarchy that it became necessary in 1637 for the combined colonies to conduct a major expedition to wipe out the Pequots. In 1639 and 1640 her emissaries made preposterous claims against the Plymouth Colony in a boundary dispute, reaching a decision quite unfavorable to Plymouth's towns after a year of haggling. In 1652 an even more arbitrary boundary settlement with New Hampshire produced the annexation by the Bay Colony of the new county of Yorkshire, extending Massachusetts' domain almost to Casco Bay. Experiences of the other colonies in the loose confederation for defense against the Indians from 1643 to 1653 were similarly distasteful, since the theocracy steadily went her own dominating way regardless of majority votes against her in the confederation.

The height of arrogance was reached by the Puritan theocracy in the 1650's in their persecution of the Quakers. The governorship of obstinate old John Endecott and the religious tyranny of the Rev. John Norton, "undeterred by doubt and unrestrained by pity," produced our national symbol for religious persecution. This inquisition outdid in savagery anything that Archbishop Laud had ever perpetrated on the Separatists or Puritans. Four Quakers were executed, three had their ears cut off, forty were whipped, sixty-four imprisoned, forty banished, one branded, and many others received inhuman punishments in the stocks, stripped naked, and subjected to lavish cruelties, while Endecott stood by shouting "I thank God I am not afraid to give judgement." So barbarous did ingenious punishments of the courageous Friends become that even the Puritans' supporters in England cried out in protesting letters to the Bay Colony's leaders. In Massachusetts anyone who criticized was subject to imprisonment.

Such extremes of inhuman barbarity were characteristic of only a few of the Puritan leaders. There were among the Massachusetts Puritans many gentle and devout Christians who deplored the whole Quaker inquisition and did what they could subsequently to atone to the survivors for their sufferings. The twin fellowships of Congregational and Unitarian churches that trace their lineage to Puritanism have become perhaps the more liberal as a result of the outrages committed by their ancestors in the name of religion. Certainly the bigotedness of the leaders of the Bible Commonwealth has discouraged any subsequent purpose to impose a state religion on the American people.

Despite the bigotedness of the administrative and religious leadership, there began to appear certain evidences of political forces that might serve more liberal groups in opposing the theocracy. These mechanisms arose almost inevitably out of the necessities of town government. The theocrats were not themselves numerous enough to supervise all the local problems. As early as 1634 it was conceded that two delegates, or deputies, from each town should sit in a lower house of the General Court, of which the Governor's assistants were to comprise the upper house. Two years later the freemen in town meeting were authorized to elect their own selectmen, and local authorities were soon allowed to control the distribution of lands, roads and schools, and judicial districts were set up to supplement the colony's courts, previously an exclusive function of the assistants. In 1641 a simple code of laws called the "Body of Liberties," compiled by Ipswich's liberal preacher Nathaniel Ward was forced through the General Court. When this was superseded eight years later by a much better compilation of law by the Presbyterian physician Dr. Robert Child, the judicial functions of the assistants, now called magistrates, became definitely limited to a government of laws, not of men. Punishments were no longer completely at the whims of the magistrates. In 1644 the General Court even voted that between sessions the acts of the magistrates must be limited by all previously existing law. Thus, gradually, the towns and their deputies began to assert their power as against the magistracy. However, since the franchise and all otherwise irreconcilable disputes were still referred to a coterie of the clergy for decision, the theocracy still held the whip hand for the first thirty-five years of the history of the colony.

The real ultimate source of democracy in Massachusetts was in the town meeting system. Local affairs necessarily were left by the General Court increasingly to the discretion of the freemen in the towns themselves. What began as informal meetings to settle local quarrels and problems soon crystallized into monthly, and then annual meetings. These town meetings elected "the chosen men," or selectmen, to administer town affairs in the interim between meetings. Soon elected constables, moderators, clerks, fence viewers, surveyors of highways, and tithingmen had to be added to departmentalize the increasingly complex functions of town government. But all these remained under the jealous review of annual town meetings, where the property-holding freemen, or heads of families, wielded their power of discussion and ballot to criticize or replace the existing officials. The town fathers had to present records of their stewardship in "Town Reports." Irregularities were therefore rare and soon corrected. The meetings opened with prayer, and followed an agenda, or "warrant," containing the various items of business, which were discussed and voted on under rules of parliamentary procedure controlled by an elected moderator, with a clerk keeping the records. The town was a miniature republic. The habit of orderly discussion and decision by majority vote which these meetings engendered in the populace spread into all their community activities, even the churches. James Russell Lowell made a pat remark on this subject: "Puritanism, believing itself quick with the seed of religious liberty, laid, without knowing it, the egg of democracy."

This republican habit of procedure, born in the Massachusetts towns, became so clearly the proper way of government to a great mass of the citizenry that it eventually strongly influenced the forms of not only Massachusetts' Constitution of 1780, but even that of the United States. Meanwhile the habit of local government participation bred a population with sufficient political consciousness to exert a strong deterrent to tyranny either by the Governor and his magistrates or by the English crown. Indeed the Committees of Correspondence about which the American Revolutionary organization was built were a close copy of the selectman and town meeting system hewed out in the Massachusetts Bay towns. Here already were the forum mechanism and the participation in popular sovereignty which have steadily produced the opinion groups by which Massachusetts is still ruled.

A further mechanism destined to be an agency for the overthrow of tyranny was the Bay Colony's emphasis on education. The concentration of educated men was probably higher in Massachusetts Bay than in any other unit of England's New World empire. The natural desire of these men to carry on their cultural tradition motivated the founding of Harvard College in 1636. Founded to perpetuate the clergy, this institution subsequently contributed greatly to the education of other community leaders as well. But perhaps even more significant for the seventeeth century was the growth of primary education. Endowed schools were started in Boston in 1636 and in Salem in 1639. The Roxbury Latin School has functioned almost continuously since 1645. But the most striking novelty was the General Court's edict of 1642 placing upon the selectmen of each town the responsibility for training or apprenticing all boys whose parents were unable to provide it, and in 1647 frankly ordering elementary schools to be set up in all towns of fifty householders and a grammar school in all towns of a hundred householders. By 1650 there were publicly supported grammar schools, preparing for college, in Boston, Charlestown, Salem, Dorchester, Cambridge, Roxbury, Braintree and Dedham. This was the first time anywhere in the world that public education of *all* boys at public expense had ever been instituted by any government. The simple faith in general education which has become so dominant a part of the American way of life was born in Massachusetts Bay under the shadow of the very bigotry and intolerance which it was best designed to overthrow. This is the best existing testimony to the strength of the liberal and democratic reaction that even then was quietly developing in the Massachusetts Bay towns.

CHAPTER SIX

The Yeomanry and the Gentry

If Massachusetts Bay were to throw off the yoke of Calvinist absolutism inherent in the fantastic marriage of its trading company charter to its Bible Commonwealth leadership, it must do so either by revolutionary social changes within its society or by pressures from mother England. As matters turned out, both methods were joined to bring about the downfall of the theocracy.

Massachusetts Puritanism was an amalgam of two separate phases of the English religious Reformation. Plymouth represented a sample of rather simple English yeomen who started as Separatists from the Anglican Church and then were exposed in the Netherlands to Congregational influences allowing considerable individualism of belief, roughly approximating Martin Luther's "priesthood of all believers." There was tolerance and kindliness among these people, exemplified by their democratic church organization and their emphasis on the New Testament rather than the Old. As we have already seen, they were willing to accept in their "Mayflower Compact" a limited consent of the governed as the basis of governmental authority. The town meeting was an outgrowth of this Plymouth viewpoint toward popular sovereignty. These developments were radical departures from the feudal attitudes still prevailing in the monarchies of Europe.

Massachusetts Bay, on the contrary, represented a slice of English gentry, brought up in the tradition of class distinction, in a period when the middle class of English business was involved in a struggle for power with the feudal nobility who had always previously controlled England. They believed in divine right, both of the King and of the Anglican Church, and while they had now rejected the absolutism of the bishops they had substituted, at least for the moment, absolutism of the clergy of the Massachusetts Bay churches. They were willing to live under the rigid, intolerant Calvinism of the theocracy with its Old Testament emphasis on sin and damnation, which allowed the individual no freedom of interpretation. The only human rights they openly defended were property rights. It seems particularly curious that they could combine the religious principles of an Oriental despotism with their Cromwellian struggles for liberalism in politics. Vernon Parrington approvingly quotes, to this point, Harriet Beecher Stowe's remark that they got their theology from the sixteenth century and their politics from the seventeenth.

It should by now be obvious that between the liberal yeomanry of Plymouth and the Massachusetts Bay frontier towns and the Puritan theocracy of the Boston Bay settlements a fundamental struggle was developing on political battlefields in town meetings and the lower house of the General Court, which must determine the eventual character of Massachusetts. It also seems apparent that the outcome of this battle must be strongly influenced by the shifting attitudes of the prosperous gentry whose growing mercantile enterprises increasingly made them sensitive to governmental control of their business interests. As new American-born generations replaced the original English immigrants, many of these men became more Yankee than Puritan. Likewise, it was now possible for Yankee yeomen, by thrift and vigorous enterprise, to become Yankee gentry in this land of opportunity, thanks to free land, free education, and hard work. Indentured servants could become property owners and by that token freemen, voters, even selectmen or deputies. The melting pot was beginning to simmer. More and more, businessmen would hold the balance of power between liberalism and tyranny.

There exists no more potent stimulus to social leveling than warfare. Massachusetts was now about to undergo her first trial at arms. It, too, played its part in the battle for popular sovereignty.

Massasoit's death in 1661 created a new situation in Indian relations. Until then the old chief had held faithfully to his treaty with the English. Under his heir, Alexander, uneasiness grew on both sides. There was widespread misunderstanding among the Indians over their rights to hunt on lands they had sold. Game disappeared as plantations grew. Unruly frontiersmen cheated Indians and haled them into court for minor offenses. Plymouth's governors grew jittery and demanded that Indians deposit their arms at Plymouth as token of good faith. After Alexander died on the way home from one of many summonses to Plymouth, his brother Philip succeeded to the leadership of a tribe that was already assembling arms for what seemed to be an inevitable clash. When in 1675 John Sassamon, a Christian Indian who had served as Philip's secretary, was murdered after revealing Philip's warlike plans to Governor Josiah Winslow at Plymouth, Winslow executed three of Philip's council thought to be his murderers. This precipitated war.

Fighting broke out at Swansea in June. Philip's headquarters on the west side of the Taunton River mouth was cushioned by friendly Rhode Island, not included in the New England Confederation's defensive alliance because Massachusetts Bay refused to deal with heretics. But to the north and east he was hemmed in by growing settlements. The war began with desultory house burnings in Swansea and Dartmouth. Philip actually warned some of his English neighbors in Swansea in time for them to seek safety in Rhode Island. At the end of June about five hundred men, mobilized at Attleboro by Boston and at Bridgewater and Taunton by Plymouth, attempted to attack Philip on the Mount Hope peninsula. He eluded them by moving his forces across the river east of Fall River. They wasted two weeks trying to make peace with the Narragansetts of Rhode Island, but the latter simply abandoned their villages and retired into the wilderness. Meanwhile Philip burned Middleboro and Dartmouth, made a lightning raid on Taunton, and then recrossed the Taunton River before the English could trap him on the Assonet peninsula.

Philip now moved north into central Massachusetts, joining forces with the Nipmuck tribe, who promptly burned Brookfield. The English added the Connecticut valley Pocumtucks to Philip's allies by attacking their village near Northampton. The result was that Northfield and Deerfield had to be abandoned, and were burned. Almost a hundred militia, including half the male population of Deerfield and fifty "flower of Essex" troopers from Cape Ann, were killed in the ambush of two supply trains withdrawing from Northfield and Deerfield. Indians burned the outlying farms, dwellings and gristmills of Northampton and Hatfield. Springfield lost 32 houses and 25 barns in a single October raid. When Connecticut troops were forced to retire southward to defend Glastonbury and Suffield, remaining Massachusetts militia in the Connecticut valley were sufficient only to defend the strongest palisaded garrisons but totally unable to keep offensive companies in the field. Meanwhile innumerable conflagrations consumed the valley farms, and even scouting parties were repeatedly ambushed and massacred. The year 1675 was a black one in Massachusetts history.

In December fresh levies of troops from Cambridge, Watertown, Roxbury, Dorchester and Weymouth joined new men from the Plymouth towns and three hundred from Connecticut for a massive attack on the great Narragansett winter village in a swamp near Kingston, Rhode Island. Fifteen hundred colonial troops attacked in waves a stockaded redoubt reinforced by hedges and ramparts, with blockhouses flanking the approaches with cross fire. Initially repulsed with heavy losses, the English finally breached the ramparts and poured in to butcher hundreds of Indians, men, women and children. Approximately 75 English were killed and about 150 wounded were brought out in a snowstorm to Wickford. The Narragansett power was hurt, but not wholly broken. The colonial force spent the month of January seizing and burning Narragansett supplies throughout Rhode Island, while the remnants of the Indians fled to join Philip at his Quebaug village near Brookfield. In February Indians attacked in turn Sudbury, Lancaster, Concord, Medfield and Weymouth. Fifty of the Lancaster garrison were killed or taken prisoner, among the latter the minister's wife, Mrs. Rowlandson, whose diary became one of the great source books of the war. There were 18 killed at Medfield, and 50 houses burned. After Major Savage's militia destroyed Philip's Quebaug village in March, the escaping Indians attacked and burned the town of Groton, which then had to be abandoned. March also saw Chelmsford, Marlboro, Rehoboth, Providence, and even a part of Plymouth attacked and burned. Ambushes continued, 6 thus losing their lives in Longmeadow, and 42 in Seekonk. In April Bridgewater, Billerica, Chelmsford, Marlboro, Weymouth, Hingham, Wrentham and Sudbury were attacked, 35 being killed at Sudbury. Haverhill, Rowley, Bridgewater, Halifax,

Middleboro and Scituate suffered attacks and burnings in May.

But Philip's campaigns were on the wane. Guerilla warfare could be continued only as long as the Indians could live on captured supplies, and these were giving out. The Narragansett sachem Canonchet was captured in April. Captain Turner's bloody attack on the Indian headquarters village at Turner's Falls killed over a hundred natives in May, and a few weeks later Philip's forces were quickly repulsed at Hatfield and Hadley. Desertions began to reduce his might. When in desperation he started back into his own Taunton River country in July, the colonial troops kept tight garrisons at all the fording places, and gradually hemmed him in. The old Plymouth Indian fighter Captain Benjamin Church finally got him surrounded, and he was shot by one of Church's friendly Indian scouts on August 12. Philip's head decorated a pole in the old town of Plymouth for a quarter century thereafter, demonstrating to all who passed how Plymouth treated an enemy.

The grisly business of mopping up proceeded. Indian captives were either executed or sold into West Indies slavery. Exiles wandered into New York or Canada. A very few made their peace and settled down wretchedly among the victors. Never again were native Indians a significant factor in the colonial life of Massachusetts; not even in the French and Indian Wars did they go on the warpath. As a component of the Massachusetts population their descendants lost the integrity of survival as a separate people and intermarried or died out. It was the extinction of a race.

Massachusetts lost at least 600 fighting men, 600 dwellings, and 50 towns in the struggle. The frontier was set back ten years or more. Plymouth Colony alone spent £100,000 in the war, an enormous sum for those days. But there were also gains in King Philip's War. No longer was there a barrier of fear on the frontier. Men of all classes had learned discipline and community feeling under suffering for a common cause. Some of the cockiness was thrashed out of Massachusetts Bay. She learned, at horrible cost, some of the errors of military unpreparedness. She learned, through many episodes, how dependent she could be on her sister colony of Connecticut. And finally, in the vicissitudes of field service, her gentry and her yeomanry learned something of the mutual respect that campaigns and campfires always produce in men of good will. Boston and Cambridge men always have something to learn from the men of Taunton and Brookfield and Northampton.

King Philip's War was only one illustration of the revolutionary social changes occuring within Massachusetts that were beginning to undermine the power of the theocracy. Warfare in the field is a great leveler, but the controversies of the market place are even more so, if, as in Massachusetts, equality of economic opportunity breeds a conviction that government should be by consent of the governed. Among second- and third-generation Yankee gentry a new ferment was stirring. Advances in standards of living had produced a new class of "moderates," men of wealth in business and commerce, outside the ruling oligarchy, but men of substance because of their business standing. In local issues these moderates were often opposed by the yeomanry and the frontiersmen. But in any contest with England, the moderate gentry held a balance of power, as against the theocrats, which might place them in a position to take over leadership of the Bay Colony and displace the religious zealots whenever any profound upheaval occurred. Such a crisis was now in the making.

Among prominent merchants in England there existed a "mercantile theory" for the newly expanding Empire. By this theory the colonies were to send raw materials to the mother country, which would manufacture them and export the finished products to the Continent of Europe or back to the colonies. According to Navigation Laws passed between 1650 and 1663, all this trade was to be conducted in British or colonial vessels and all cargoes from Europe to the colonies must be landed in an English port en route. The principal purpose of these laws was to forestall such nations as the Netherlands from competing in this lucrative commerce. For Virginia the system worked very well, because its staple crop, tobacco, fitted perfectly into the theory. But Massachusetts produced no staple crop that England wanted. Continental Europe was the best market for New England's fish, ship timber and spars, pork, corn, wool and iron, and the West Indies colonies of nations other than England greedily bought Yankee horses, dairy products, flour, oatmeal, peas and biscuit. Likewise returning Massachusetts vessels found in Boston itself a ready market for Continental Europe's wines and brandies, fruits, oils, silks, laces and linens, the Dry Tortugas' salt, and the West Indies' sugar, molasses, indigo, cotton, logwood and silver. In Massachusetts, indeed, the Mercantile Theory worked in reverse, for very soon New England small industry began to produce textiles and iron hardware which competed with English industry in the same markets. For twenty years the Navigation Laws were not enforced, and hundreds of small Massachusetts vessels made fortunes for their owners carrying Yankee goods to Virginia and the islands, tobacco to Continental Europe, and European products back to Boston.

By 1675 increasing outcries from English merchants at this illegal Yankee commerce induced Charles II to establish the Lords of Trade to regulate the problem. Edward Randolph, sent several times to Boston to secure enforcement of the Navigation Acts, reported to the King that Massachusetts' Governor Leverett had insisted the laws of Parliament did not apply to Massachusetts! The General Court concurred by repeated delays in taking action on the matter. When Randolph was made collector of customs for the port of Boston in 1679, the Governor's collusion with local merchants steadily nullified Randolph's attempts to enforce the laws. Taken in conjunction with many other evidences of Massachusetts' disobedience to royal and parliamentary criticism in matters of religious intolerance, failure to allow appeals to English courts or even to recognize the jurisdiction of King and Parliament over the colony, the result was inevitable.

In 1684 King Charles abrogated the colony's charter and arranged for a royal governor to take over control of Massachusetts Bay. So at last the whole rickety structure of the theocracy, governor and General Court, came tumbling down.

Joseph Dudley, son of an earlier Bay governor but himself a moderate, was made interim "president," with an appointed council of moderates to govern until a new frame of dominion government for New England should be worked out. His brief period of crown colony government of Massachusetts was a progressive one, although he was cordially hated by the theocrats for accepting the royal appointment. Associations of merchants were formed who worked out compromises that strongly stimulated colonial commerce, and under his regime such great land companies as the Atherton Company and the Million Purchase Company promoted resettlement of frontier towns. Had Dudley's administration been allowed to continue, an even better demonstration of the moderates' capacity for wise leadership and liberal evolution of the colony's economic and social affairs would have resulted. But the Lords of Trade were not satisfied.

After the death of King Charles, Sir Edmund Andros was appointed governor of a newly organized Dominion of New

England, which included, through forfeiture of the Connecticut and Rhode Island charter, all of New England and New
York also, of which he was already governor. His appointed
council of twenty-eight men was made up of well-chosen
influential men of all these colonies, mostly of the moderate
group. Unfortunately Andros, a blunt and officious soldier,
with no understanding of the colonial mind, alienated everybody. Only in military affairs was he successful. But in
domestic matters he made mistake after mistake. He reduced
the ownership of land to anarchy by a legalistic insistence on
rewriting all deeds to include the royal seal, charging a quit-
rent in cash sufficient in the case of large undeveloped frontier
tracts to demand a quarter of their value. This, in an area
where barter of farm products was the usual legal tender (a
couple of sheep was good for a year's tuition at Harvard),
placed an impossible burden on much of the population. He
decreed that dissenters from the Puritan church need no
longer contribute to the maintenance of the minister, not perhaps realizing that this diminished support to schools and
Harvard College. Most Puritans refused jury service rather
than follow his decree that they must kiss the Bible before
being sworn in. He permitted festivities on Saturday night,
which was a part of the Puritan Sabbath, and insisted on the
celebration of Christmas, likewise anathema to the Puritans.
Probably his most resounding blunder was to force his way
into Boston's Old South Church to attend Anglican services
while the Puritans waited outside for the hated English service
to be done with before they could hold their own. But he
really brought about his own downfall when he responded to
a public clamor against taxation without representation by
issuing a Local Government Act abolishing all town meetings
except for annual election of town officers!

The impossible situation resolved itself when the news

arrived in Boston of the Revolution of 1689 in England. Representatives of all the disgruntled groups in Massachusetts were already in London petitioning for a change of administration. In Boston armed bands made prisoners of the King's officers, set up a provisional rebel government consisting of some members of the old General Court, and formed a Committee of Safety. Andros and his officers were held as prisoners for several months until the new King William recognized the rebellion as a friendly gesture toward the new dynasty and requested that Andros and his associates be returned to England.

Massachusetts never returned to the theocratic system. The political power of the Puritan church leaders and the religious qualifications for voting were essentially broken. The bases of the English common law were recognized. The moderate group, long the chief economic support of the colony, secured the share in government which they deserved. From here on Massachusetts' stubborn insistence on government by representative assemblies made its mark on many other colonies, whose charters were amended to obtain this privilege after 1689. Henceforth a measure of local autonomy became a recognized pattern in the English colonial system, matching the autonomy of Parliament at home. While this local autonomy was balanced by the royal appointment of colonial governors, the colonial assemblies retained the power to control the Governor's salary and by this device usually succeeded in preventing arbitrary or oppressive conduct by a governor. The yeomanry and the gentry, by their combined efforts, had struck the first blow for freedom.

CHAPTER SEVEN

Expansion and the Canadian Wars

With the exception of the brief campaigns of the Pequot and King Philip's Wars, Massachusetts had had the good fortune to grow up during sixty years of peace. Yeomen and gentry had been able to apply themselves uninterruptedly to their internal problems of politics, religion and commerce without much concern for the rest of the world. The revocation of the charter and the Andros rebellion had indeed brought them to grips with England, but the substance of these controversies was still centered in the domestic social and economic revolution going on within Massachusetts Bay. Even the three years of interregnum after the accession of King William, during which a new charter was being hammered out in England, must have seemed to the colonists themselves largely a continuation of the profound internal struggle between the old theocracy and the new business class.

A dramatic example of this continued concern with largely outworn domestic problems occurred in 1692. Quarrels between his parishioners and the Rev. Samuel Parris, new minister in Salem Village, now Danvers, became focused on the behavior of certain adolescent girls who had been meeting at his house. There they had become fascinated with slave Indian John, and especially with his half-breed wife, Tituba, who delighted in performing various West Indies tricks of necromancy, contortions and convulsions. The children soon learned to imitate these stunts for the edification and horror of their parents. Learned divines, including the Rev. Cotton Mather, were called in, and became convinced the children were possessed by the devil. In the absence of regular courts, the new charter being then under negotiation in England, special courts of oyer and terminer were set up for witchcraft trials of the children and some of their neighbors. The judges, including William Stoughton, lieutenant governor of the colony, acted themselves as prosecuting attorneys, allowed the accused no counsel, proceeded to fill the jails with suspected witches, and actually convicted and hanged twenty citizens of the neighborhood as witches. Since criticism of the procedure came to be represented as possible evidence of guilt, few dared to protest. Many people believed in witches, and the public hysteria assumed such feverish proportions that certain industrious citizens, including the Rev. Parris, assiduously hunted their communities for clues to incriminate new victims. A few courageous men, like Nathaniel Saltonstall, Robert Calef, and the ministers of Andover, Francis Dane and Thomas Barnard, boldly protested the disgraceful methods by which the testimony and convictions were obtained. Governor William Phips, who had been away on colony business, promptly disbanded the witchcraft courts on his return, releasing the 150 accused still awaiting trial. But this did not prevent the wanton execution of twenty poor neurotic victims of a public mania that remains alongside the Quaker persecutions as an ineradicable judgment on the excesses of Massachusetts Puritanism. Twenty years later the Commonwealth made restitution to those accused who were still living, and to the heirs of those executed, in the amount of £578.

Perhaps this final insanity of the theocrats was a dying

convulsion. Certainly the inbred thinking of most people was changing, whether of its own initiative or by the inevitable pressure of events. Massachusetts had spent too long in self-centered arrogance. External affairs were moving on in ways that cried for resolute colonial action. Massachusetts herself was increasing in population, and this increase was bringing about some of the outward-looking problems that must concern her in the second sixty years of her growth. Even Governor Andros, in 1688, had had to put down Indian rebellion among the Abenaki in Maine. In 1689 Dover, New Hampshire, was sacked, Pemaquid abandoned to the natives, and the frontier settlements withdrawn to Portland. In the next year Frontenac's terrible massacre of the colonial outpost at Schenectady and a French assault on Falmouth, Maine, made it quite clear that the French were bent on widespread envelopment of the northern English colonies. French privateers were even capturing Boston shipping in New England waters.

To meet these threats the first intercolonial congress to include colonies outside New England met at Albany and agreed to attack Montreal and Quebec by the twin routes of Lake Champlain and the outer St. Lawrence. The Lake Champlain attack failed for lack of supplies and Iroquois support. Massachusetts' Sir William Phips captured Port Royal in Nova Scotia but promptly lost it again by providing an insufficient garrison to hold it. His naval force subsequently bombarded Quebec for a week without making a successful landing. A second Boston expedition against Port Royal was captured by Villebon, leaving all the Bay of Fundy in the hands of the French. Bloody Indian raids continued on Massachusetts outposts at York and Wells, and even as far south as Haverhill on the Merrimack, until the Peace of Ryswick in 1697 temporarily stopped the fighting. Massachusetts went heavily in debt to support her part in these fruitless campaigns. She tried to rebuild burned forts and replenish garrisons along her ravaged frontiers during a period when her government was weakened by corrosive bickering for control of the purse strings between successive royal governors and her General Court. Meanwhile Nova Scotia-based French privateers reduced her fishing and trading fleet. It was only too obvious that Canadian wars would shortly be resumed and that the French, claiming most of Maine and given Nova Scotia by the Ryswick treaty, would soon again be hemming in the only territories into which the expanding economy of Massachusetts could grow. This was no time for witchcraft trials.

The opening of Queen Anne's War in 1703 was coincident with the arrival in Boston of Governor Joseph Dudley, who had in 1686 been interim "president" before the Andros regime. He proved to be the first efficient executive to take charge of the colony in ten years, which was fortunate, since events demanded a strong war governor. For in 1703 war parties of the Abenaki, organized by Canada's aggressive new governor, Vaudreuil, slaughtered no less than 300 English on the Maine frontiers. In February, 1704, a war party of French and Indians made a surprise assault on Deerfield, massacred 50 inhabitants, and marched more than 100 of its remaining survivors through 200 miles of winter snows to Canadian imprisonment. New England rose to this butchery, and under Governor Dudley's leadership all the colonies co-operated in rebuilding forts at Saco and Casco, sending snowshoe parties attacking the Indian villages, and supplying convoys against privateers that had appeared even in Connecticut waters. For four years matters remained stalemated, but in 1708, when 35 New England vessels were captured by the French and 473 Yankee prisoners were taken to Port Royal, the General Court began to draft soldiers and impress sailors for an expedition against Port Royal. In 1610, supported by English frigates, this army of 1,400 Massachusetts men, aboard 30 transports, bombarded the town and secured its surrender. The place was renamed Annapolis and has remained under the British flag ever after. For Massachusetts this victory not only removed French pressure on her territory of Maine but in large measure restored her ocean commerce and fisheries, which had been badly hurt by French piracy for nearly twenty years. The fact that a grandiose English naval expedition of 12,000 British troops aboard more than 70 ships, provisioned at Boston, failed in 1711 even to penetrate the St. Lawrence on a projected assault on Quebec, because of the incompetence of its leadership, could not destroy the glory of the Massachusetts achievement at Port Royal. For Acadia and Newfoundland remained in British hands in the 1713 peace treaty of Utrecht, even though France was crafty enough to retain Cape Breton, on which she subsequently developed her Louisbourg naval base. Massachusetts' provisioning of the ill-fated British Quebec expedition cost her £40,000, half again the amount of her annual budget at that time. But no longer could the French stop Yankee expansion and Boston's trade up the Bay of Fundy. Vaudreuil and his able Jesuit lieutenant Father Ralé continued to incite the Abenaki to attack English trading posts and settlements in the 1720's, but a surprise English attack on Norridgewock, in which Father Ralé was killed, and Captain Lovewell's raids on the Pigwackets of New Hampshire eventually wiped out Indian resistance, and the power of the French to control them.

The disappearance of French ability to harm New England produced rapid resettlement and expansion of all the frontiers. Before 1692 few towns in central and western Massachusetts existed other than those already mentioned in connection with King Philip's War. Most of these were reoccupied after that war. But the Deerfield experience hardly encouraged new pioneers until Queen Anne's War was over. By 1715 Leicester, Oxford, Rutland and Sutton had been laid out in what was to become Worcester County, and Northfield and Sunderland in Franklin County. During the same period (1692–1715) seventeen new towns were established in the eastern counties. But between 1715 and 1742, in years of peace, the western settlements grew rapidly. Worcester County added fifteen new towns: Sturbridge, Shrewsbury, Grafton, Hardwick, Lunenburg, Southborough, Westborough, Uxbridge, Upton, Bolton, Leominster, Holden, Harvard, Warren and Dudley. The modern Hampden County gained two towns: Brimfield and Blandford, thus with Springfield and Westfield totaling four. Berkshire County established its beginnings at Sheffield and Stockbridge. During the same period the eastern counties added twenty-five new communities, all separated from previously existing towns. Of these Barnstable County gained Provincetown; Bristol added Raynham, Easton and Berkeley; Plymouth acquired Kingston, Hanover, Halifax and Wareham; Middlesex added Acton, Bedford, Holliston, Stoneham, Tewksbury, Townsend, Waltham, Westford and Wilmington; Essex gained Methuen and Middleton; and Norfolk acquired Bellingham, Stoughton and Walpole. Chelsea was separated from Boston.

The impetus of the Anglo-French struggle for the control of North America was just as vigorous during the years of peace as during the recurrent wars. This expansion of the English inexorably outward from their commercial centers was of more lasting significance for their eventual victory than the military campaigns, violent as they were. A unified military command under brilliant leaders often made the French more effective in war than the English, at least on land, but nowhere had France concentrated any such commercial and industrial base for operations as had the English in New England. The French colonists never had got their economic roots deep enough into American soil to be ineradicable. The devious harassing tactics of the French, nipping at the flanks of New England, hitting and running, had driven the English back repeatedly, but the French never could follow these up by major assaults in force at the center. Only such major assaults could really determine the issue, and for these the steady growth of population and commercial prosperity in Massachusetts and New York and Pennsylvania began to place the balance of power in English hands. Thirty years of peace that now followed Queen Anne's War were sufficient to build an economy capable of generating a sustained and final drive on Canada.

The establishment of fifty new Massachusetts towns was therefore not just a statistic. It meant new sawmills, gristmills and iron forges set up on innumerable new millponds, providing the lumber, the cornmeal, and the hardware necessary to build farmhouses, stock crossroads stores, and send a surplus for export to busy harbors in exchange for European goods. Every new farm meant an added center of production, not only of corn and pork but also of countless domestic industries. Every house was cluttered with tools by which Yankee industry turned the long winter into productive effort. There were shoemaker's tools, branding irons, mortars and pestles, candle molds, harness, cider presses, butter churns, carpentry and blacksmith outfits, looms, spinning wheels, axes and adzes, hayrakes, plows and harrows, fishing tackle, grindstones, flails, reaping hooks, wheat sieves, ox yokes, shovels and scythes. The strange combination of woodcraft, agriculture, seamanship, industry and commerce on which Massachusetts' prosperity grew led men to become Jacks-of-all-trades. This is still a Yankee characteristic. For centuries now Yankees have been able to apply their hands by turns to the varied techniques of

fishing, farming, carpentering and boatbuilding. This constituted a striking change from the guild and apprentice system of the English, which tied a man to his craft for life, with no hope of transfer. This American social revolution freed men from the economic group into which they were born, and produced a fluid society. With ability a man could strike out into a new career. Whether Puritan or liberal, yeoman or gentry, the Yankee was above all industrious to begin with, and urged on to more stubborn industry by a climate so rigorous that it punished him with frozen fingers if he didn't provide himself with those creature comforts of which he was capable. The whip of necessity was always over his back. It produced a breed of men singularly ambitious for advancing their lot, by the use of brawn, wit and resourcefulness. What brawn would not produce, trade and inventiveness could.

The result was that in most towns homespun and buckskin began to be supplemented with imports of Holland lawn, Osnaburg linen and Spanish poplin. Clapboarded salt-box houses replaced the thatched plank structures of the pioneers. Plaster, or even imported wallpapers, took the place of simple paneling, and local carpenters grew skillful in supplying carved trim, cornices, stair rails and newel posts. Endless varieties of mantels, corner cupboards and beamed ceilings graced the interiors. The wealthy began to import mahogany furniture, silver plate, copper and china. Those moderately affluent had delftware and a few silver spoons and porringers. Only the poor still got along with pewter, earthenware and wooden dishes. There were almost no desperately poor, unless they were lazy. The old Puritan distaste for such frippery as necklaces, sunbonnets and parasols was beginning to disappear.

Winthrop, Dudley and Saltonstall had probably visualized a Massachusetts set up on the English model of large estates farmed by tenants and hired labor. To their surprise, the New England towns, based on freehold and free labor, appeared instead. The depression of 1640, which forced Massachusetts to find overseas markets for its goods, had firmly established fishing, shipbuilding and overseas commerce as the basis of the otherwise agricultural economy. By 1750 almost every small harbor from Newbury to Taunton had an active shipyard and was sending sloops, lateen-rigged ketches and schooners to Nova Scotia, the West Indies, and Europe. Ironworks in Pembroke and Hanover were already supplying ship fittings to yards on the North River that built vessels up to 400 tons. Ropewalks, sail lofts, cooperages and ship chandleries thrived around all the larger harbors, and in Newburyport, Salem, Boston and Plymouth countinghouses began to be necessary for the exchanges of domestic and foreign commerce handled by merchants who were beginning to prosper and found family dynasties. Massachusetts was beginning to become a teeming school of occupational training in all the arts of shipping and commerce, marine insurance, banking and investment. Men could start as ship carpenters, become shipowners, sea captains, and even merchant princes, all in one lifetime in one small town.

The same thing occurred in early Massachusetts industries. A classical instance can be cited in the ancestral family of Abraham Lincoln. Mordecai Lincoln, the great-great-great-grandfather of the Civil War President, was a son of an indentured servant. Born in Hingham in 1657, he was apprenticed to a blacksmith. In 1691 he bought for the modern equivalent of about $35 a half interest in a waterfall site on Bound Brook in Cohasset, on the boundary between Massachusetts Bay and the Old Colony of Plymouth. Here he built a sawmill. Not content with this, he dammed the same brook twice more, upstream, and built first a gristmill and later a forge with a triphammer. He hammered out ironware on

Monday and Tuesday, ground corn on Wednesday and Thursday, and on Friday and Saturday sawed boards, using the same water over again three times each week. When he died he left an estate of £3,099, which meant that he was a wealthy man in those times. Yet he was the son of an indentured servant.

This sort of fluidity of economic opportunity was producing a new form of class society. For, while poor men by their own thrift and industry were able to become pillars of their towns, some of them were also establishing for their families dynasties of wealth that propagated their estates into business empires. This process, dependent on commerce, segregated itself in the larger seaports. Especially Boston, the largest town in the American colonies at this period, had become the trading capital of America by its control of the largest network of packet and intercolonial shipping through which foreign goods could be distributed along the eastern seaboard. The Yankee farmer prospered, together with the merchant, because his barreled beef and pork, bowls, buckets, brooms, oxbows, ax handles, hewn lumber and barrel staves accompanied Cape Ann and Cape Cod fish to foreign markets. But the merchant had the advantage of extending his interests to continually new ports, entering the slave trade from Guinea, the West Indian molasses trade out of which Massachusetts built sixty-three full-time rum distilleries, the Honduran mahogany trade, and privateering enterprises.

By 1730 Boston had built its lighthouse on the Greater Brewster and its 2,000-foot Long Wharf extending from State Street to deep water. Boston-owned Nantucket whalers were active off Brazil and in the Arctic. Its population of 17,000 now included French, German, Dutch, Scottish and Irish, some of whom themselves set up merchant families: Faneuils, Delanos, Crowninshields, Wendells and Magees. Along with Salem Derbys and Ropes and Marblehead Lees and Hoopers, these wealthy merchants became a vital influence on Massachusetts politics and social life. They built the mansion houses of Ipswich, Beverly and Salem. They owned the trading companies, the ships, the fishing vessels, and often the banks, insurance companies and land companies. By a single remark they could swing town meetings. Their counsels were often decisive in legislative matters. They set standards of elegance and the social graces. From having been a "moderate" opposition in 1690, they were a ruling class by 1740.

Thus in half a century Massachusetts had overthrown a religious oligarchy and had in turn enthroned an aristocracy of wealth. In this process the general population had not been depressed, but had also greatly improved its condition. The prosperity was general. Freedom of opportunity was still the ruling passion. But there were beginning to be sources of discontent between the small pioneers of the frontier and the merchants of the coastal towns. The time would come when these differences, and those also between the journeymen workers of the seaports and their employers, would produce violent explosions. But for the moment all participated in the general prosperity.

It was against this vastly expanded background of commercial progress and extension of Massachusetts population that war clouds portending a resumption of the struggle for Canada began to appear in the 1740's. The renewed outbreak of war in Europe was followed by French capture of the English fishing settlement at Canso in northern Nova Scotia. Boston reinforcements foiled Duvivier's attack on Annapolis, but that attack made Massachusetts Bay flame with ambition to take Louisbourg from the French. An expedition of 4,000 colonial militia landed from 96 vessels at Freshwater Cove below Louisbourg in April, 1745, under command of William Pepperrell, a Maine trader. With improvised equipment he got his artillery ashore, laid effective siege to the fortress, and with the help of a British naval squadron pounded the town for six weeks before Duchambon was forced to surrender. New England's joy knew no bounds. It was the first demonstration of her capacity to mount a major military campaign with her own resources. France sent two fleets in 1746 and 1747 to recover Louisbourg, but each came to disaster through storm and through defeat by British Admirals Anson and Warren in European waters. Failure of naval support stymied a Massachusetts project for another expedition against Quebec. But what French fleets could not accomplish, diplomacy achieved: the Treaty of Aix-la-Chapelle in 1748 returned Louisbourg to France, in exchange for Belgium. Massachusetts never entirely overcame her resentment against the mother country for this deal, which coolly canceled out the most glorious military contribution New England had ever made to the Empire. Men from towns like Hingham never forgot their sufferings in hauling cannon, 200 men to a gun, under fire, to place them in position before the walls of Louisbourg.

England, however, had merely declared another truce. She reimbursed Massachusetts £183,649 for the expenses of the Louisbourg expedition and forthwith began at Halifax to build a great new naval base from which Governor Edward Cornwallis vigorously enforced firm control over the French Acadian population of Nova Scotia, which culminated in their tragic expulsion in 1755. England's policy was becoming more aggressive in America following Anson and Warren's destruction of the core of the French fleet, and it was becoming obvious that she must use her newly won command of the seas to check the French advances in the Ohio valley, now grown too extensive for colonial militia to handle alone. The next war must be for keeps, and would require the full force of British regulars and navy, using the American colonies primarily for supply bases. In the new Seven Years' War thousands of colonial militia participated in the great campaigns of the Lake Champlain and Ohio valleys, but they were no longer the prime movers. The major forces of both home countries made the decisions and did most of the fighting.

In America the war really opened in 1754, two years before it was declared, with George Washington's Ft. Duquesne expedition of the Virginia militia. Braddock's defeat there in 1755 was followed by Sir William Johnson's success in stopping Dieskau's southward penetration at Lake George. But between 1756 and 1758 Montcalm defeated English colonial forces in turn at Oswego, Fort William Henry and Ticonderoga and it seemed as though the French were on the march to cut the colonies in two.

With William Pitt in Britain's War Office, however, the picture began to change. In 1758 Jeffrey Amherst and James Wolfe's 20,000 men recaptured Louisbourg, with Admiral Boscawen's squadron assisting, and Bradstreet cut Quebec's communications with the west by capturing Fort Frontenac on Lake Ontario. In the fall Forbes' capture of Fort Duquesne brought the entire Ohio country into British hands. Matters were now prepared for an assault on the Quebec bastion. In 1759 Admiral Saunders brought his enormous fleet of 250 vessels carrying 30,000 men. General Wolfe's two months of bombardment and maneuver finally culminated in the successful landing of 5,000 men at the Foulon Cove and an all-out battle on the Plains of Abraham that resulted in the slaughter of 4,000 French and the mortal wounding of both generals, Wolfe and Montcalm. The English colors that rose that night over the citadel of Quebec have stayed there ever since.

In the summer of 1760 General Lévis and Governor Vaudreuil were gradually hemmed in at Montreal by the remorseless advance of British forces simultaneously approaching from Quebec, Lake Champlain and Lake Ontario, and French Canada fell to the British.

In all these campaigns Massachusetts men took part. But it was British sea power and British regulars that won the battles. The planning and strategy were those of William Pitt, Jeffrey Amherst, Boscawen, Wolfe, and Saunders. Only when these elements were added to the sick spectacle of losses by colonial militia in the first three years of the war did the tide turn. Yet one should not belittle the colonial contribution because of that. Massachusetts spent the enormous sum of £1,039,390 on the prosecution of the war. During 1758 she had 6,925 men in the field in addition to many on ships and performing other supply functions. A single town, in this instance Abington, had militiamen fighting in Nova Scotia, Lake Champlain, Lake Ontario and at Quebec. At the end of the war sixty Abington veterans petitioned for a land grant in Maine as a reward for war service.

From Georgia to Hudson's Bay the continent was now an English domain.

CHAPTER EIGHT

Prologue to Revolution

In Massachusetts rebellion against established authority was no new principle. Both Plymouth and Massachusetts Bay were settled by protesting minorities. The Bay Colony was no more than eleven years old before it fought for, and won, a "Body of Liberties" from its own governor and magistrates. For thirty years after 1660 Massachusetts chose to ignore English Navigation Acts, therefore lost its charter in 1684, and still was in 1689 so stubborn in civil disobedience as to hold its royal governor, Andros, a prisoner for several months. The American Revolution in Massachusetts was in one sense only a culmination of a century of grievances similar to those which had produced the Andros rebellion. This time, however, these grievances were ably cultivated by a few zealous colonial leaders and strongly abetted by the stupidity of an incompetent British ministry. The Revolution was certainly no sudden creation of the embattled minutemen of Lexington and Concord. Its roots went deep into commercial competition with the mother country, into innumerable quarrels with England over campaigns and finances during the Canadian wars, and perhaps especially into a pervading colonial social revolution through which conservative merchants were losing political control to what Governor Bernard called in 1768 "a trained mob." It was often a disciplined mob, despite its violence, and it was so astutely led that it had a frame of government already in being before its revolution actually began. This was no anarchist plot; it was the deliberate building of a new nation.

We have already hinted at the extraordinary expansion of trade that had collectively made of Boston merchants, coincident with their military activities, a major unit in the British imperial system. We have touched on the development of divisions in colonial society based on the building of an aristocracy of wealth in the great commercial towns and the discontent which this tendency produced among the still largely disenfranchised farming and laboring populace. Many merchants found it to their advantage to co-operate with the revolutionary movement in order to protect their commerce from English attempts to hurt it. It was this wedding of economic power with a popular uprising which alone provided the leaders of the Sons of Liberty with any hope of success against the strongest nation in the world.

The prodigious struggle for markets and raw material that attended the world-wide commercial expansion of the eighteenth century was the dominating motive of all the nations involved. Beneath the easygoing picture of belles and fops and elaborate court life lay an unremitting struggle for supremacy in trade. All the wars had been fought primarily for this objective. To meet the enormously expanding administrative problems of its spreading empire, England had only a coterie of complacent bureaucrats. Many of these men never had really administered their offices, but had entrusted their duties to some ill-paid secretary while they spent the salaries pleasantly amid the social glitter of life at court. Oftentimes customs collectors for ports in American colonies had never left England, but carried on all duties of the office through a deputy overseas. Such officials were quite incom-

Reference

1. Corps Hill Burying Ground (Copp's Hill)
2. Christ Church (Old North)
3. Paul Revere's House
4. Old North Meeting
5. Faneuil Hall
6. Boston Massacre occurred here in 1770
7. State House
8. Old Meeting
9. Prison and Court House
10. King's Chapel
11. Granary Burying Ground
12. Valley Acre Hill
13. Beacon Hill
14. Mount Whoredom
15. Old South Meeting
16. Trinity Church
17. New South Meeting
18. Fort Hill
19. Boston Tea Party occurred here in 1773
20. Fortifications on Boston Neck

Back Bay

```
0            ¼            ½
|------------|------------|
      Scale of Miles
```

The Common

The Mall

Common St.

L

Beacon St.

Pleasant St.

Frog Lane

Clough St.

Hog Alley

Winter St.

Newbury St.

Orange St.

Marlbo

16

Boston Neck

20

Causeway

South End

Gibbon's Ship Yard

Essex St.

Pond St.

Summer St.

20

17

Long I

South St.

Co

Belche

A Plan of
the Town of Boston

Based on a map drawn by Lieut. Page
[His Majesty's Corps of Engineers] in 1775.
Areas filled in since 1775 are blue.
White areas show the present-day water line.

Windmill Point

19

Fort Point Channel

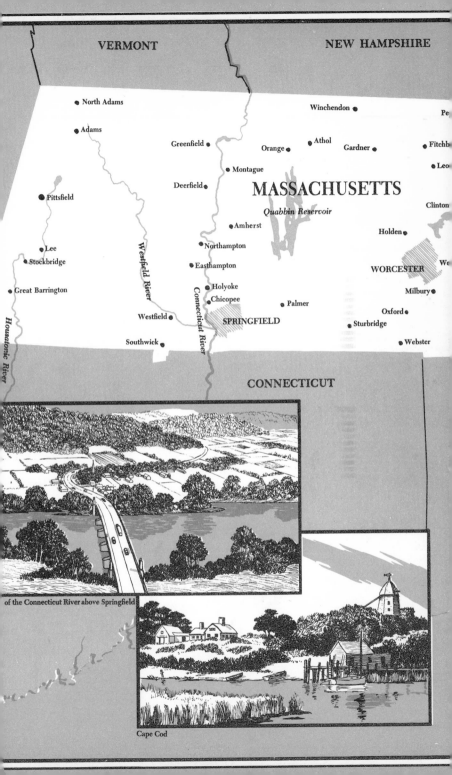

VERMONT

NEW HAMPSHIRE

North Adams

Winchendon

Pe

Adams

Greenfield

Orange

Athol

Gardner

Fitchb

Montague

Leo

Deerfield

MASSACHUSETTS

Pittsfield

Quabbin Reservoir

Clinton

Amherst

Holden

Northampton

Westfield River

WORCESTER

Lee

Easthampton

We

Stockbridge

Holyoke

Connecticut River

Chicopee

Milbury

Great Barrington

Palmer

Westfield

Oxford

SPRINGFIELD

Sturbridge

Housatonic River

Southwick

Webster

CONNECTICUT

of the Connecticut River above Springfield

Cape Cod

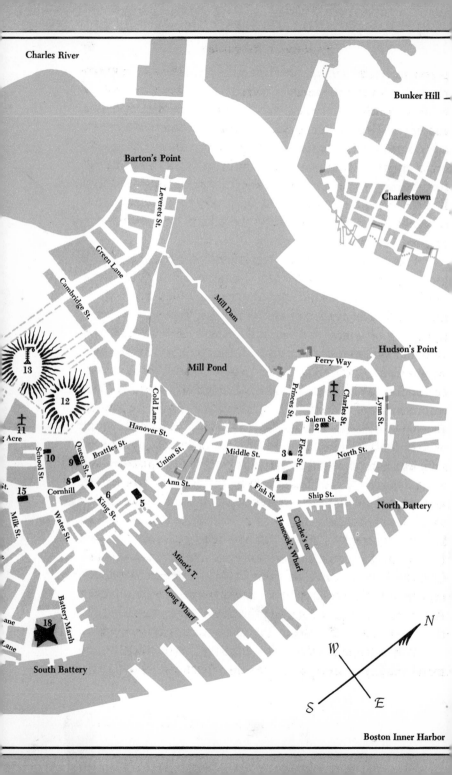

petent to render policy decisions on such matters as impressment of American seamen, currency problems, review of colonial legislation, Indian policy, debtor-creditor relations, and appeals from colonial court decisions. There were indeed a good many conscientious royal governors in American and other empire service who even dissipated their own private fortunes in the attempt to administer colonial affairs efficiently. But the general atmosphere of corruption and bureaucracy throughout the system defeated the efforts of this minority of good executives.

This rottenness in the administrative structure of the growing imperial system was, at bottom, responsible for many of the grievances on which the American Revolutionary movement grew. The evasion of customs duties, bribing of officials, smuggling of wines, molasses and French West Indies goods were but symptoms of the general disrespect for English law with which American colonists responded to English official corruption. Whenever a point was reached where a strict enforcement of the evaded regulations should be insisted on and new and sterner regulations imposed the colonial stage was set for an explosion. For the colonies were by now self-sufficient and possessed of fierce pride. Their population was about a quarter that of England herself. They had built strong, with that bold frontier individualism and self-assertion of which we have spoken before. They had taken Port Royal and Louisbourg without much English help, and had held the frontier lines on militia duty while the English regulars took Quebec. Few of them, or their fathers or grandfathers, had ever been to England, and they had grown to be distinctively Americans, no longer English in their outlook or thinking. On the whole, they hated what they had seen of British regulars.

It is a familiar story. The fundamental question of the moral validity of imperialism has never been solved and probably never will be. There is involved too deeply the irreconcilable opposites of freedom and empire, of human rights and commercial exploitation. There was an impossible gulf between the ruling class of England and the common people of America. And the system of representative assemblies subject to the authority of royal governors was an impossible one to maintain, for it perpetually reminded every American colony of that fundamental and irreconcilable conflict in the imperial mechanism.

These perhaps were the principal disintegrating forces that made revolution eventually inevitable. But among the common people of Massachusetts there were many special causes of grievance that tended to the same end. There was the recurring fear that the Church of England and its hated bishoprics might be re-established or strengthened. There was the matter of the King's Woods, where the best timber was reserved for the Royal Navy. The colonists had risen to the evangelical revivals of Jonathan Edwards and Whitefield, which had split the church. This religious struggle eventually strengthened religious tolerance and tended to inject democratic ideas into the aristocratic church. And as they went off to war over and over again, and suffered all the brutalities and insecurities of those explosive years, they came back home full of resentment against privilege of all kinds, whether of military rank, English bureaucracy, extravagent living among the wealthy, or the tax collector.

The conquest of Canada only intensified the disintegration. Faced with the necessity of setting up a new colonial administration and new policies, in a vast country still populated by Frenchmen, England must incur enormously increased expenses for defense of the new territory. Carrying a tremendous war debt, she turned to the colonies for aid in financing the new garrisons. But all attempts to get the colonies to unite on any over-all plan for financing or administering such continental problems had always ended in jealous bickerings between the separate provincial governments, and England had no better success now. Only in war had there been produced even grudging co-operation between Massachusetts and Connecticut, New York and Virginia. Many attempts over seventy-five years to produce regional administrations even of New England and New York under a common colonial governor had failed, and in the Albany Congress of 1754 the colonial assemblies had rejected a project of federation of the colonies drawn up by Benjamin Franklin and favored by a Massachusetts delegation led by Thomas Hutchinson and by all other delegations except Connecticut. From the empire viewpoint the impasse was clear. If the colonies could not of themselves produce plans of co-operation in matters of defense and Indian policy and taxation, then such plans must be imposed on them by Parliament and the Ministry.

The problem was immediately accentuated by the outbreak of the Pontiac Indian war on the western frontier, for which England maintained the entire cost of 10,000 troops and got no help from the eastern colonies, even Pennsylvania refusing to take part in the suppression of raids on her own borders.

After due warning to the colonies, Parliament passed a new Molasses Act in 1764 reducing the duties to threepence, but providing for strict enforcement by the navy, and imposing new duties on sugar and wines. This was followed in 1765 by the Stamp Act, requiring a tax in the form of stamps on all legal documents, newspapers, licenses, and pamphlets. The Molasses Act was significant in that its prohibitive rate of duty was for the first time set frankly for the raising of revenue instead of merely for the regulation of trade. But the Stamp

Act went much further by extending this principle of raising revenue to the interior of the colonies as well as the ports. Hitherto only the colonial assemblies had laid taxes other than duties payable at the waterfront on imported goods.

The Molasses Act produced depression and bankruptcy among some merchants, and immediately brought many of this conservative group into antagonism with England. The Stamp Act added to the merchants an extremely articulate group of newspaper editors and lawyers, whose protests filled the broadsides now so generally being published in large towns. And since the Stamp Act struck directly at the pocketbook of every small landholder or debtor who needed legal papers and had little hard money available in the postwar inflation, the protest of the populace was immediate. In Virginia Patrick Henry became spokesman for all frontiersmen in the famous Virginia Resolves, which were soon resounding in the agitator press of all the colonies, their dramatic appeal for revolt arousing everywhere the greatest enthusiasm on the part of the common people. Under the skillful demagoguery of Sam Adams and the eloquence of James Otis the Boston Town Meeting became a sounding board for radical speeches and appeals against the hated taxes, and these appeals were echoed immediately in resolutions pouring from other town meetings throughout the province of Massachusetts. Associations of merchants organized to boycott British goods in New York and Boston, forming tight nonimportation agreements that soon began to hurt British trade. Two hundred fifty Boston merchants signed such an agreement in December, 1765. In almost every town Sons of Liberty were organized among the radical groups, and they soon began to use violent means, tarring and feathering merchants or tax collectors who attempted to carry on normal trade or collect taxes. Committees of Correspondence were set up to exchange information and new techniques of protest between the towns of one colony and the others. Mobs paraded the streets and demonstrations were general throughout the colonies. The courts of justice were closed and kept closed by mob interference. A Stamp Act Congress was called in New York and under James Otis' leadership drew up strongly worded resolutions summarizing the colonial grievances. These were passed by the colonial assemblies and sent to Parliament and the King.

Samuel Adams wrote to Christopher Gadsden, the formulator of most of the resolutions of the Stamp Act Congress, that he considered the Stamp Act a blessing in disguise, in that it united the colonies for the first time. Certainly this was its significance, for what neither the French wars nor the colonies themselves had been able to do the Grenville ministry accomplished. "Taxation without representation is tyranny!" became a war cry.

In Boston the Stamp Act protests took the form of riots in August of 1765. The newly appointed stamp distributor under the act, Andrew Oliver, was hanged in effigy from the Liberty Tree at the corner of Washington and Essex streets and his office and house were broken into and ransacked. The house of the registrar of the Admiralty was similarly plundered and the records of the Admiralty Court destroyed. Chief Justice and Lieutenant Governor Thomas Hutchinson's magnificent house on North Square was thoroughly gutted, his library scattered, and only by good fortune was his splendid manuscript, *History of the Colony and Province of Massachusetts-Bay*, picked up and preserved from the mud of the street where it had been thrown. Mobs rescued their leaders from the jail in which Governor Bernard had incarcerated them, and prevented the sheriff from performing his duties. Governor Bernard ordered out the militia, but so general was the protest that the men refused to muster.

It can be seen that control of the governmental structure itself was already being threatened ten years before the actual Revolution. What has been called "beer hall politics" was already strong in Massachusetts, and these riotous phenomena taken together with the town meeting actions, the Sons of Liberty, and Committees of Correspondence, are evidence of the degree to which popular action was beginning to take the place of aristocratic government. No doubt the mobs were in part under the influence of lawless and undisciplined toughs, but the connivance of such men as Sam Adams, James Otis, John Hancock, and even some members of the Massachusetts Council, who were using the mob as one instrument in the orchestra of rebellion, indicates the shift in balance of political power that was occurring. A similar shift was taking place in Connecticut and in Virginia.

The efficacy of this method of protest was now demonstrated. So disastrous were the effects of nonimportation agreements on the business of English merchants that they too began to protest to Parliament, and in March, 1766, the Stamp Act was repealed and the Molasses Act amended to reduce the duty to one penny. The English Ministry fell and was replaced in June by a new one under Pitt, who was, however, so ill that he never controlled the policy of the new administration. Rejoicing in the colonies knew no bounds, and the feeling of victory only added to the self-confidence of the radical leaders in the colonies.

But rejoicing was short-lived. The new chancellor of the exchequer, Townshend, an erratic and stupid minister, perpetrated a series of new import taxes on the colonies, the revenue to be used not only for defense but to pay the costs of courts and civil government. These tariffs on such needed commodities as lead, glass, painters' colors, tea, and paper proved to be "a fatal and irretrievable blunder." The Townshend Acts threw the colonies into a depression during which many merchants failed, farms were mortgaged, and bills remained unpaid. What had previously seemed to many conservatives a mere administrative dispute over revenues now was rapidly growing into a fundamental conflict for political and economic control of the colonies. For many years the popular houses of the colonial legislatures had successfully restrained their governors and judges by control of their salaries. It began now to be clear that the British Ministry intended to usurp this power. Townshend rapidly enlarged the customs service and cracked down on smuggling. Boston mobs responded by unloading contraband wines from incoming ships in defiance of the collectors. The Massachusetts Assembly voted to send a circular letter, written by Sam Adams, to the other colonies suggesting united action to oppose English payment of the judiciary and civil officers and protesting the injustice of taxes levied for revenue only. When in June, 1768, a mob unloaded a wine-laden vessel of John Hancock's by force, Governor Bernard seized the ship and anchored it under the guns of the Royal Navy ship *Romney*. The mob then attacked the collector's office and ran wild in the town, forcing the English officials to take refuge aboard the *Romney* and in Castle William. The Boston Sons of Liberty demanded that the Governor send the *Romney* away, and such men as John Adams now refused to acknowledge the authority of Parliament. Hillsborough, the new British secretary of state for America, demanded that the Massachusetts Assembly rescind its action in circularizing the other colonies or be dissolved. The Assembly refused, and Governor Bernard forthwith dissolved the session and wrote to General Gage in New York asking for British troops to protect the Massachusetts government.

All the popular support of the disbanded Assembly now

rallied around the Boston Town Meeting. Delegates from ninety Massachusetts towns, called together by Boston, petitioned Governor Bernard for a new Assembly session, but this was of course refused. Everywhere the Sons of Liberty, usually with the approval of town meetings, took over local administration. The arrival of troops in Boston only added to the popularity of the radical groups. Nonimportation agreements were enforced by the mobs. Where conservative merchants did not co-operate, they were tarred and feathered. The class of conservatives who had successfully retained political power for seventy-five years now completely lost it and it seemed that anarchy might follow.

But the time was not yet ripe for outright revolution. The recall of Governor Bernard, now obviously useless in Massachusetts, in July, 1769, followed in 1770 by the repeal of the Townshend Acts, except that on tea, brought another lull in the crisis. Trade was resumed and merchants began to prosper again, losing their principal cause for quarrel with England. The Boston Massacre, a bloody little skirmish between a Boston mob and the King's troops, in 1770, was followed by the wise withdrawal of troops from Boston streets, and both sides retired to lick their wounds. John Adams' unpopular but quite just defense of the British soldiers involved in the "massacre" was a sobering influence. For two years affairs in Massachusetts quieted down. Sam Adams sometimes found difficulty in keeping his radical groups active. He had for a long time now been intent on independence from England. From 1765 to 1770 the British authorities had played into his hand, providing him provocation after provocation to build his conspiracy stronger. He had squandered his inheritance, let his business go to pieces from neglect, and ignored the needs of his family to build a career of politics. He had developed in Boston to the highest degree all the modern techniques of the political club caucus—the "smoke-filled room," yellow journalism, the intellectual fringe, and gangster violence—to serve his purpose. He wrote political diatribes under many assumed names, kept the Boston papers full of insinuating personal attacks on his enemies, supplied town meetings with inflammatory resolutions, and corresponded regularly with leaders in other colonies who held similar views. He kept a constant feud going in the press, the town meeting, and the Massachusetts Assembly with his chosen enemy, the new governor, Thomas Hutchinson, whose correct but nepotistical aristocracy provided an ideal counterirritant to his rabble-rousing theories.

In 1773 Sam Adams perpetrated "an irresponsible piece of reckless bravado designed to precipitate a crisis," which was disapproved by many colonial leaders and would ordinarily have proved to be an overreaching of his talents. But the imbecilic British Ministry came to his rescue. News that the East India Company was being allowed to dump its surplus tea on the American market at a reduced price reached Adams. He saw in this a renewed opportunity to inflame the merchants, and he persuaded the Committees of Correspondence to prevent the landing of the tea. When the news reached England that Adams' Sons of Liberty had boarded a British ship, thinly disguised as Indians, and dumped the tea into the harbor, Lord North, the prime minister, lost his temper and made a worse blunder than had Adams. He promulgated the Boston Port Bill, closing the port of Boston and removing its customhouse. Other bills called for the appointment of councilors in England, the removal of court trials to England, and the abolition of town meetings. General Gage soon arrived as the new governor, and the stage for inevitable revolution was complete.

If the Stamp Act was a blessing in disguise to Sam Adams,

the series of bills just described were a masterpiece of folly. Injudicious as his Tea Party undoubtedly was, it proved to be Sam Adams' shrewdest trick. The burst of quick temper into which Lord North's ministry degenerated in the attempt to punish Massachusetts was echoed by an equally deafening outburst of rage and sympathy with which the colonies forthwith began to arm themselves for the coming conflict. This was the climax of Sam Adams' career. Never again were his counsels of surpassing influence in the formation of the United States; those events called for more balanced judgments than his. But the master agitator had fulfilled his function. He had brought the whirlwind into being.

Boston asked for help through the Committees of Correspondence. By oxcart and wagon the answer came. Salem and Marblehead took over the functions of Boston's port, and food and commodities were painfully trundled overland across the fording places of Saugus and Medford and Cambridge. Muddy River, now beginning to be called Brookline, became a caravan town as long supply trains from all directions converged on Boston Neck. Shiploads for the relief of Boston came from as far as South Carolina.

Meanwhile in Taunton and throughout the province radical posses hunted down hated "mandamus councilors" and Gage found it impossible to assemble a government in Boston. But town meetings in every other town chose delegates to a provincial Assembly to meet at Concord. Judges were prevented from holding court and jurors refused to serve. The structure of the royal province government simply disappeared everywhere, and there was substituted the extralegal Provincial Congress at Concord. Responsible citizens in most of the towns began to join the radicals. It was realized that anarchy was no substitute for tyranny. The machinery for orderly reaction to the crisis had long been ready, despite the mobs. Delegates began to be chosen for a Continental Congress to discuss the crisis. What had happened to Massachusetts could happen to any of the colonies. Wise heads must make the next decisions.

On September 6, 1774, delegates from the nineteen towns of Suffolk County, then including all of modern Norfolk County, assembled in Dedham and made Dr. Joseph Warren chairman of a committee to frame suitable resolves to the new governor, General Gage, protesting the outrageous punishments inflicted on Massachusetts by the Boston Port Acts. Three days later the meeting reassembled at Daniel Vose's house in Milton and adopted these Suffolk Resolves, which were forthwith not only dispatched to Governor Gage but carried also by Paul Revere to the Continental Congress, just then assembling in Philadelphia. Promptly adopted by the Continental Congress, these resolves became a rallying cry to all the revolutionary groups in the colonies. Not only did they protest the infringements on civil rights included in the Boston Port Acts, but they denied that any "obedience is due from this province to either or any part of the Acts," and they declared that judges holding office under these acts were "unconstitutional officers" and advised all disputants to submit their quarrels to arbitration outside the courts. They called on collectors of taxes to refuse to pay over public money to the province or county treasurers and demanded that mandamus councilors resign. They recommended that town meetings appoint militia officers and muster the militia under arms once a week, although "determined to act merely on the defensive, so long as such conduct may be vindicated by reason, and the principles of self-preservation but no longer." They reinforced arrangements to boycott English goods and appointed a committee "to encourage arts and manufacturers amongst us by all means in our power." They gave complete support to the Continental Congress and to the Provincial Congress. Finally they confirmed and strengthened the Committees of Correspondence organization and threatened to "seize and keep in safe custody" the leaders of the "present tyrannical and unconstitutional government throughout the country and province" should any move be made to apprehend their own patriot leaders.

If revolution consists of defiance of the existing governmental authority, calling the people to arms, and setting up the framework for a new government, then Massachusetts was already in revolution. In the attempt to interfere with the town meeting system Lord North had only revitalized the Massachusetts towns. The Suffolk Resolves were a symbol of the sort of response the towns were making. The town meetings of all the Old Colony towns from Orleans to Rhode Island were by now dominated by radical patriots. In Danvers, where he lived during the summer of 1774, General Gage considered it necessary to have two companies of regulars watching over him all that summer. After England stopped shipments of arms to the colonies in October, royal supplies of ammunition were seized by patriots in Rhode Island and New Hampshire. In February Gage sent a detachment of British under Colonel Leslie to seize a patriot store of powder in Beverly, but the mobilization of a threatening force of patriots to protest it induced the colonel to retire without securing his objective and without bloodshed. Colonel John Glover's famous Marblehead regiment stood by as the British reembarked for Boston. Plainly, it was now only a question of where the first shot would be fired.

Plymouth, Essex, Middlesex, and Worcester counties had all held county conventions and had passed resolves as unanimously supported by their towns as Suffolk's. The House of Representatives meeting in Salem in October was not attended by the Governor, and after awaiting him vainly for a day, the House elected John Hancock chairman and Benjamin Lincoln, of Hingham, secretary, and promptly converted itself into a Provincial Congress. Its later meetings at Concord and Cambridge were well attended and included such able men as Joseph Warren, Elbridge Gerry, William Prescott, and Artemas Ward. Sam Adams, John Adams, Thomas Cushing, and Robert Treat Paine were already sitting in the Continental Congress at Philadelphia, and thus were not at Concord and Cambridge. The most significant action of the Provincial Congress was to recommend the taking over from sheriffs and collectors of taxes all public funds in their possession in order to purchase ordnance and military stores needed by the province. Thus, at a blow, the patriots took over from the British not only the effective government of all Massachusetts outside of Boston but the tax structure and military control as well.

It is a matter of unusual interest that in Massachusetts the provisional government was organized and functioning before any military outbreak occurred. Just as, many years before, Massachusetts had been politically mature enough to force the formation of a bicameral legislature by pressure from local town meetings, so now a provincial congress was in orderly session and taking over state functions again, through town meetings and county conventions, six months before a blow had been struck for liberty.

CHAPTER NINE

Call to Arms

The year 1774 had proved Massachusetts' determined capacity to mobilize a provisional government and emergency supply system in her political and economic crisis. Whether the province would respond to a call to arms was still in the balance. Minutemen totaling more than 15,000 were drilling on almost every village green, and were even storing powder and ammunition in the church meetinghouses. The British Ministry, and General Thomas Gage, had stirred up the hornet's nest. In Boston some loyalist collaborators assisted his 4,000 troops in every way possible, but many other Boston citizens set fire to supply wagons entering Boston Neck and to piles of lumber for building soldiers' barracks. And as for the rest of Massachusetts: when Gage had successfully seized a provincial powder supply at Somerville in November, he was told that 40,000 Yankees had started to Boston on the false rumor that six patriots had been killed in the encounter. Plainly, any bloodshed would trigger some kind of armed uprising. Yet Gage felt that he must continue doing something to maintain his disappearing authority over the province until the requested reinforcements should arrive. So now he picked as his secret objective the military stores the minutemen had been assembling at Concord. Since the rebellious Provincial Congress had been meeting at both Concord and Cambridge only a few months previously, this was indeed a sortie into enemy country.

Despite all attempts at surprise, William Dawes and Paul Revere were galloping through Brookline and Charlestown before the British midnight troop movement was well begun. Through Medford and Cambridge they awakened almost every home. At Lexington Revere warned Sam Adams and John Hancock at the house of Parson Jonas Clarke. A reconnaissance group of British officers sent ahead of the British columns to prevent alarms on the road to Concord captured Paul Revere, but, learning that the countryside was already on the alert, let him go and galloped back to North Cambridge to warn Major Pitcairn's advance force of six British companies that trouble lay ahead. Already the sound of guns and church bells confirmed the news. Pitcairn waited there for Lieutenant Colonel Francis Smith's main force to join him, ordering his men to load muskets but not to fire without an order. Smith also had heard the church bells, and sent back word to General Gage, asking the reinforcements that ultimately saved his troops from annihilation. Then the combined force of 700 Grenadiers and Light Infantry marched forward toward Lexington Green. It was now early dawn.

There on the green, drawn up in two columns, stood about seventy men of Captain Jonas Parker's company of minutemen. Neither commander intended to molest the other; indeed Parker ordered his men to disperse and not to fire. But some held their ground. No one knows who fired that first shot, the one "heard round the world." Once it had been fired, the shooting became general. The British fired two volleys before Pitcairn could get them under control. Only one of the British was wounded, but eight patriots were killed and ten wounded. This was the bloodshed which might call the province of Massachusetts Bay to arms. Few would have forecast a new seven years of intercontinental war.

For hours the Concord militia had been burying and hiding the best of their powder and ammunition stores. The British found little but some shovels, flour, gun carriages, and two cannons. While they fanned out in the village, minutemen of seven surrounding towns marched in to join the Concord company under command of Colonel James Barrett. Totaling perhaps 400 men, they assembled on the hillside of the Buttrick farm a few hundred yards northwest of Concord Bridge, the hilltop screening them from view of a British detachment guarding the bridge. When his sentries reported columns of smoke from the burning supplies in the center of Concord, Colonel Barrett supposed the invaders were setting fire to the town, and decided to fight his way down into the town to protect it. Ordering his men to put new flints in their muskets, he led them down the hillside against the three British companies at the bridge. The British opened fire but broke ranks when half their officers were wounded, and fled into the town. This famous Concord Bridge fight lasted perhaps two minutes. The militia crossed the bridge and advanced to the crown of the cemetery ridge overlooking the town, and stood their ground there unable to interfere with the British because Colonel Smith sent flankers to clear the ridge. After several hours the regulars began to retreat along the same road by which they had come. But this long British delay in preparing to retreat was disastrous. Minutemen from more distant towns continually kept arriving. They first converged at the bridge at Meriam's Corner and raked the British with deadly flintlock fire. From there on the "running fight" was continuous. Patriots ambushed the redcoats from every stone wall, house and tree. The disciplined regulars stayed in ranks, taking severe punishment from embattled farmers who gave them few targets to fire at, yet picked off soldier after soldier from close range. About thirty-five hundred patriots fired flintlocks at the British that day, pouring in from Billerica, Woburn and Reading, Framingham, Sudbury, and other more distant towns. The British became demoralized. Their flanking parties sometimes caught the Americans from behind along the fields, but more often failed to cover the column. All the British wasted powder in futile wild firing. After three miles, their ammunition was running low. Pitcairn tried to rally them at Fiske Hill but, when his frightened horse threw him, the infantry broke ranks and passed Lexington Green almost at a run.

Lord Percy's relief brigade of 800 men, after disgraceful delays in Boston and the further necessity to replank the Charles River bridge over which they had to cross at Cambridge (the patriots had torn up the planking), finally made contact with Smith's exhausted force just east of Lexington, giving them an hour to reorganize and rest. In Arlington the patriots under General Heath fought the British to a standstill but had to give way when Lord Percy brought up artillery. Colonel Pickering with 300 Salem militia again stopped them at Somerville, but likewise had to fall back before cannon fire.

Ferried back to Boston under the guns of the fleet, the British found casualties of 273 men. There were 93 dead and wounded among the patriots. Neither General Gage nor his successor, Sir William Howe, ever again tried a sortie from Boston into the surrounding countryside. It was their first experience of the punishing lesson the British had to learn over and over again during the Revolution, that in partially wooded country determined militia, even though poorly organized, can nevertheless take the measure of trained regulars if they can produce accurate fire from available cover and concealment. Long experience against French and Indians had taught Americans in an entirely modern school of tactics, which, after the bayonet was added to their armamentarium, proved extremely effective in stopping regulars well trained in the close-order tactics of Frederick the Great. But perhaps the most surprising lesson was learned by the British regulars, that the despised colonial rabble did not run away when fired on. The British headaches in Boston that night were even more ominous than the British wounds.

British headaches continued the next day. When General Artemas Ward arrived on April 20 to take over command of the colonial forces from General Heath, he found Colonel Stark's New Hampshire troops already in Medford, General Israel Putnam's Connecticut forces in Cambridge, and General Nathanael Greene's Rhode Island men in Jamaica Plain. A total of 16,000 men hemmed in the British in Boston, leaving no doubt of the resolute revolutionary spirit throughout New England. Even General Gage wrote that they were "joined with an uncommon degree of zeal and enthusiasm."

All the towns from Medford to Milton now went to work on the problem of billeting and feeding soldiers, while General Ward organized effective siege lines controlling all the land approaches to Boston. On May 10 the Continental Congress at Philadelphia adopted the besieging army and began to raise troops for it from the other colonies. The New England revolt thus became an American revolution.

The month of May was used by both adversaries for digging in. The colonial forces bolstered their lines with earthworks and mats of brush but, lacking artillery, could only pick off occasional British with desultory musket fire. The arrival of Pennsylvania riflemen for a time took toll of numerous British officers who were careless in failing to take cover. Flurries of cannon fire from British 24-pounders set up on narrow Boston Neck opposite the provincial entrenchments on Meeting House Hill in Roxbury occasionally produced patriot casualties. But no real forays in strength were possible from either side. The situation remained a stalemate. The British scoured the islands of Boston Bay and the neighboring shores for food and fodder. On May 27 the patriots put a stop to this by two small expeditions from Winthrop and Milton, removing cattle and burning the grain on the harbor islands. The larger of these, led by General Putnam and Colonel Stark, also burned an armed British schooner in Chelsea Creek and got her 4-pounder cannon and swivel guns. The smaller, under Major Vose, removed the lamps and burned the lighthouse at the entrance to Boston harbor. But British batteries on Boston Common, Copp's Hill, Batterymarch and Castle Island, and the guns of the fleet, prevented any penetration of the city itself. Similarly General Gage made no attempt to attack the American redoubts in Somerville and Roxbury, or the patriot lines that stretched across Cambridge, Watertown, and Brookline. He did not even consider it necessary to occupy the dominating heights of Bunker and Breed's Hills in Charlestown, nor Dorchester Heights in South Boston.

Yet the initiative was slowly passing to the Americans, as they consolidated their positions and gradually built some sort of organization out of their polyglot militia units. By mid-June the Massachusetts Provincial Congress thought the forces were ready for more concerted action. In response to a rumor that Gage was contemplating the fortification of Charlestown, a thousand Americans under command of Colonel William Prescott were sent to occupy Breed's Hill on the evening of June 16. No definite provision was made for reinforcement. Tactically it was a foolhardy project, since the position could easily have been outflanked by the British had they chosen to move ships up the Mystic River and attack it from the rear.

During the night the provincials dug a redoubt eight rods

square at the top of the hill and extended a long breastwork from it down the north slope away from the Boston side to a stone wall and rail fence that carried the line to the Mystic River shore. When General Gage studied the new position in the morning he missed completely the real opportunity the situation presented him, of cutting off the foolhardy maneuver from the rear, and thought only of the magnificent chance it offered for a frontal assault. At last, to his mind, the Americans had got themselves into a fixed position where a charge of solid ranks of British regulars could demonstrate once and for all what concentrated British firepower could do to un-disciplined rabble dug in in a hayfield. Actually, the greatest strength of the American position lay in its concentration of *accurate* firepower against just such an assault as Gage was contemplating. For when British regulars charged, they ad-vanced firing with "the head upright" and "the muzzle a little lower than the butt," taking only a general aim in the direction of the enemy. Against a solid rank of opponents this produced a heavy musket barrage that was extremely effective in the open field. But against Americans who took careful aim from the cover of a fortified position it could be disastrous. Ameri-cans generally supplemented their larder with wild game and took pride in their marksmanship. Turkey-shoots were a favorite form of recreation.

During the morning about 2,500 British troops were ferried across to the easterly end of the Charlestown peninsula under cover of bombardment of the American redoubt from the fleet and Copp's Hill battery. Colonel Prescott got a few American reinforcements from Colonel Stark's New Hamp-shire companies, who joined Knowlton's Connecticut troops along the rail fence. Colonel Prescott was in personal com-mand at the redoubt and breastwork, with the help of Boston's tireless physician patriot, General Joseph Warren, who volunteered without command. The total American force was about 1,500. The British bombardment put out of action the few available light fieldpieces on the hill but, since the heavier British cannon got mired near the bottom of the hill, field artillery took no effective part in the action anyway.

Heavily burdened with full field packs and three days' provisions, the British advanced slowly in close order, company front, up the steep hill. They fired ineffectual formal volleys, mostly over the Americans' heads. Until they were within sure range, the patriots held their fire. Then the sudden deadly, accurate volleys of the Americans took such toll of the British that they broke ranks and retreated, leaving many dead and wounded on the field. Out of range, they re-formed, still in company front, advanced, and were met again with the same intensive burst of precision fire, which stopped them and again made them fall back. They were reinforced, and General Howe ordered them to remove knapsacks and to re-form in column. This time the attack was to be concentrated on the redoubt itself, ignoring the breastwork and picket fence, bringing over General Pigot's troops, hitherto on the right, into the central assault. This type of attack the provincials were not prepared to resist, with a smaller target to fire at, ammunition nearing exhaustion, and few bayonets for hand-to-hand fighting. Dr. Warren was killed, the patriots fell back with considerable losses, and the British took the redoubt. But even then the defenders of the breastwork and rail fence were able to cover the retreat of the main force, and the exhausted British did not pursue the Americans beyond adjoining Bunker Hill. Late-arriving American reinforcements ensured that the provincials escaped over the narrow isthmus into Somerville. The British burned the town of Charlestown and set up their own fortifications on captured Bunker Hill.

The British victory was a hollow one. Well over 1,200

regulars, including a high proportion of officers, were killed or wounded. But no Tory or Britisher could any longer call the provincial troops an undisciplined rabble. No one had dreamed that militia, outnumbered almost two to one, could exact such frightful slaughter from the King's forces before falling back. To the victors, it was a disaster.

Many American officers were punished for the confused planning and poor preparation of Bunker Hill. But the story was soon a proud legend throughout the colonies as the realization grew that the defeat was a glorious one. The skirmishes of Lexington and Concord had been an indication only of the will to fight. Bunker Hill was a test of military power, in which the losers came off with all the glory. This was the signal that the American Revolution was not a small revolt to be easily put down by limited action. Both sides now knew they must stand and fight with all available resources. The gauntlet was thrown down. There could be no turning back. Americans were trying to throw off the English yoke. It was liberty or death. They were throwing their lives into the fight to become an independent nation.

CHAPTER TEN

Struggle for Independence

No adequate understanding of Massachusetts' part in the American Revolution can be obtained without consideration of her first citizen, John Adams. For, while he often exemplified the pompousness and arrogance that other colonies complained of in the Massachusetts character, he had also such qualities of genius that he was one of only three or four men who persuaded the country into independence, and he became the work horse of the Continental Congress, a founder of its foreign affairs, and a brilliant inventor of our constitutional system. Before the Revolution his immense legal knowledge had enabled him to provide the basic patriot arguments against the Stamp Act and against the judges who accepted royal salaries. He also had contributed steadily to the anti-British propaganda sedulously promoted by his firebrand second cousin, Sam Adams. Both had become acquainted with other colonial leaders through their service at the First Continental Congress in 1774.

At the Second Continental Congress, which met while all the colonies were still aflame with indignation at the recent battles of Lexington and Concord, John Adams rapidly surged into a position of leadership. He strenuously opposed further petitions to the King, and proposed immediate preparation for the inevitable conflict. His power over the congress was based on his absolute conviction that the die was cast, that matters had gone beyond any possibility of reconciliation. With the help of other radicals, like Jefferson and the Lees of Virginia, he persuaded the Congress to adopt the provincial army besieging Boston. Though he was inclined to be jealous, to lose his temper and be impetuous in argument, his fluent speech, his enormous vocabulary, and a passionate conviction could make him an extremely effective orator at times. In the memorable debates leading up to the adoption of the Declaration of Independence, which Adams helped to write, Jefferson afterward said: "John Adams was our colossus on the floor. Not graceful, not eloquent, not always fluent in his public addresses, he yet came out with a power both of thought and expression which moved us from our seats." He eventually served on more than ninety committees in the Congress, and was chairman of twenty-five. He fought for opening relations with foreign governments, struggled as chairman of the Board of War to organize a military establishment, worked like a beaver to get a navy built, and was one of the most sought-after consultants on the drafting of constitutions. Everywhere he won the admiration of the other great leaders of the Congress for his solid ability and his capacity for hard work.

One of the greatest examples of his brilliant thinking was his nomination of George Washington of Virginia to become commander in chief of the army besieging Boston. Coming from a Massachusetts man, in the critical days just before the battle of Bunker Hill, this stroke of diplomacy at one blow ensured the unity of the colonies in the fight for independence. The tall Virginian, who appeared as a delegate at the Congress in the uniform of a colonel of militia, had made a profound impression and, both then and in the days following his election as commander in chief, comported himself in a manner that won the confidence of all the colonies in his leadership. It was a master stroke on Adams' part, and one of the great contributions to the eventual success of the Revolution. Along the route that Washington traveled from Philadelphia to Boston it became increasingly apparent to the crowds who turned out to cheer him that here was the leader they were looking for.

George Washington arrived to take over his command at Cambridge on July 3, 1775, barely two weeks after the Bunker Hill battle. The battle had only intensified the impasse of the siege. Still the two fortified lines glared at each other. Neither had what it took to overthrow the other. The Americans lacked artillery to dislodge the British; without the power to maneuver, the British could accomplish nothing against the provincials. Like all fixed sieges, it remained a war of attrition. General Gage urged the British Ministry to abandon Massachusetts and transfer the army to New York. When he was recalled in October, General Howe merely repeated Gage's recommendation and tried further to tighten his defenses.

Washington calmly and tirelessly applied himself to the task of overcoming personal quarrels, jealousies, and profiteering which he found disunifying the "mixed multitude of people" in the blockading militia companies. His single-minded efforts to weld the chaotic rabble of the several colonies into an integrated provincial army of three divisions began gradually to bear fruit as winter approached. Even the obvious hazards of the crisis did not prevent wholesale desertions, stupid incompetence, and disobedience among the ranks. Only Washington's stubborn insistence on continuous field training, better staff work among poorly trained officers, and rigorous discipline, with which he filled the dreary months from July to March, could have produced the unified force that fought the vigorous later campaigns of the Revolution.

The Commander in Chief's pre-eminent contribution to this early phase of the struggle was his firm but patient mastery of the human obstacles. He personally detested the equalitarian democracy of the Yankees, their choosing of officers by ballot, and the fraternization of officers with men in the ranks. Yet by steady insistence on subordinating all local or regional differences to the common cause of the United States as a whole he succeeded in welding unity into an army of the most diverse origins. This was perhaps more essential to patriot success in the struggle than any battle victory.

Another brilliant aspect of General Washington's organization of the besiegers was his determined effort to improvise a colonial navy. The raids of May 27 had by no means cut off supplies to the 18,000 British in Boston. Transports and armed merchantmen regularly arrived under the guns of Commodore Banks' Boston harbor fleet with reinforcements and provender for the besieged army. Finding among the Massachusetts companies Colonel John Glover's Marblehead regiment, composed almost entirely of trained seamen, Washington issued army commissions to certain skippers and manned their sloops and schooners with detachments from the Marblehead regiment. The little fleet thus provided during the fall of 1775 did important damage to British supply during that winter. Captain Nicholas Broughton's schooner *Hannah* is most often remembered, because she was first to be commissioned and therefore constituted the founding of the United States Navy. But the schooner *Lee*, Captain John Manley, was of more significance, since she captured the large British brigantine *Nancy* in November, 1775, with 2,000 muskets, 31 tons of musket shot, 3,000 round shot, several barrels of powder and a brass mortar, and brought her into Gloucester. Similarly Captain James Mugford in the schooner *Franklin* brought into patriot hands 75 tons of powder and entrenching tools from the British ship *Hope*. More than thirty such British prizes were taken by Washington's little Massachusetts Bay navy before the British naval squadron finally abandoned its hold on Boston harbor in June, 1776. Some of the prizes were later recaptured by the British frigates *Milford* and *Renown*, which subsequently patrolled the Massachusetts coast in the attempt to blockade its harbors, but the record of the little schooner navy in the first critical year of the war was a good one.

Yet captured ammunition, even when supplemented by a further supply of shot seized in the King's storehouse in New York, could not break the siege of Boston until cannon were found to fire them from. Without a siege train of heavy artillery Washington could scarcely hope to drive the British out of Boston. Even an investigating commission, sent by the impatient Continental Congress to urge Washington to assume the offensive, could see that. A former Boston bookseller and amateur artilleryman, Colonel Henry Knox, however, had a plan. Ethan Allen's capture of Forts Ticonderoga and Crown Point on Lake Champlain the previous May had been followed by the expeditions of Montgomery and Benedict Arnold against Canada. Montgomery had captured Montreal, only to be killed in the disastrous colonial defeat at Quebec in December. But a hundred or more heavy cannon, mortars and howitzers still sat unused in the ramparts at Ticonderoga.

Willing frontiersmen, whom Henry Knox hired, wrestled 59 of the fort's cannon, even huge 16- and 24-pounders, down the steep slopes of Ticonderoga and the Lake George portage into waiting gundalows, on which they were sailed, sometimes through breakable ice, southward to the head of Lake George. There they were dragged on to forty-two heavy sleds, and when snow and ice had sufficiently accumulated, eighty-one yoke of oxen and many horses drew them slowly over the wilderness hills to the Hudson. One 6-pounder broke loose and fell through ice at the mouth of the Mohawk, and another at Albany. From Claverack oxen hauled the sleds up over Berkshire's drifted mountain trails to Great Barrington, Monterey and Blandford, and thence down the slopes to Springfield. After fifty days of bitter winter toil, in which both New York and Massachusetts frontiersmen participated, the strange cavalcade reached Washington's lines in Dorchester.

For days shovels, barrels, and mats of brush had been collected by muffled oxcarts in Dorchester with which new redoubts and emplacements could quickly be built on the heights of South Boston. Masking his maneuver with three days of severe cannonading of various British positions and a diversionary preparation for attack from Cambridge, Washington sent 4,000 men to Dorchester Heights on the night of March 4. Working all night, with much better preparation than at Bunker Hill, the Americans presented to the British on the morning of March 5 a virtually impregnable fortress high on the hill, from which their cannon and mortars commanded not only the town of Boston but the whole anchorage of the British fleet before the town. The inadequate force that General Howe put aboard transports to test the new American position never attacked. After a severe storm had delayed the landing for several days, Howe changed his mind. Washington withheld his heaviest fire in order not to destroy the town, awaiting negotiations, and these began on March 8. Howe got the promise of safe evacuation in return for assurance that the town would not be burned. On March 17 all the British, together with a thousand American loyalists who chose exile, sailed off to Halifax, never to return. In the bloodless battle of Dorchester Heights, with an assist from Henry Knox, George Washington won the first great American victory of the Revolution. This was the last garrisoning of

British troops in Massachusetts, the end of British occupation in the province where the war began. Massachusetts men would fight long and hard in other colonies, battle it out at sea, and rot in British prisons for yet another seven years. But Massachusetts was now free.

A squadron of the British naval forces, under Commodore Banks, remained in lower Boston Bay for three months longer, supported by seven transports loaded with Scottish Highlanders. General Benjamin Lincoln of Hingham organized several thousand militiamen, many of them from South Shore towns, and set up some Ticonderoga artillery on Point Allerton, Long and Peddock's and Moon Islands, and Hough's Neck in Quincy. The cannonading began on the morning of June 14. The British squadron was hit, and reluctantly hoisted sail and withdrew from the best naval base Massachusetts afforded. Throughout the remainder of the war these patriot batteries, and similar ones in all the harbors from Newburyport to New Bedford, were tediously manned by local militia companies exempted from drafts for the Continental Army. The *Milford* and *Renown* periodically made nuisance raids on Massachusetts harbors. Early in 1777 the little Massachusetts navy was disbanded in order to free it for foreign duty. The only major naval attack on a Massachusetts port occurred in September, 1778, when General Grey's 4,000 British troops in a 20-vessel squadron commanded by Captain Fanshawe landed at New Bedford. There and at Fairhaven they set fire to 26 storehouses, two ropewalks, about 70 vessels, and 42 homes and shops of ardent patriots, in retaliation for the extensive privateering activities carried on in the two ports. Then they sailed away. The damage was extensive, but privateering continued out of that harbor.

When Washington moved his army to Long Island after the evacuation of Boston, most of Colonel Glover's Marblehead regiment and many other Massachusetts units accompanied him. Glover's marine troops saved the surrounded army on August 30 after the Battle of Long Island by their skillful night evacuation of the whole army in small boats across the East River from Brooklyn. On Christmas night their special skills were again called on in the crossing of the ice-filled Delaware above Trenton. No less than 2,400 soldiers, with all their equipment, were transported in a snowstorm across the swollen river, enabling Washington to surprise and capture almost a thousand Hessians in Trenton and a few days later to strike Cornwallis a hard blow at Princeton, thus re-establishing the American hold on New Jersey for the winter. Glover's troops again distinguished themselves in hard fighting at Saratoga, and were appointed to escort Burgoyne's surrendered army to Cambridge in the fall of 1777. General Benjamin Lincoln commanded 2,000 New England troops in the Saratoga campaign, in which he was wounded. Later in the war Washington assigned to him the difficult holding operation against strong British forces in South Carolina and Georgia. He received Cornwallis' sword at the Yorktown surrender, and later became secretary of war in President Washington's Cabinet.

Massachusetts men took part in most of the land campaigns of the Revolution but, once the theater of action had left New England, their contributions at sea grew to be perhaps the more important portion of their service. From all the colonies it has been estimated that at least 70,000 Americans were at one time engaged on the sea against the enemy. The Continental Navy never exceeded sixty vessels, and in the latter years of the war these almost disappeared from the sea as the British captured or destroyed the few frigates Congress could afford to build. But tremendous damage to British supply lines was inflicted by thousands of American privateers and letter-of-marque ships which combined lucrative cargo carrying through the blockade with attack and capture of British merchantmen at sea. While the losses in such shipping were extremely high, the profits accruing to their owners when they succeeded were so enormous that astute merchants and crews alike, sharing the prize money, developed by such private means a fighting fleet immeasurably more effective than the infant nation could afford with public funds. Massachusetts led in this type of warfare, providing more than 1,600 such ships during the war. When in 1777 Silas Deane, the American agent to France, so far persuaded French Foreign Minister Vergennes of the advantages to France of the American rebellion that the French court secretly set up Hortalez and Company to ship large quantities of military supplies to the French West Indies, it became possible for American ships to transfer these cargoes from Martinique and St. Eustatius to American ports. Soon American privateers were allowed to take British prizes into European French and Spanish ports. These ports thus became bases for American vessels attacking British merchantmen around the British Isles themselves, where their concentration was greatest and their protection proportionately weaker. Since the British then had to provide naval protection for their merchantmen in European waters, the number of Royal Navy vessels available for the American blockade was sharply reduced. This really hurt the British economy and its military supply line.

As early as March, 1777, the Massachusetts Board of War sent the state navy brigantines *Tyrannicide*, Captain Jonathan Haraden, the *Massachusetts*, Captain John Fiske, and the *Freedom*, Captain John Clouston, to cruise off the coast of Ireland, England and France. Accompanied by privateers, these vessels captured twenty-five prizes along European coasts. Many Boston and Salem ships participated in these activities, or in privateer cruises along southern American shores and in the Caribbean. During 1777 alone, 474 vessels were captured from the British. American losses were heavy also, but since the British vessels were usually larger, the relative losses in British tonnage were far greater than the American. Captured British vessels were promptly refitted as American privateers, further increasing the United States' striking power. The exploits of John Paul Jones in the *Ranger* and *Bonhomme Richard* in actually raiding Scottish and English coasts brought the war to the enemy with stunning impact, and when France brought her fleet and army into the war against England the colonial rebellion was converted into a new test of the balance of power in Europe.

Admiral d'Estaing's French fleet destroyed a British squadron at Newport, Rhode Island, in 1778, and had intended to support General Sullivan's attack on the long-standing British occupation forces in Newport. To New England's consternation he failed to accomplish this, when Admiral Howe's New York fleet pursued him into Rhode Island waters. A sudden storm so damaged both fleets that the engagement never took place and d'Estaing sought refuge for repairs in Boston harbor, where his fleet stayed at anchor from July to November accomplishing nothing more than the destruction of the Newport squadron.

The Revolution wore on, often stalemated for long periods. The British occupied Castine, Maine, in 1779, and from that base raided New England shipping all the way from the Grand Banks to Boston. A Penobscot Expedition of 2,000 Massachusetts men in 40 vessels failed to dislodge them. They then evacuated Rhode Island, which was soon occupied by a French force, itself promptly blockaded by a British fleet under Admiral Arbuthnot. Finally in 1781 the combination of circumstances which Washington had been working with

might and main to bring about actually happened. With Cornwallis' southern army in Virginia and the large French fleet of de Grasse in the West Indies, Washington succeeded in effecting a junction of his own army with Rochambeau's Newport forces, which together were moved rapidly south to hem Cornwallis into Virginia's Yorktown peninsula. The French Newport squadron got free of Narragansett Bay and brought heavy artillery to the Chesapeake, where de Grasse fought off the British combined fleets and likewise entered Chesapeake Bay. Cornwallis was trapped and had no alternative but to surrender. Had the British been able to put together sufficient sea transport, they would gladly have evacuated the United States at any time from this point on. All they held was New York.

The real contributions of American seamen to the Revolution were in diverting to the Continental Army essential munitions and supplies intended for British forces, in keeping the sea lanes open for American commerce when it was desperately needed, and in cementing the effective French alliance without which Washington could not have defeated his major antagonist at Yorktown. In all this, Massachusetts seamen played a glorious and overwhelming part. Particularly did the names of such Salem privateers as the *General Pickering* and the *Grand Turk* earn a valorous niche in America's maritime history.

John Adams, after three grueling years in the Continental Congress, was sent in 1778 to join Benjamin Franklin and Arthur Lee as commissioners to France. Taking with him only his 10-year-old son, John Quincy Adams, he sailed from Nantasket Roads in the frigate *Boston*. Escaping one British ship and capturing another en route, the *Boston* arrived at Bordeaux in April. The establishment of the French alliance and the sending of d'Estaing's fleet were results of the commissioners' work at Paris. Adams returned home in August, 1779, just in time to be assigned by the Massachusetts constitutional convention the task of writing a constitution for the commonwealth.

The draft of the Massachusetts Constitution that John Adams wrote is basically the one, with subsequent amendment, under which the commonwealth still functions. The Adams principles, which were widely copied by other states subsequently, have stood up well over the years. They include a complete separation of the three governmental powers, executive, legislative and judicial, with a bicameral legislature originally designed to represent the popular voice in the lower house and the aristocracy and property owners in the upper. The judiciary was to be completely independent of control by the others, and Adams insisted on a strong single executive with veto power over the Legislature. This was to be, in his words, "a government of laws and not of men." With minor changes, Adams' draft was adopted by the convention and by Massachusetts' towns in 1780. Perhaps the greatest tribute to John Adams as a constitutionalist is the fact that the structure of government outlined in the Constitution of the United States in 1787 mirrored almost precisely the principles he had written into the Massachusetts Constitution eight years before.

In four months he was off to Europe again, this time to join Franklin and John Jay in negotiating with a weak British Ministry a treaty of peace which secured for the new nation an independence of action that became a source of wonder and celebration to American patriots. In this accomplishment great credit was due to Adam's Yankee stubbornness, for he refused to let the new United States be a tool in the hands of France for continued harassment of England. His reward was to be appointed ambassador to England, the first of those uncomfortable missions to the Court of St. James's in times of crisis at which the Adams family have specialized.

So at long last the independence of the United States was solid and sure. In Massachusetts the rebellion began. Massachusetts invented a model for provisional government, showed the way to rid itself of royal domination, and convinced the nation to adopt that program. Its leaders and its common soldiers and seamen suffered through the battles, endured the necessary hardships, and built the nation strong. These were stubborn and individualistic Yankees, like John Adams himself, too hot for the British to handle. It was because of their arrogant tenacity that they were so effective in crises, on sea and land, and in the Congresses. Such characters were needed to secure liberty for a new nation. That there were loyalists, profiteers, and deserters among them is not surprising. The wonder is that these Yankee individualists found among themselves enough community loyalty to work not only together but joined with aristocrats and patroons, merchants and Frenchmen through defeat after defeat, and still outlast and beat down the mightiest nation in the civilized world. Massachusetts made no heavier sacrifices than many another colony; in fact her territory remained immune from the years-long ravages of war that scorched the earth of New York, New Jersey, and the South. But her record of initial rebellion, statesmanship, and military and maritime courage is a proud one among the many colonial contributions to the birth of the new nation.

CHAPTER ELEVEN

Rags to Riches

Only after the achievement of liberty did the full weight of its cost really strike hard at Massachusetts. The peace brought rejoicing; it also brought the most profound economic depression the Bay State ever experienced.

During the last years of the war the powerful British blockade had destroyed virtually all of the state navy, a large proportion of Massachusetts' privateers and fishing vessels, and most of New Bedford's whaling fleet. England promptly closed her home ports and her West Indian harbors to Yankee shipping. French and Spanish colonies did the same. Even the Americans themselves set up state tariffs that discouraged coastwise trade. Meanwhile British ships poured into Boston harbor cargo after cargo of European goods of just the types most needed to overcome the shortages generated by seven years of war. Eager speculators bought these up on credit and held them for high prices to greedy buyers, producing a flight of scarce hard money that only accentuated an already severe war-born inflation of the currency. The weak Confederation government could do nothing to control or correct the financial crisis that these profiteering practices produced. The inevitable result was chaos. Debts piled up among farmers, small businessmen, and war veterans who could least afford to pay their bills and taxes. Some states resorted to unsecured issues of paper money; prices went up and all the evils of uncontrolled inflation appeared.

Under normal circumstances the West Indies trade would have balanced out this profiteering: exports of Yankee products would have brought in sufficient Spanish silver to keep specie circulating. After a time various subterfuges were invented to help bring this about, through registering Massachusetts vessels out of Nova Scotian ports or by securing admittance to West Indies harbors in pretended distress or emergencies. But these tricks took time to develop. Meanwhile the Massachusetts economy grew desperate. Boston creditors were dunning country storekeepers and farmers for money they did not have. State tax collectors began to throw citizens into jail for nonpayment of heavy wartime taxes. It was also customary at that time for courts to sentence debtors to terms in jail. Families began to lose their homesteads and farms. The courts were jammed with suits. To upstate war veterans this seemed an intolerable reward for their recent patriotic services.

In country towns in 1782 and 1783 these veterans began to adopt an old revolutionary technique. They re-formed the Committees of Correspondence. They met and protested in county conventions. They memorialized the legislature. And when these traditional maneuvers failed to produce any relief, they began to occupy the court houses and prevent the judges from sitting. But this time it was not British colonial judges they were obstructing: it was the courts of their own newly won government they were rebelling against.

George Washington, greatly concerned at the situation, wrote to Henry Lee: "Know precisely what the insurgents aim at. If they have *real* grievances, redress them if possible; or acknowledge the justice of them, and your inability to do it at the present moment. If they have not, employ the force of government against them at once." But the Massachusetts legislature vacillated, did nothing effective, and the ugly disturbances grew more intense and widespread. The old patriot leaders were for the most part no longer in office. The responsible commercial aristocracy who had fought the war had now been often displaced by men of the profiteering class whose motives were less concerned with the welfare of the community than with that of their speculative gains.

In Hampshire County seven conventions were held by the insurgents, sometimes including representatives of fifty towns. Mobs of several hundred men attacked the jails in Northampton and Hatfield to force the release of prisoners. Only militia mobilization or abandonment of court sessions prevented similar outbreaks at Springfield, Worcester, Taunton, Concord and Great Barrington. The magnitude of the protest can be judged by such evidences as that there were 4,000 lawsuits in Worcester County in 1784–85 in a population of 50,000. In Groton every fourth man was subjected to from one to twelve suits for debt between 1784 and 1786. In Concord in 1786 three times as many prisoners were jailed for debt as for all other causes combined, and in Worcester County twenty times as many.

By 1786 county conventions in Essex, Middlesex, Worcester, Hampshire and Berkshire counties had met and taken various actions of protest, and by correspondence had so coordinated their leadership that it was obvious a major threat existed to the integrity of the commonwealth, and its constitution. While the laborers, mechanics and farmers who mostly made up the rebels were sometimes disenfranchised by the property qualification for voting then prevailing, their interference with orderly government in the courts of common pleas was a serious one. The fact that most of the rebels and their leaders were veterans of the Revolution made their plight a particularly appealing one. The legislature did make some concessions, consisting mostly of legalizing the payment of debt by goods instead of specie, but these were no real answer to the problems.

By 1785 some of the militia were refusing to muster to protect the courts. Obviously some concerted action was necessary. Governor Bowdoin in 1786 therefore ordered General Benjamin Lincoln to lead an expedition to crush the insurgents. Lacking any appropriations to finance the troops, Lincoln went to a club of Boston gentlemen, warned them it was advisable to lend part of their wealth to save the rest, and within twenty-four hours raised enough money to finance his expedition. After protecting a meeting of the court at Worcester, he marched to Springfield to reinforce General Shepherd in his defense of the federal arsenal there against an assault by the insurgents under their principal leader, Captain Daniel Shays. He then attacked and dispersed another rebel force nearby led by Luke Day, and quickly made a forced march to Petersham, where 150 of the Shays rebels were surprised and captured. This broke up the main body of the rebellion, though Lincoln pursued other bands for a few weeks longer in Berkshire County. At the next election three quarters of the legislature were displaced, sometimes by members of the insurgent bands. Along with the general amnesty that followed, numerous measures were passed to alleviate the sufferings of the debtors. But before this was accomplished, hundreds of pioneer families abandoned their farms and moved to Vermont or to New York, starting the emigration movement that continued to transfer discontented Massachusetts farmers to "western lands" for the next century. There were no liberalizations made, however, in the property qualifications for the franchise.

Shays' Rebellion, as this rather pitiful episode has come to be called, was evidence that the old Massachusetts contention between the yeomanry and the gentry, between the propertied seacoast class and the democratic townsmen, had by no means been resolved in the American Revolution, however equalitarian that struggle had seemed in its statements of principles. Men were indeed "created equal," but men of property still held the upper hand. Even the Massachusetts Constitution of 1780 has been described by Samuel Eliot Morison as "a lawyers' and merchants' Constitution directed toward something like quarter-deck efficiency in government, and the protection of property against democratic pirates." And in Shays' Rebellion property owners won out over Jeffersonianism in Massachusetts in the first real test. This set the stage for Massachusetts' forces of law and order to secure the state's ratification of the Federal Constitution in 1788, though by a bare majority.

There was beginning to be a solid economic reason for the victories of Federalist merchants in this political arena. Yankee shipmasters were already meeting Caribbean islanders' needs for New England lumber, codfish and whale oil by smuggling through Dutch, Danish and Swedish islands. Reappearance of an export market for farm produce and home industry gradually assuaged the economic causes of Shays' Rebellion. But, more significantly, Massachusetts merchants were beginning to invade a larger world of commerce where neither West India regulations nor European embargoes could hamper them. Boston and Salem boldly began to challenge Britain in the farthest reaches of the enormously lucrative Far Eastern trade by which the monopolistic British East India Company had for years supplied the world with tea, spices, India cotton and silk.

In 1783 Hingham's little sloop *Harriet* already had set out for China. But at Cape of Good Hope alarmed British merchants eagerly bought Captain Hallet's cargo for double its weight in tea to forestall his intention of first carrying the American flag to the Orient. That honor was reserved therefore for the New York ship *Empress of China*, which Boston's Major Samuel Shaw took to Macao the next year. There he secured a profitable cargo and the following year, 1786, established Shaw and Randall at Canton, the first American commercial firm in China. He was soon visited there by Salem's wartime privateer *Grand Turk*, Captain Ebenezer West, the first Massachusetts vessel to reach the Far East. She was followed by Elias Hasket Derby's *Astraea*, Captain James Magee, and Derby's bark *Light Horse*, Ichabod Nichols master. These vessels proved that enormous profits could be obtained in this direct trade with the Orient, through by-passing onerous duties charged by the Dutch and English on Oriental commodities. Tea, silks, chinaware and nankeens now began to flow through the Salem warehouses of the Derbys and Crowninshields, the Perkinses and Pickmans and Cabots, and decorated Salem mansions. For the next forty years Salem ships became as common as the British in the Dutch East Indies, Manila, China, both coasts of Africa, and the Southwest Pacific. Madras chintzes, Bombay ginger, Sumatra pepper, Batavia and Mocha coffee, Arabian senna, and Manila hemp and indigo soon were piled high on Salem's wharves and paid for McIntire mansions on Essex and Chestnut streets. Often half a dozen voyages of these rugged shipmasters earned them enough to retire to Salem in their thirties, continuing the leisurely management of their mercantile enterprises from counting houses near their homes. Not Harvard men, these weather-beaten executives ran their homes and offices like quarter-decks, and often merited, like Elias Hasket Derby, the nickname "King."

Boston's China trade began in 1787 when John Kendrick of Wareham and Robert Gray of Tiverton sailed the ship *Columbia*, built on the North River in Scituate, around Cape Horn to Nootka Sound, on Vancouver Island, and thence to

Canton and around the world to Boston. This first Cape Horn voyage, and first circumnavigation by an American vessel, established the northwest fur trade as a second avenue of trade to China, where furs were in great demand in exchange for Oriental goods. Along variants of this route Yankee captains were soon smuggling supplies to Spaniards in Chile and California, and collecting fur seal in the Falklands, Chile and Santa Catalina, and sandalwood in Hawaii. By 1805 American imports at Canton reached $5 million annually, and were exchanged for 10 million pounds of tea. Some of these voyages netted $200,000 on a total investment of $40,000.

Boys went to sea at sixteen, and sometimes were shipmasters at twenty. It was a rough life, involving dirty weather off Cape Horn and sudden warfare with Indians or Malay pirates. Some ships disappeared with all hands. There were castaways and mutinies, scurvy and occasional tyranny. But there were also idyllic sojourns on Pacific islands. The pay was high. The crews were New England men from top to bottom, and those who could take it thrived on the life at sea. The masters and business agents were usually gentlemen, and were so considered in foreign ports. They rapidly developed new skills and new branches of learning, devouring source books on the history and commerce of the Orient, Europe, and the Levant. Marine societies and philosophical libraries sprouted in Boston, Salem and Newburyport, collecting logs, market reports and navigation information for the benefit of their members. Nathaniel Bowditch's new *Practical Navigator* so far surpassed any previous guide to navigation that it remained the bible of American shipmasters for more than a century. His work was to ships entering harbors what instrument landings are to airplanes today. With its principles Bowditch himself brought a ship from Sumatra into Salem harbor on Christmas Eve of 1803 in a blinding snowstorm without having picked up a single landmark.

The fabulous success of Massachusetts' China trade completely transformed the commonwealth's economy. That it happened to coincide in time with the ragged rebellion of Daniel Shays is one of those curious paradoxes that add spice to history. Within a decade the whole Bay State economy and political system somersaulted into a Federalist paradise. The national government built lighthouses, and raised tariffs against foreign shipping. Every conceivable encouragement was given to shipbuilding, by which Massachusetts multiplied its merchant and fishing fleet almost ten times bewteen 1789 and 1810. Shipyards sprang into feverish activity at Newburyport and Salem, the Mystic River at Boston, on the North River at Scituate and Hanover, and in smaller ports like Ipswich, Essex, Quincy, Cohasset, Duxbury, Wareham, Wellfleet and Mattapoisett. Especially along the North River there were spawned families of craftsmen in all the shipbuilding arts, who built there more than a thousand vessels, and graduated apprentices who set up new shipyards in South Boston, New Bedford, Barnstable, Kingston and Medford. In the Federalist period an average of twenty-three vessels were completed each year in North River yards. Now only a few crumbling retaining walls are left of all that feverish industry. It is difficult even to visualize the busy clatter of adze and calking iron, or the excited pageantry of a launching. It now seems inconceivable that brisk little forges and ropewalks and cooper shops in all the now peaceful surrounding towns were then in frenzied activity turning out anchors and spars, cordage and sailcloth, blocks and capstans and hogsheads for the score of shipyards that lined the lazy stream. The same was true around every harbor from Newburyport to Taunton. Only at the fish piers of Gloucester, Boston or New Bedford can one still recover a somewhat dieselized smell of the halcyon days of New England maritime life. Only in Old Dartmouth's Whaling Museum or in Salem's Peabody Museum can one really reconstruct something of the China trade days from the painfully accumulated relics there displayed.

But every coastal town on the Bay State's shores remains branded with the worldly wisdom, the good living, and the sophisticated wealth of those prosperous years. Walk down the Main Street or around the Common of any maritime village from Newburyport to New Bedford and look at the "Early American" houses the merchants built. Go inside the houses and see the carved mantels, the stairways, the blue chinaware, the lacquered Chinese desks, the India prints, and the Paisley shawls. The Puritan was growing up. He had his portrait painted in a foreign port. He decorated his house with a porch with fluted columns. He had money for a fine clock, for a Chinese Chippendale table and a brass-handled bureau, and some porcelain pitchers with his ship emblazoned on them. He had his ship carver place a screaming eagle over his doorway.

The domestic arts quickly developed to match the challenge of the imports. Every little town soon had a silversmith, a fine cabinetmaker, and a house carpenter expert in moldings, dentates and paneling. The Willards learned how to build tall clocks. Silversmith families began to provide fine flagons, communion sets, porringers, beakers and teapots. Andirons, table silver, fine furniture and ormolu mirrors were fashioned by home craftsmen for the merchant princes. By the same token water power began to be used for larger enterprises than the classical sawmill, gristmill, and triphammer-forge of the earlier days. Cotton mills were appearing at East Bridgewater, Beverly and Acushnet. Paper mills, tanneries and printing presses were growing in numbers not only in Greater Boston but also in New Bedford, whose whaling industry was as prosperous as the China trade.

In Boston the changes brought about by maritime expansion were prodigious. Three times the size and importance of Salem, Boston's port frequently held as many as 450 sail at one time. State Street was crowded with banks and insurance companies. Charles Bulfinch was rapidly transforming the town with his plans for the new State House, brick mansions on Beacon Hill, the South Meeting House, the Tontine Crescent, and India Wharf's great countinghouse. New wooden bridges were built to Charlestown, Cambridge and South Boston. The crest of Beacon Hill was shoveled off to fill the North End's Mill Pond. Plans were afoot to extend Beacon Street across the mud flats of the Back Bay.

Boston was becoming a complex society, dominated as much by wealthy shopkeepers, capitalists and politicians as by merchant princes. Many cliques divided the aristocracy. The Essex County Lowells and Higginsons did not move in the same circle as a politician like Josiah Quincy or an Anglophile speculator like Christopher Gore. The Puritan oligarchy was gone. The common bond of the aristocracy was its loyalty to Federalism, already a reactionary creed outside of New England. There were many gentlemen's clubs, formal dinners, and parties at country estates. A hereditary wealthy class was already drawing comfortable luxury from the assured profits of invested capital. Younger men were on the make, sailing the ships and developing new enterprises but with the aim of establishing great fortunes like their elders. Banks, insurance companies, commodity exchanges and countinghouses were entrenching the wealthy in a hereditary class that would dominate Boston's character for a century. Salem was in its glory also, but as ships grew larger her shallow harbor would transfer her commerce to build still further the concentration of wealth in the port of Boston. The gap between the very rich and the very poor was widening.

CHAPTER TWELVE

Overseas Entanglements

Massachusetts had again extricated herself from economic depression, just as she had originally done in 1640, by going to sea. The glory of her new China trade was qualitatively no different from that of her previous maritime exploits in nullifying the Navigation Acts of 1675, the French depredations of 1710, the Townshend Acts in 1770, and the British blockade of 1776. Economic prosperity rarely makes a society popular among its neighbors, though in the previous instances Massachusetts' commercial successes had served a continental purpose in agreement with a popular protest against oppression. But the Federalist merchants of 1800 found themselves operating in a quite different national climate, full of resentment at their entrenched wealth and their reactionary philosophy. While Massachusetts was forcibly wiping out Shays' Rebellion, other states were removing the property qualifications for voting. And as quarter-deck efficiency glorified property rights above human rights in Massachusetts, underprivileged Bay State farmers began to desert their gravelly fields and look for a better livelihood on western lands. The new democratic frontier thus grew in population at the expense of Massachusetts.

The relative importance of New England in the national scene had been declining for more than a century. From half the colonial population in 1650, New England had shrunk, relatively, to one fourth of the United States total in 1790. In half a century Boston had grown by only 2,000, reaching 20,000 in 1790, while New York and Philadelphia, each with 13,000 in 1750, had grown by 1790 to 46,000 and 55,000, respectively. Only nine communities in Massachusetts had more than 4,000 inhabitants in 1789, most of them seaports. Meanwhile an extensive emigration was in process toward western New York State, Ohio and Pennsylvania. Fugitives from Shays' Rebellion were joined by the discontented of every stripe, escaping westward from the domination of seaboard merchants and taxgatherers. The sons of solid citizens, tired of hauling boulders off Massachusetts fields to build yet more stone walls, eagerly abandoned their fathers' farms for a new start in the opening West. Massachusetts' share in the nation's growth was rapidly being eroded.

These changes are well symbolized by the political experiences of Massachusetts' first citizen, John Adams, whose stubborn honesty and independence of judgment was always above party considerations. After eight years of diplomatic service in Europe, culminating in the uncomfortable ambassadorship to England, he returned to Braintree in 1788 to find himself within a few months elected vice-president under President George Washington, inaugurating the United States system under its new Constitution. He was entirely unprepared for the changes that had occurred at home. Instead of the collection of provinces driving, however falteringly, toward nationality, which he had left in 1779, he found a disjointed assemblage of political cliques whose rivalry in strife for power and local privilege was the keynote of its activity. This was of course the inevitable result of the painful emergence of the two-party system from the futile weakness of the rejected confederation government. During his absence a sharp line of cleavage had developed between the Revolutionary leaders, mostly of the propertied aristocracy, and the still disenfranchised little people who had profoundly suffered in the Revolution and the postwar inflation. Adams was no democrat, but he did believe in the philosophy of equalitarianism quite as much as did Thomas Jefferson. Federalist political forces, however, threw Adams into public antagonisms with Jefferson, who had become the symbol of equalitarianism. Adams' tragic experiences in his presidency were the result of his being caught between the Federalist treachery of his own Cabinet and a Jeffersonian opposition with which he often, in principle, agreed.

As vice-president he at first basked in the universal popularity which the Washington administration enjoyed. But, since he had developed a jealousy of the President, Adams was not called into Cabinet councils and, as partisan controversy grew, the deciding vote he cast twenty times as presiding officer of an equally divided Senate did not help his popularity. Since his party was now dominated by Washington's Federalist Cabinet leaders, with whom Adams had not established close liaison, Adams' political future rested in their hands. The Cabinet's most adroit political administrator, Alexander Hamilton, had never forgiven Adams for replacing Hamilton's father-in-law, General Philip Schuyler, by General Gates just before the American victory over Burgoyne at the Battle of Saratoga. Hamilton had already tried to block Adams' election as vice-president. Now he attempted to interfere with his election as president. But Adams' popularity throughout the country was too great, and all Hamilton succeeded in doing was to reduce Adams' effectiveness as president. Adams was elected by only a three-vote majority in the electoral college, with Jefferson as his vice-president.

John Adams' greatest weakness was his poor judgment

of men and a consequent inability to build around himself a loyal group of followers. As an individual he was brilliant to the point of genius, but this brilliance was accompanied by an impatient egotism that often alienated associates who might have become his strongest allies. In this he perhaps only mirrored that Puritan arrogance which had gotten Massachusetts into trouble with her sister colonies time and again a century and a half before.

Having developed no staff of his own, Adams now reappointed most of Washington's Cabinet. This was the greatest blunder he ever made. For, although Hamilton himself was no longer a member of the Cabinet, his successor, Wolcott, and two other members, Pickering and McHenry, were more loyal to Hamilton than to the President. It took Adams a long time to discover that these three men regularly leaked confidential Cabinet discussions to Hamilton, who was now not even an official of the government but only a New York lawyer in private practice. The lonely President was then forced back upon his own individual judgment in matters where the national welfare was opposed to the particular interests of the Hamilton bloc. Meanwhile the growing popular party led by Jefferson sniped at Adams as an aristocrat and as an opponent of the French Revolution. What Adams really objected to in the French Revolution was the political immaturity of its leaders. Adams himself, supported neither by his supposed Federalist associates nor by his Jeffersonian antagonists, became a president without a party.

Curiously enough the major crisis of those years was one which required just the lonely, nonpartisan good judgment which the Massachusetts President pre-eminently possessed and for which his successive services at the courts of France and England had particularly well prepared him. Whether England or France was the more shabby in its treatment of the new United States at that time is a tossup. Both indulged in piracy on American commerce and both habitually insulted American diplomats. Without the firm, cool hand of George Washington the nation might already have been at war with France over the Genêt incident. The close ties of Federalist merchants to England were opposed by equally strong bonds of sympathy of the Jeffersonian Republicans for the new French Republic. Massachusetts' Fisher Ames had again probably prevented war in the 1795 crisis over the humiliating Jay Treaty by his extraordinary speech in Congress. Had Jefferson been president, such a premature disastrous war with England could scarcely have been avoided. Though humiliating, the treaty was as good a compromise on the British commercial and frontier problems as could have been obtained. To France, however, it was a body blow. Her corrupt Directory refused to accept retiring President Washington's appointment of Federalist Charles C. Pinckney as United States minister and threatened a break in diplomatic relations. Congress supported Adams in his appeal for appropriations for harbor defenses and a new militia and navy to meet the French threat of war. Construction of the new frigates *Constitution* and *Constellation* was completed under this legislation. John Adams confirmed Pinckney's appointment, adding John Marshall and Elbridge Gerry to the French mission, and stood fast against Talleyrand's disgraceful attempt to blackmail the United States with bribes and threatened attacks on the American coast.

Exposure of the infamous French blackmail offers by President Adams' publication of the XYZ correspondence threw the United States into a patriotic frenzy. Singing "Hail, Columbia" the people demanded an immediate declaration of war against France. John Adams was momentarily elevated to a pinnacle of popular approval. George Washington was made commander of a new army, with Hamilton and Pinckney and Knox recalled to serve as major generals under him. Military stores were accumulated, privateers commissioned, and the war at sea already begun. Here was a chance for Alexander Hamilton to conquer Louisiana, even Mexico, and annex them to the young republic. The people wanted war. Every interest of the ruling Federalist party demanded war.

Only John Adams kept a cool head. He had learned confidentially that the French were completely taken aback at the American war preparations. He now had indisputable proof that Talleyrand had changed his mind and would receive a new American minister with the courtesies properly due the representative of an independent power. He realized that the war would be extremely unpopular with the Republicans, and even with many moderate Federalists, especially if it were later revealed that overtures for a peaceful settlement had been available. So the Federalist President did not bother to consult his Federalist Cabinet. He acted. He simply announced to the Senate that he was appointing a minister to France.

No more devastating blow was ever administered by its chief to his own party. It split the Federalists from top to bottom. During months of haggling every possible obstacle was placed in the way of completing the mission to France. But the mission sailed. So obvious did the treachery of Pickering and McHenry, the secretaries of state and war, become that Adams dismissed them. Furious and unreasonable Federalist enforcement of Alien and Sedition Laws against their Republican opponents became so flagrant that the country reacted in sympathy for the Jeffersonians. The Federalists thus completed their own destruction. The election campaign of 1800 was a particularly nasty one. John Adams went down to defeat knifed in the back by a notorious Hamilton letter alleging Adams' "unfitness for the station of Chief Magistrate." He was thus pushed out of office by the same extralegal genius who had hounded and beset every statesmanlike move he had tried to make during his presidency. He retired, embittered, to his Quincy mansion, cordially despised by his Boston Federalist friends for the crime of having, singlehanded, prevented a war. "I desire no other inscription over my gravestone," he later wrote, "than: Here lies John Adams, who took upon himself the responsibility of the peace with France in the year 1800."

So the old man retired to his Quincy study, placed on the shelf by the Republic he had served so well. His friends, the common farmers and fishermen of New England, always stood by him. But the Anglophile merchants of State Street and Essex County defended English impressment of American seamen and were outraged by Jefferson's embargo. Adams approved the embargo, though believing an eventual war with England was inevitable. They could not approve Jefferson's purchase of the huge Louisiana Territory; he applauded it. It was natural that finally a reconciliation occurred between the two elder statesmen. Thomas Jefferson, like John Adams, was a liberal and a rebel. Both men were scholars. Their subsequent old age was filled with correspondence about philosophy and religion.

As Adams' successor in the Presidency, Jefferson did not at first interfere with Massachusetts' maritime prosperity. Few changes were made in the Federalist system of tonnage duties, tariffs, and fishing bounties. In 1804 the Bay State actually cast its electoral votes for Jefferson. Conditions changed, however, when England renewed her war with Napoleon. Each nation tried to control neutral shipping to the other's ports by searches and confiscations that became a violent restriction on Yankee commerce. In 1807 the British ship of war *Leopard* attacked the U.S. frigate *Chesapeake*, killing or wounding twenty-one of her crew and impressing four seamen. This was a culmination of many such acts perpetrated by both French and British, but more flagrantly and oftener by the British. Had Jefferson called for war with England in 1807 he would have had an enraged and unified nation behind him. Instead, he declared an embargo, forbidding any American vessel to sail for a foreign port, and enforced it in American ports with federal troops. Despite enormous smuggling activities on the Canadian and Florida borders, he managed to keep a fairly tight lid on foreign commerce for a year and a half.

This proved to be a disastrous policy. The penalty was placed now not on the warring nations of Europe but rather on the most enterprising segment of the American economy. The China trade, which was not really involved in the war, was penalized along with the rest. New England exports declined 75 per cent; shipbuilding dropped to a third that of the previous year; and prices of farm produce dropped 50 per cent. As merchants went bankrupt and unemployment grew, popular resentment at the artificially produced economic slump became universal. Contempt for the embargo produced inevitable clashes between revenue officers and mobs of people. The moribund Federalist party, out of power everywhere except in Connecticut, bounced back to life. A few extremist leaders even contemplated secession from the Union. Twenty Massachusetts towns petitioned the President to remove the embargo. Gloucester, Worcester, Newburyport, Rowley, Cambridge and Beverly began to plan Committees of Safety like the Revolutionary ones, protesting troops quartered among them in times of peace. The Rhode Island legislature termed the enforcement act oppressive and tyrannical. In Connecticut Governor Trumbull refused the use of the militia to assist customhouse officers in suppressing riots. So great became the pressure that Jefferson had to give in. In March, 1809, a few days before Madison's inauguration, the embargo was repealed. For two years matters quieted down and trade was encouraged. Republicans again returned to power in New England, though it was obvious that serious dissension still existed, on the one hand, between maritime New England and the agricultural South and West and, on the other, between two partisan groups in New England over contrasting philosophies in government. A further crisis would only rekindle these dissensions.

In 1811 the sectional dissension was set aflame over the question of admitting Louisiana to the Union as an eighteenth state, the first state to be set up from territories not a part of the original Union. The jealous partisan strife which this controversy started was only accentuated and continued by the cry of the Republican War Hawks for war with England. The true origin of the War of 1812 was the desire of the West to settle its serious Indian problem by driving the English out of Canada. No regard in those days was paid to the fact that England, despite our grievances with her, was defending the rest of Europe against the military despotism of Napoleon. Impressment of our sailors was a relatively minor issue: France had in fact injured our commerce more than England. Napoleon certainly directed his diplomacy toward tricking us into declaring war on England.

Contrary to their feeling in 1807, the majority of New England people were now opposed to what they called "Mr. Madison's War" and did not support it. Massachusetts, Connecticut and Rhode Island refused to place their militia at the disposal of the federal government, except for local defense. In the newspapers there was open debate on dissolving the Union. New England failed utterly to subscribe more than a token amount in war loans, and since the region possessed a large proportion of the nation's available money, there was eventually a national financial crisis. Contrary to the story in the Revolution, Yankees contributed far less than their share to privateering. In the inland counties a minority of patriots supplied regiments of volunteers and a few co-operative merchants like the Salem Crowninshields contributed in a maritime way. But for a state owning more than a third of the nation's registered tonnage, twice that of New York, her nearest competitor, Massachusetts lagged badly. Her frigate *Constitution*, partly outfitted by William Gray, won outstanding victories over the *Guerrière* and the *Java*. The Crowninshields' ship *America* and the Boston-owned Salem brig *Grand Turk* gave good accounts of themselves as privateers. Boston's Captain David Porter did well in the Pacific in the frigate *Essex*.

But the major events of this somewhat inglorious war scarcely belong in this book, so little part did Massachusetts men play in them. Even the much-trumpeted secession movement leading up to New England's anticlimactic Hartford Convention of 1814 hardly concerns us, since the extreme Federalists of the Essex Junto, a club of wealthy merchants who spearheaded this movement, could never carry their supporters further than mere nullification of government policies that seemed mainly foolish or mistaken. The Federalists never attained a majority without including a group of moderates that repeatedly returned to Republicanism when crises quieted down. These moderates never were persuaded that either the embargo or the war was sufficient cause for dissolving the Union.

Massachusetts' actual role in the war is perhaps best described by a review of some of the minor incidents that occurred along her coast. Massachusetts was not a military objective other than as a part of the thinly maintained British blockade of the American coast. In 1813 Captain James Lawrence, who had conducted in 1812 a successful cruise in the sloop *Hornet*, took command of the 38-gun frigate *Chesa-*

peake in Boston harbor and was almost immediately challenged by Captain Brock, of the British frigate *Shannon*. Sallying from Boston with a green crew, the *Chesapeake* was soon overwhelmed by the superior gunnery of the *Shannon*. Lawrence was killed, and his frigate captured and taken to Halifax. Residents of South Shore towns watched the unequal struggle from hilltops, as it occurred just off the Scituate shore. Three frightened North River boys had an even closer view from their little Scituate fishing boat.

While Massachusetts volunteers were serving in the battles of Chippewa, Lundy's Lane, Fort Erie and Lake Champlain in 1814, the British began to tighten their blockade along the coast. Two British frigates, the *Junon* and the *Teredos*, actually chased the *Constitution* into Marblehead harbor in 1814. Massachusetts shores had to be garrisoned by 35,000 well-armed militia to forestall raids by British landing parties from the blockading squadrons. Between June and November, 1814, artillery companies from such inland towns as Hanover, Milton, Dedham and Clinton stood guard in the defenses of Plymouth, Scituate, Cohasset, and Forts Warren and Independence at Boston. Forts at Salem and Marblehead were enlarged and reconstructed. Booms were placed across harbor mouths and trenches manned on promontories. Field guns were set up to rake entrance channels and schooners were pulled up in salt marsh creeks for protection.

Despite such precautions, two British men-of-war from anchorage in Buzzards Bay sent six boats ashore at Wareham, where 200 men landed and destroyed buildings. Anchored vessels in Scituate harbor were burned on June 11 and those in Annisquam on June 13. Twice small British raiding parties entered Boston harbor by night and destroyed sloops and schooners almost as far up as the Battery. They set their watches by the Gloucester town clock, sent flags of truce on shore at Salem to exchange prisoners, and even sent letters ashore to be published in Boston newspapers. They even indulged in such horseplay as playing ninepins at the Baker's Island lighthouse and hunting running cattle with muskets on Cape Ann.

The other side of the picture is less entertaining. American collaborators, especially on Cape Cod and Nantucket, regularly supplied the British squadron with fresh vegetables, beef and mutton, for a good price. Provincetown harbor practically became their naval base. The selectmen of Provincetown, Truro and Wellfleet freely went abroad British frigates and sold them beef at seven pence per pound. Yet literally scores of packet boats and coasting schooners were captured or burned by the four or five frigates and the dozen or more armed schooners and privateers in the blockading squadron. They thus completely disrupted Massachusetts commerce for most of the year 1814, bottling up the American frigates *Constitution* and *Independence* in Boston and the *Congress* at Portsmouth for long periods. In Massachusetts' province of Maine, they landed and occupied Eastport and Passamaquoddy Bay, and then Castine and Belfast, dominating Penobscot Bay. At Hampden they captured the crippled frigate *Adams*, and then proceeded to take possession of Bangor.

At home, Massachusetts seems to have prospered. In the early years before the blockade was tightened there was a scarcely concealed extensive trade with the enemy, through Halifax, the West Indies, and Spain. This was conducted with British licenses passing the American vessels through the blockade. Massachusetts was by no means alone in this treacherous practice, for such licenses were openly bought and sold in New York and Philadelphia also. Americans sold supplies as freely to other blockading squadrons, even in Chesapeake Bay, perhaps even while the new capital city of Washington was being burned. Trade was therefore far more active during the war than it had been during the embargo. Furthermore, shortages of British goods stimulated American manufacturing. The absorption of British energies in the Napoleonic struggle removed British competition from Yankee industrial enterprises with the result that cotton and woolen mills, ironworks, and other new industrial experiments flourished even when shipbuilding and commerce began to languish. Inland transportation began to supplement coastwise trade: roads were built, and ox teams slowly hauled new goods overland to southern markets.

It should by now be apparent that the War of 1812 arose from no universal burning issue that stirred the nation; it was rather imposed from the world outside. Such strange and paradoxical behavior as substantial people indulged in during the war scarcely suggests a nation fighting for freedom, or for wholehearted protest against anything in particular. Indeed the United States seems to have been a bystander caught up in the furious struggle of world politics, and maneuvered somewhat halfheartedly into taking sides. There is some doubt as to whether the chosen side was the proper one. In the preliminary bouts under Washington and Adams the nation came close to choosing the opposite side on two occasions. And in the end even the peace came suddenly, because it served England's purpose to get rid of an annoyance on her flank. The treaty negotiated by John Quincy Adams made no changes from conditions that existed at the beginning. Probably the whole thing was a mistake. Probably George Washington's admonition about avoiding entangling alliances might well have been extended to avoiding entangling enmities also. It seems problematical which was more disgraceful, Massachusetts' failure to support the nation or the nation's unwarranted attack on England.

CHAPTER THIRTEEN

Cultural Renaissance

In the United States as a whole, the thirty years that followed the War of 1812 were marked by prodigious economic and physical expansion. The South of King Cotton was on the make. New York and Pennsylvania spent fortunes on canals and railroads, and thus captured half the Mississippi valley's markets. The combined discoveries of iron ore and anthracite built western Pennsylvania's Pittsburgh into a burgeoning colossus. Pennsylvania by 1810 was producing half the cast iron in the nation. Down the Ohio she shipped nails and builders' and agricultural tools in unending streams to supply the limitless needs of homesteaders swarming into the fertile valleys of Kentucky, Indiana, and on across the plains. Syracuse salt displaced the New England product; Merino sheep in the middle states, imported from Spain, began to capture wool markets previously held by Yankee farmers. As we have already noted, Yankees themselves abandoned their farms and joined the emigration.

In 1815 and 1816 England repeated her post-Revolution maneuver by dumping in American seaports an accumulation of her manufactured goods, at loss prices, in an attempt to kill prosperous new American industries which embargo and war had fostered. Should the United States become industrially self-sufficient, the loss of the American market would be a catastrophe to English manufacturers. The English maneuver did succeed in closing up much of the *seaboard* American iron industry, along with some sheep raising, woolen mills, cotton, textile and cordage plants. But its major effect was to produce an outraged demand on Congress for a high protective tariff to save American industry. The fact that the greater part of the importing business of Massachusetts merchants and ship-owners would disappear under prohibitive tariff rates scarcely concerned manufacturers in Pittsburgh or Syracuse, or grow-ers of wool or hemp in Ohio and Kentucky. New England was whipsawed between her own merchants' desires for a low tariff and her manufacturers' demands for a high one. But the middle and western states invariably wanted protec-tion. Inevitably they got it in the tariff of 1818. Just as in-evitably, foreign commerce shrank to half the volume of 1816, and American tonnage fell to the level it had attained twenty-five years before. The proportion of foreign trade carried in American ships continued to drop another 10 per cent between 1826 and 1840. In Massachusetts, in order to protect Francis Cabot Lowell's wonderful new power loom, which spun, weaved and printed coarse cottons in his Waltham factory, the East India trade in cottons was cut in half. Lowell himself, like many other merchants, transferred his investments from ships to factories. Except for the California trade revival which built the great clippers of the 1850's, the golden days of Yankee foreign commerce were done. Massachusetts was now practically committed to a future in industry instead of ocean commerce. By 1828 Daniel Webster, her great champion in the Senate, had switched his ringing oratory to favor the protective tariff. Massachusetts' maritime supremacy was over.

This development, marking a profound historic change in the direction of the New England economy, constituted the end of one era in Massachusetts and the beginning of another. It meant a retreat from the maritime life in which Massachusetts had for two centuries surpassed all other regions of the nation and a new substitute destiny in industrial competition with other areas that often held greater advantages in such competition than did New England. It further isolated Massachusetts from the main currents of change in the nation and further diminished her already waning proportionate influence in the national life.

To be sure, Massachusetts' achievements already attained in industry were not inconsiderable. The seed sown by John Winthrop the younger in his founding of the Saugus Iron Works in 1643 had been transplanted many times in the form of new forges and iron "bloomeries" wherever bog iron ore, water power, and inherited skills coincided to enable men to produce the hardware necessary for machines. The dynasty founded by Winthrop's technician, James Leonard, who set up the Taunton ironworks in 1656, kept ironware in continuous production for fully two centuries through five generations of the Leonard family. In the critical inflations of the American Revolution, Taunton people used a form of hard currency that never depreciated in value. Instead of worthless continentals they bought and sold goods for *pounds of iron*. The Leonards grew rich in iron, paid their stockholders in iron, and Deacon Elijah Leonard in 1750 built a mansion from the profits of iron. And because the Leonards for years had been training Taunton valley men to use water power to fashion iron to their particular needs, there were men available all over southeastern Massachusetts who could invent and manufacture clocks and watches, tack-making machines, cotton gins, shoe sewing machines, spinning mills, and eventually power looms. All these devices were in operation in Taunton, Bridgewater, Brockton or Fall River before

1820. There were concentrated in this area to an extraordinary degree the Yankee assets of initiative, great inventiveness, and technical skill. It was men with these characteristics who rapidly developed laborsaving devices enabling Americans to undersell the British in world markets. With the added advantages of a protective tariff and rapidly expanding western domestic markets, Massachusetts men repeatedly accumulated large fortunes on relatively small investments in many lines of manufacture. Wherever Yankees possessed superior technical skill their industries thrived despite any or all geographic disadvantages. Many former shipbuilding skills were now turned to equal industrial proficiency. But, by the same token, skilled artisans from Massachusetts, like Abraham Lincoln's ironmaster ancestors, sometimes migrated to New Jersey or Pennsylvania, where raw material shortages and geographic hazards were not as great. Massachusetts lost inevitably, as time went on, some of her original pre-eminence in competitive capacity. In later chapters we shall have occasion to comment in greater detail on this trend.

From nothing in 1825, Lowell grew by 1840 to a population of 20,000. In the same years Fall River expanded 328 per cent, Chelsea 272, New Bedford 206, and Cambridge 155. Between 1810 and 1837 cotton factories increased in number in Middlesex County from 4 to 34, in Bristol County from 13 to 57, and in Norfolk County from 10 to 32. Such precipitate population increases as these brought a host of new social problems, soon intensified by immigration of hundreds of thousands of unskilled workers fleeing Ireland's potato famine.

The industrial city was a completely new phenomenon in Massachusetts' society. The old communities had been rather simply organized with a minimum of restrictions, designed to allow individual freedom except as needed for the general welfare. Fire departments were voluntary associations or clubs. The only police were a sheriff or constable. Other public services were improvised as needed by voluntary organization: certain academies, libraries and museums had been thus formed. All the communities were essentially small towns, some of them now grown large and wealthy enough to have stimulated a variety of community associations of the voluntary type. Starting with Phillips Academy at Andover in 1778, twenty-seven incorporated academies had been founded before 1820. The idealists of the Revolution had propagated many "good works" in the form of community associations formed to carry out the responsibilities of free citizens in the new Republic. Among these were the Massachusetts Humane Society (1786); the Boston Dispensary (1796); the Massachusetts General Hospital (1811) and its branches, McLean Hospital (1818) and the Massachusetts Eye and Ear Infirmary (1820); Perkins Institute for the Blind (1830); and the Handel and Haydn Society (1815). Timothy Dwight, Yale's president, noted that by 1812 Boston had the American Academy of Arts and Sciences, American Antiquarian Society, Massachusetts Medical Society, Massachusetts Historical Society, Boston Library Society, Massachusetts Agricultural Society, Boston Athenaeum, Boston Mechanic Association, and eight other charitable or missionary societies.

In such a list we have a hint of the method already used by Massachusetts towns to meet civic needs. Out of Puritanism a type of civic religion had emerged, concerned not so much with creed or belief as with insistence on good works. Its hallmark was responsibility and concern for the welfare of the community, expressed as volunteer service by organized associations or societies. This kind of civic religion was already established as the outward form of what may be loosely identified with the liberal or Unitarian branch of the Congregational Church of that period in its conduct of community affairs.

This therefore was the type of community organization that was available to be utilized in individualistic Massachusetts as it attempted to digest the problems of the industrial revolution.

Politically this same liberal movement successively amended the state constitution in 1820, 1833, 1836, 1840 and 1857 in order completely to divorce the state from the Congregational Church. Compulsory church attendance was abolished, along with compulsory taxation for support of the church. Religious requirements and religious oaths for officeholders were done away with, and also property qualifications except the poll tax. Thus all denominations and all economic classes were placed on an equality before the commonwealth. State senators and governor's councilors were now to be elected by popular vote, and liberal methods of amending the Constitution were achieved. Such distinguished jurists as Joseph Story, Isaac Parker, Lemuel Shaw, Levi Lincoln and Daniel Webster contributed to this campaign of liberalization of the state system. Even venerable John Adams participated in the first of these conventions, vindicating opinions on religious toleration which he had expressed in 1780 but in which he had then been overruled. But he would never have approved the popular election of the State Senate which he had visualized as a carefully chosen, appointed group of "the rich, the wise, and the good." Yet this new generation was now ready to take on all the hazards, and the virtues, of full electoral democracy.

Horace Mann's liberal improvements in public education during this period have become classical. Starting with the first state schools for the blind, for the deaf, and for wayward boys, he thereupon began campaigning for public high schools and for the training of teachers in normal schools. His enormous energy forced these projects to success after 1837 while he was secretary of the State Board of Education. His brilliant annual reports in this office influenced educational policies in many other states and in Great Britain, and won him the enthusiastic support of prominent men like Edward Everett, president of Harvard, Josiah Quincy, liberal mayor of Boston, the great jurist Rufus Choate, the statesman Charles Sumner, and intellectual leaders like Samuel Gridley Howe, John G. Carter, Edmond Dwight, and the poet John G. Whittier. Through Mann's persistent efforts Massachusetts became world renowned as a pioneer in public education in secondary schools, and in the founding of the world's first normal schools at Bridgewater, Westfield and Lexington.

Such Massachusetts contributions in the fields of community institutions, political liberalization, and public education were a direct outgrowth of the American Revolution. These were all a natural refinement of the theories of community responsibility and individual liberty first espoused by the great Revolutionary leaders. They represented an extension to the unpropertied classes who had fought the Revolution, of some of the privileges hinted at by the rabble rouser Sam Adams and formulated by his heroic cousin John Adams into a constitutional system. Too gradual in their development to have prevented a Shays' Rebellion, they nevertheless were accomplished and functioning in the much more profound potential crisis of the industrial revolution, whose hordes of illiterate immigrants needed above all the education and the participation in civic activities which the Massachusetts reforms extended to them.

The outward and visible social improvements just discussed were really only some of the by-products of one of those brilliant intellectual and spiritual renaissances that occasionally decorate human progress. Massachusetts in this Golden Age was prolific in her contributions to the nation. For two centuries New England's religious libraries had been filled with heavy sermons and hopelessly academic Puritan controversies. American contributions to any humanly valuable segment of world literature or philosophic thought had been lacking until the great state papers of the Revolution and the successive provocative issues of *The Federalist* let loose a galaxy of original minds who began to produce masterpieces of literature. The American Revolution produced a sharp break in traditional standards, and its liberalized thinking acted like wine in the veins of certain children of the new Republic. The same thing happened in Massachusetts that had appeared in the vital young republic of Rome or in sixteenth-century Europe of the Reformation. Suddenly the floodgates of frustration let go, and out poured a whole generation of men of genius.

The forerunners of this phenomenon were William Ellery Channing and Theodore Parker, whose first questioning of long-accepted Puritan dogmas in the Congregational Church laid foundations for the Unitarian schism in Puritanism. But Ralph Waldo Emerson carried this questioning to its logical conclusion by breaking away even from the Unitarian wing of the church. "Cast behind you all conformity!" he demanded, proclaiming in "The American Scholar" and other challenging essays and poems a new humanism, a liberty of self-improvement built on the value of the individual man's own thinking. Drawing on Teutonic and even Oriental literatures, he for the first time formulated a philosophical and spiritual freedom for the individual alongside the political and social freedoms built into the new American Republic. Where Puritanism had fled the tyranny of the bishops, he was demanding an escape from that of the brethren, or Puritan clergy, and exaltation of the individual's right to think for himself. Henry David Thoreau, his Concord neighbor, ably seconded this search for individual spiritual freedom and provided an almost monastic illustration of such living in his lonely hermitage beside Walden Pond. The lesser lights of the famous "transcendentalist," or Concord, group further exemplified this philosophy in the short-lived Brook Farm experiment, where Margaret Fuller, Bronson Alcott, George Ripley and their followers established a cult of free thought that contributed a somewhat lunatic fringe to the thoughtful and far-reaching contributions of Thoreau and Emerson. The definitive work of Emerson, particularly, has stood fast for over a century now as a major philosophical base on which all subsequent American thinking about individualism in philosophy has to some degree rested. Its influence has been world wide, wherever men participate in thoughtful conversation.

The singular and brooding genius of Nathaniel Hawthorne, which was only briefly touched by these Concord surroundings, went on to pen in prose fiction the finest portrayals of the somberer side of Massachusetts village life ever produced. His portraits of the frustrations of Puritanism probably served to further alienate his readers from the more morbid characteristics of the older culture. The Quaker poet John Greenleaf Whittier brilliantly reproduced the folklore of Middlesex and Essex counties in volumes of lyric verse whose contemporary popularity made of New England country life a perpetual legend. His limning of a snowstorm has become a national symbol. Similarly many of the folk tales in verse of Henry Wadsworth Longfellow of Cambridge, especially his rather imaginative *Courtship of Miles Standish*, have become and remain a solid segment of the nation's tradition. The same is true of Richard H. Dana's *Two Years before the Mast*. Both James Russell Lowell and Oliver Wendell Holmes caught admirably in verse the twang of Yankee humor, along with some of its shrewd wisdom. Dr. Holmes, in his *Autocrat of the Breakfast Table* astutely recorded much of the more practical individualism of which the new intellectual aristocrats were capable. In historianship, Bancroft, Prescott, Motley and Francis Parkman set standards so firm that all subsequent American historians enter the field with a certain trepidation. In the almost extinct art of oratory, Edward Everett, Charles Sumner, Wendell Phillips, and the giant of them all, Daniel Webster, so far surpassed any more recent novices in the field that they now serve chiefly to symbolize, along with the other giants just reviewed, what can only be looked upon as the Golden Age of American literature.

All these contributions of the renaissance of Massachusetts culture are intangibles. One cannot compare them statistically with the enormous increase in the nation's wealth, its industrial expansion, or its commercial growth. But the coincidence of their occurrence along with the fulminating westward expansion of the young Republic unerringly carried these fresh, new intangible ideas coursing across the continent, profoundly influencing every new settlement in the golden West. A cultural emigration from New England accompanied Pittsburgh's iron hardware down the Ohio and across the plains. The canalboats, railroads, stern-wheelers and wagon trains carried not only the Yankee trader's gadgets, bolts of cotton cloth, and grandfather clocks but also people, carrying in their packs copies of the new books and in their heads ideas of the new America they were going to build.

The streams of migration that proceeded across Tennessee into the deep South and on into Texas carried the lore of King Cotton and the traditions of the aristocratic South. As the plantations of the southern tidewater lost their fertility, they were transplanted over the mountains into new bottom lands where increasing hordes of black slaves could plant new acres and send out through Mobile and New Orleans enormously multiplying cargoes of bales of cotton for markets in the British Isles and New England. This was one phase of American cultural migration. From Maryland, Pennsylvania and New Jersey there swept another stream of back-country farmers, traveling salesmen and ironworkers along the Cumberland Road and the Pennsylvania canals into the Ohio country. Farms, towns and industries sprang up along the rivers, on into the opening vistas of the new Northwest. They carried with them all their fierce antagonisms against the rich merchants of the wealthy seaboard, their former landlords and creditors. From New England and New York State descendants of Shays' Rebellion and forsakers of the worn-out farms of the New England hill country similarly sailed the Erie Canal to Buffalo, and by lake boat or overland merged gradually with the Ohio migration to fill the northern half of the Mississippi basin, eventually pushing on over the Donner Pass or up the Oregon Trail to California and the Pacific Northwest. Soon they were joined by others who came by sea, around the Horn.

Modern scholars are gradually tracing the innumerable rivulets of legend by which the American way of life, in the heads of migrating people, was carried from region to region along the intercommunicating network of this stupendous migration. How was it that schools and colleges, libraries and lyceums, churches of every stripe, musical associations, charitable and literary organizations, philosophers, teachers, poets and novelists happened to erupt throughout the Ohio valley, the Great Lakes country, and on to the ultimate Pacific coast? Original Massachusetts migrations led by such promoters as Manasseh Cutler and Rufus Putnam were shortly followed by leaders like Lyman Beecher at Cincinnati and Andover's "Iowa band," the founders of Iowa College. Horace Mann himself became Antioch College's first president in 1853. Kansas will not soon forget Amos Lawrence and the New

England Emigrant Aid Society. In the sciences, in medicine, in librarianship, museum administration, railroad promotion and financing, in journalism and law, the stamp of Massachusetts men on the character and development of the West was enormous. The works of Longfellow, Emerson and Parkman were well known even at the end of the Oregon Trail. And as time went on progressive ideas of political and social reform, the care of the insane, and many policies in higher education, scientific investigation, and developments in the fine arts came to be among the most significant exports of Massachusetts to other states of the Union. So pervasive was the general seeding of the intangible products of her Golden Age of literature and education on the mentality of the opening West that the grandchildren of the old West consider the word "culture" a byword somehow synonymous with Boston. They still come back to Massachusetts in droves, either to study or to imbibe, as tourists, some faint relic of the enchantment with which Massachusetts culture held their grandsires spellbound.

Massachusetts herself, despite her welter of intellectual improvement, remained curiously provincial. Though her scholars plundered Europe for new books and ideas, building up the Harvard Library to 84,000 volumes before 1850, Boston alone among major seaports failed to establish a through railroad route to the West. Massachusetts had built, in the Middlesex Canal, the first such waterway; the first post road; and the first horse railroad, carrying Quincy granite for the Bunker Hill Monument. But the Boston to Worcester railroad was unflatteringly regarded as "a forty mile extension of Boston Wharf," and when the Great Western was built through to Albany, in 1841, New England forcefulness was not adequate to the task of securing through traffic co-operation with New York's Buffalo and Albany Railroad. Remnants of this inadequacy still persist to plague Boston's port development after more than a century. A Massachusetts man, William F. Harnden, more enterprising than his state, founded a guard service for Boston and New York freight out of which grew the Adams Express Company. A New York associate carried the idea further in establishing the Wells Fargo Company, progenitor of the American Express Company.

Despite her lofty intellectual renaissance, in the national political arena Massachusetts was no wiser than her immediate self-interest seemed to dictate during these years. This was a period of sharpening intersectional rivalries in the national government. Massachusetts saw her relative influence steadily declining with the admission of each new western state to the Union, and she jealously opposed the extension of American autonomy to Texas and California, just as her Federalists had opposed the purchase of the Louisiana Territory. She was naturally disturbed by the extension of slavery, even though her cotton manufacturers were averse to any change in the system of producing cotton, which seemed to require slavery. Massachusetts' liberals, led by William Lloyd Garrison, grew increasingly rabid for abolition, but political compromise with the South was carried on as long as possible by leaders like Webster, who considered the threat to the Union to be worse than the evils of slavery.

A bright constellation in the political firmament of these years was the career of John Quincy Adams. During the difficult Napoleonic years he had upheld European respect for American diplomacy while serving successively as minister to the Netherlands, Germany and Russia. He was chairman of the United States Peace Commission negotiating the Peace of Ghent with England and became, like his father, minister to England. In all this foreign service his performance was of the same austere, incorruptible pattern as his father's. He was a good secretary of state under President Monroe, securing the annexation of Florida from Spain and formulating the Monroe Doctrine, a century-long basic part of American foreign policy. But, like his father also, he came to the Presidency in 1824 poorly equipped by temperament and political training to make use of the party system. His principle of never refusing office, but never actively campaigning for it, seems to us now almost like a fairy tale. He was probably the last of our presidents whose every decision was made on the merits of the issue. This naïve honesty and lack of political expediency exposed him to unbridled attacks by his Jacksonian political adversaries, who were never handicapped by such scruples. He therefore went out of office, again like his father, embittered and discouraged that the nation was falling into the hands of the mob. But, unlike John Adams, the son swallowed his humiliation and returned to Washington for eighteen years of continued service in the House of Representatives. There his stature as a public servant was steadily enhanced by his long successful battle for the establishment of the Smithsonian Institution, on the principle that such government encouragement of scholarship was necessary to a democracy, since an ignorant people could not govern itself. His lonely, stubborn fight for the constitutional principle of free petition, an aspect of the slavery controversy, also earned him the admiration of all his colleagues in the House. His death, at his seat in the House of Representatives, was to many a symbol of an end of the old aristocratic principle that a public servant should vote as his individual conscience guided, rather than as a voice of his party. Such a symbolism highlights the significance of Massachusetts' newly won role as a center of national culture. The Adamses, father and son, had bequeathed to the United States a burning appreciation of the need for informed, scholarly solutions of great problems. If party politics were to take only the form of the spoils system, under the new conditions of extending the franchise to all male citizens "free, white and twenty-one," it seemed possible indeed that the United States might meet its doom at the hands of an illiterate majority.

The new cultural renaissance in Massachusetts was therefore of a significance far surpassing its mere prestige as a spellbinding enchantment to its admirers. A much greater question was at issue. Could a galaxy of individual stars, Emersons, Adamses, Horace Manns, Choates, Sumners, Websters, Channings, Parkmans and Garrisons, bring sufficient teamwork to bear on educating a democratic electorate to prevent its destroying itself with its newly won democracy? The brilliant founders of the Republic were all dead now. Could a nation, now overspreading a whole continent, develop a civic religion sufficient to provide throughout its explosively expanding regions the academies, libraries, museums, the Smithsonians, colleges, and civic associations necessary to allow free-thinking individualism in a society part pioneer, part immigrant, rich and poor, slave and free, all facing a developing industrial revolution, an impending struggle over slavery, and a tendency to believe that "to the victors belong the spoils"? If so, only a cultural revival like that of Massachusetts could turn the trick. There were many thoughtful people who doubted it could be done. Most European students of the United States believed its democratic tendencies would destroy the young Republic. Certainly if it were to be saved it must be through education, and not only through the free elementary public schools pioneered by Massachusetts in the 1640's but also through precisely the public high schools, academies and colleges that the New England cultural revival was fostering all over the United States. This was the real meaning of New England's nineteenth-century contribution to the national life.

In this contribution Massachusetts' cultural leaders played a major part. If their earnestness and missionary zeal sometimes lacked a sense of humor, and subjected their "culture" to the charge of pompousness, nevertheless their purpose was ultimately served and the educational system of the nation stands as their monument today.

CHAPTER FOURTEEN

Wind and Water, to Steam

The technical uses to which man puts the forces of nature sometimes establish unerringly the character of a whole period in history. Such a period was the middle third of the nineteenth century. Beautiful wind-propelled sailing ships in foreign trade were gradually displaced by sooty steam-driven ocean packets. The sturdy coastwise schooner, the slow-moving canal barge, and the river boat gave way to the puffing steamboat and to the railroad's iron horse. Diversified small-town mills powered by water wheels beside pretty little rivers grudgingly succumbed to enormous steam power plants driving huge multiple factory complexes filling the industrial areas of large cities. From the simplicity of clean wind and sparkling waterfall, civilization progressed to the lurch and pound and scream of coal furnace, walking beam, and belt drive. It was against this background that New England's cultural renaissance struggled.

Not all of these evolving changes, however, proceeded at the same rate of speed. While high tariffs did rapidly reduce foreign trade, for instance, they did little injury to the thriving coastwise sailing trade by which schooners and sloops continued to transport products of industry and commerce from large distributing seaports to smaller harbors not yet served by rail. This domestic trade, in fact, did not reach its height until mid-century, when the prodigious stimulus of the "coast-wise" California trade brought it to its peak. And even past the end of the century windjammer schooners continued to carry most of the freight cargo to and from the less developed commercial harbors of the nation.

Obviously the many little shoal-water harbors of Cape Cod and Massachusetts and Buzzards bays never could compete in overseas commerce with Salem, Boston, New Bedford and Nantucket. Whether in the China trade or in whaling, they had neither wharfage, moorings nor channel room for the great sailing ships needed in these enterprises. But the little seaports were ideally suited to fishing and to coastwise distribution, in schooners, of the products of the great trade routes. An occasional brig or bark out of their enterprise did occasionally enjoy the glory of great voyages, but fishing and coasting were their particular specialty. And many of them turned to shipbuilding, on the theory that a new-built hull was shoaler draft than a full cargo. In this respect skill could overcome all geographical disadvantages. And they naturally excelled in building vessels best fitted for their own type of commerce.

In the little harbor of Hingham, for example, cordage by Fearing, blocks by Leavitt, and sails by Marsh and Mayhew enabled the Barkers to build a whole fleet of fishing schooners. That such industry was established early is demonstrated by the fact that nearby Scituate harbor built thirty vessels between 1783 and 1812, all schooners except a brig, one brigantine, and a full-rigged ship. Cohasset, during the same period, built sixty-two schooners, two brigs, and a ship. Quincy distinguished herself by constructing the *Massachusetts*, a great 800-ton ship whose commercial failure in China long prejudiced Boston against such large vessels.

On the North River in Hanover, Pembroke and Scituate

there developed a shipbuilding industry entirely independent of the limitations of local commerce. The North River's market for vessels was as big as the commerce of New England. Before 1813 the North River yards turned out 25 sloops, 164 schooners, 42 brigs, brigantines and barks, and 112 ships. Building came to an abrupt halt during the embargo of 1808 and again during the War of 1812, but revived briskly after the cessation of hostilities. In the entire career of North River's two dozen shipyards, more than 900 vessels were produced.

The intricacy of the marine transportation system which the period following the War of 1812 produced can best be illustrated by examining the versatility of commerce in any one of the little ports of the Massachusetts coast. It happens that quite detailed information is available about one of these small harbors, Cohasset, which is not readily found in others equally distinguished by the manifold maritime activities of this period. It comes to many as a surprise to learn that little harbors of refuge like these, whose only industries were mackerel fishing and shipbuilding, yet shared actively in the tremendous boom that Yankee industry and the nation's growth together produced. Cohasset's fifty home-built schooners and her dozen or more small barks and brigs spent only the summer season in fishing enterprises from Cape Hatteras to the Bay of St. Lawrence. In winter many of them were kept busy freighting Yankee notions to Richmond, Savannah, Charleston, Mobile and New Orleans. From Charleston they transshipped rice or hard pine lumber to Havana, Paramaribo or Santo Domingo; from Mobile or New Orleans cotton to New York, Boston, Antwerp or Liverpool; and brought home to Boston, Gloucester or Portland molasses, coconuts, corn, coffee, logwood or barrel staves from the Gulf, or railroad iron, wine, prunes, crockery or salt from Europe. Innumerable examples might be cited of the careers this trade produced from Newburyport, Chatham, Hyannis or Wareham, but again Cohasset provides eloquent examples of the trend and thus rounds out a unified picture. Francis Pratt of Cohasset went to sea a poor boy in 1826, aged eight, and retired at twenty-five to a newly bought home in Cohasset, in 1843, having served as mate or master of a bark, seven brigs and six schooners. He had sailed 78,000 miles in seventeen years, and among others had visited every port in the trade routes just described above. Yet he had gone fishing out of Cohasset almost every summer during those same years and owned two fishing schooners when he "retired."

Inevitably such a town produced master mariners for the great ships in world-wide commerce. This was as true of Wellfleet, Marblehead, Ipswich or Mattapoisett as of Cohasset, but it is again useful for illustration to use a single such harbor. By 1824 a Cohasset master, Captain Philip Fox, held one of the ocean records. In that year he drove the little Boston-built ship *Emerald* of the Boston and Liverpool Packet Company from Liverpool to Boston in seventeen days. So amazed were his owners at his return that they assumed he had not reached his destination. Only when he handed them the Liverpool newspapers would they believe his story. This record was only once broken, and then by a clipper ship.

Cohasset's Captain James Collier began his illustrious career in 1834 at the age of eighteen by bringing a cargo of coal in the little Cohasset-built schooner *Profit*, 66 tons, from Norfolk to Weymouth, from which oxcarts took it across country to Oliver Ames' shovel factory in North Easton. During the subsequent fifty years Captain Collier commanded many ships roaming all the world's oceans. For thirty years he was master of vessels of over 1,500 tons, including the clippers *Storm King, North America, Tecumseh, Pharos* and *Highland Light*. A sea chest of his, found in a family attic, revealed years later a list of his voyages to such ports as Coquimbo, Maracaibo, Queenstown, Malaga, Antwerp, Chincha, Valparaiso, Bordeaux, Buenos Aires, Montevideo, Mauritius, Rio de Janeiro, Melbourne, Bombay, Callao, London, Calcutta, New Orleans, Liverpool and San Francisco. The last nine of these he visited from two to ten times each. Few, if any, commanders of the American clippers ever surpassed Captain Collier in number of vessels commanded, and voyages made. Yet he made his start, like Francis Pratt, by presenting to his parents at the age of nine the common cabin boy's ultimatum: "Let me go fishing, or I'll run away!"

This sort of maritime tradition existed in all the little fishing ports of Massachusetts as a constant accompaniment and companion theme to New England's industrial revolution. The early railroads were east-west routes. Through rail freight service along the coast was not available until later. Only seaborne commerce connected industrial New England with its markets and raw materials. The coasting schooner was the railroad of the nation for the entire eastern and Gulf seaboards until the Civil War. And until transcontinental railroads were well established it was also ships that opened up the supply to California.

James Collier owned a wharf and six schooners during his early career. Like him, many master mariners and many shipbuilders invested their sailing profits in the business, often thus combining the functions of skipper, builder, owner and merchant. The great Salem and Boston countinghouses were not the only ones who played this game. A classical example was that of the Ezra Westons of Duxbury. A dozen small shipyards had launched sloops and schooners into Duxbury Bay before 1764 when the elder Ezra Weston began at the age of twenty-one to build larger vessels in the Benjamin Prior yard at the Nook. By 1798, when his son Ezra joined the firm, the older man had already produced a commercial empire that earned him the name of "King Caesar." After the old man died in 1822, Ezra II continued to enlarge the business. Fourteen shipyards lined the Duxbury waterfront, employing more than nine hundred men. Most of the later Weston ships were built in a 10-acre yard on the Bluefish River. Lloyds of London listed more than a hundred ships owned by Ezra Weston, making him one of the largest shipowners in the world. Timber was hauled by Weston oxen from Weston forests in Duxbury, Bridgewater and Middleboro, and in Weston schooners from Maine. Weston sailing packets brought other supplies from Plymouth and Boston. Cordage was made in Weston ropewalks, anchors in the Weston forge, sails in a Weston sail loft, and tools in a Weston tool forge. Salt was imported from Cadiz in Weston ships for the Weston fishing fleet. Five warehouses handled overseas cargoes on the Weston wharf, and the vessels were provisioned from the Weston farm. Even the banking was done in a Duxbury bank of which Ezra II was president. In 1837 seventy-one ships were built in Duxbury yards. All this empire the Westons presided over from their great Duxbury house on Powder Point and their Boston countinghouse on Commercial Wharf. For a time Duxbury vied with the North River as a training ground for shipwrights. The great Samuel Hall, who began his career on the North River, worked in the Weston yards for a time and opened his own Duxbury shipyard before moving on to his outstanding successes as the pioneer master builder of East Boston clippers.

The clue to the migration of North River and shoal harbor shipbuilders to larger shipyards as the nineteenth century progressed is to be found in tonnage statistics. L. Vernon Briggs in his *Shipbuilding on North River* lists only five ships of over 400 tons built on the river, and none of these after

1815. The largest was only 464 tons. Larger hulls could not be maneuvered out of the river. Some of the North River builders used Duxbury, Cohasset and Scituate harbors for 600- or 700-ton vessels, the largest of these, the 788-ton double-decked ship *Greenwich*, 160 feet long, being launched at Cohasset by Thatcher Magoun in 1850. How they ever got her out of that little harbor is a mystery to this day. N. Porter Keen launched a 650 ton schooner, the *Henry J. Lippett*, at Duxbury in 1874, but had so much difficulty in digging her out of the marsh across the river, after the launching, that he moved his yard to Weymouth the next year.

Large shipbuilding reached a noncompetitive basis in the smaller ports long before 1850. The Ezra Weston firm closed its books in 1857. The little harbors and river mouths never reached the clipper ship era except through their master mariners, who commanded them, and their master builders, like Samuel Hall and the Briggs brothers, who went on to the great yards in East Boston, Medford, Newburyport, Fairhaven or New Bedford.

Tribute needs to be paid to the fishing industry, which was the perpetual work horse that kept the other enterprises going. In good years such ports as Gloucester, Wellfleet, Hingham and Cohasset each packed more than 40,000 barrels of mackerel. Four or five voyages were commonly made each summer, following the mackerel northward as their "schools" migrated. Often the first voyage in May found mackerel off Cape May, New Jersey, and a June voyage off Block Island. The midsummer voyages were short, in New England waters, but fall frequently found the schooners traveling as far as Bay of St. Lawrence. In port, the wharves were busy as the already split, gibbed and salted fish were packed in barrels by boys in their early teens at 25 cents per day. Local cooper shops made the barrels, and local saltworks evaporated much of the salt from sea water. Each schooner had a crew of about ten men and boys. Originally these were all New England born: by mid-century a considerable immigration of Portuguese seamen were prospering in the fishing trade, many of them becoming masters of schooners with the encouragement of Yankee owners.

The hazards of the life were enormous. On August 16, 1846, the Cunarder *Hibernia* cut in two the Cohasset schooner *Maine* in fog in Massachusetts Bay, with the loss of six of the crew of eleven. Only six months after the 1851 storm, which destroyed the new iron Minot's lighthouse off the South Shore, another tempest wrecked three Cohasset schooners, the *Henry Knox*, the *Charles Augusta* and the *Naiad Queen*, off Nova Scotia. There was also economic disaster. In 1858 the topsail schooner *Tower* (on which Francis Pratt was second mate) sailed to Provincetown for salt, then to Nova Scotia. Near Sable Island she passed through a fleet of vessels taking 30 barrels of mackerel each, but could get none herself. She kept on through the Strait of Canso and into the Bay of Chaleur, still finding no fish. She tried the Magdalen Islands and Newfoundland. No mackerel anywhere. On the voyage of three months the crew nearly starved to death, and arrived home each owing the vessel, on shares, $27.

Boston's foreign trade had changed somewhat. The old Northwest fur trade dwindled away, but was soon replaced by active trade in hides from South America and the Mexican Empire in California, thus supplying Massachusetts' growing shoe industry. Both South America and the West Coast were good markets for New England textiles. Brazil's coffee, the Argentine's wool, hair, sheepskins and tallow, and Chile's copper and nitrates afforded exchange for three quarters of New England's sheeting and domestic cotton goods. European substitutes forced out Chinese crockery and nankeens from the American market, but the tea trade steadily increased. Boston merchants established busy agencies in Canton (Russell & Co.), St. Petersburg (William Ropes), Fayal (Charles Dabney), Genoa (Robert Gould Shaw) and Honolulu (James Hunnewell). Enterprising Frederic Tudor's prodigious salesmanship extended markets for Essex County ice to South America and the Far East, thus preserving a means of exchange for the disappearing trade with India for such items as jute, indigo, linseed, shellac, saltpeter and gunny sacks. Thomas Wales and Nathaniel Emmons sent barrel staves to La Rochelle in exchange for brandy. The Ropes family bought Russian hemp and Baltic iron at St. Petersburg with American cotton and Cuban sugar. Nicholas Reggio and Joseph Iasigi, merchants of Smyrna, by settling in Boston as merchant shipowners obtained for Boston practically a monopoly on eastern Mediterranean goods. New Bedford whalers provided commercial ships with cargoes of oil and whalebone in Honolulu and Fayal, thus affording merchants profitable return cargoes while avoiding a trip home by the whalers. Such crosscurrents and exchanges among our ships and merchants continued to keep trade on the move despite tariffs and foreign competition. But the discovery of gold in California produced a wave of seaborne traffic such as the United States had never known.

The forty-niners themselves cared little what kind of vessel they used to get around Cape Horn. But the mushrooming problem of supplying the suddenly overpopulated gold fields with food, clothing, and tools enough even for bare subsistence called for the fastest cargo carriers afloat. The earlier Baltimore clippers of the 1830's had failed commercially because their cargo capacity was too small. The same was true of some of the saucy schooners and brigs built at Medford for opium smuggling into China. Mystic builders had likewise improved the waterlines of their East Indiamen, though they were still bluff bowed, not real race horses. In New York, under stimulus of steam Cunarder competition, Donald McKay had built some fairly fast express packets for the Liverpool trade in the 1840's. Some of these had been used in Enoch Train's Boston to Liverpool service. But none of these were clippers. New York builders did produce, however, a few small clippers for the China trade between 1845 and 1849. One of these, *Sea Witch*, now proceeded to dramatize the California situation. With flour, eggs, potatoes and lumber selling for fantastic prices in San Francisco, thirty-three vessels arrived there in the month of July, 1850, averaging 159 days out of New York or Boston. But *Sea Witch* stood in to the Golden Gate only 97 days out of New York!

All the large shipbuilders went to work on this new problem. Samuel Hall, trained in North River, Mystic, Penobscot and Duxbury yards, soon launched his *Surprise*, fully rigged, into Boston harbor. Designed by Boston's 23-year-old Samuel H. Pook, and sailed by Maine's great China trade skipper Philip Dumaresq, she knocked a day off *Sea Witch's* record to California within a year.

Donald McKay now entered the game at Boston, having completed his Liverpool packets. From that moment he was never surpassed by any other builder. His first clipper, *Stag Hound*, still holds the sailing records of nine days from San Francisco to Honolulu and thirteen days from Boston Light to the equator. His second, *Flying Cloud*, though she lost main and mizzen topgallant masts on the way, made the Golden Gate in 89 days, a record never beaten except by her own performance three voyages later. Under Josiah Perkins Cressy, her hard-driving Marblehead master, she posted record after record, a day's run of 374 miles and an average speed of 13.5 knots for four days, performances never till then approached by either sail or steam. These were the largest

American cargo carriers, 1,500 and 1,700 tons, ever built up to that time, so that they were enormously profitable to their owners. McKay had solved the long-standing riddle of how to combine speed with cargo capacity. He proceeded to enlarge steadily the size and rig of his vessels, and their speed and the romantic names applied to them brought him world fame. In succession, *Flying Fish, Westward Ho!, Sovereign of the Seas, Empress of the Seas, Glory of the Seas, Romance of the Seas,* and *Great Republic* continued to carry increasing cargoes at speeds completely outclassing the merchant marine of any other nation. Even his smaller ships, *Lightning, Champion of the Seas, James Baynes,* and *Donald McKay*, all built for the Australian Black Ball Line after the California crisis was over, were extremely fast, yet were over 2,000 tons burden each. His *Great Republic* reached the sailing ship's greatest tonnage of 4,556, with the top of her main skysail mast 276 feet above the deck and her mainyard 120 feet long. Though she carried an acre and a half of sail, she was as swift and lean as the fastest of the smaller clippers.

The great era of the clipper builders lasted only six years, 1850 to 1855. Massachusetts builders made most of the records, though New York built more ships. Massachusetts-built clippers made ten of the twenty-one known voyages to California in less than a hundred days, six of these by McKay-designed vessels, three by Samuel H. Pook's *Surprise, Witchcraft* and *Herald of the Morning,* and one by Samuel Hall's *John Gilpin*. Of the twelve all-time longest recorded day's runs by sailing vessels, all over 400 miles, all were made by Massachusetts vessels, five designed by McKay and one by Pook. The fastest was *Lightning* in 1854, 436 miles in 23½ hours. But dozens of other almost equally capable clippers were built by Medford yards of the Delano's, J. O. Curtis, Hayden and Cudworth, and Samuel Lapham, by the Briggs brothers of

South Boston, by Jackson and Ewell, A. and C. T. Sampson, by J. M. Hood of Somerset, and John Currier of Newburyport.

Life at sea, however, was already undergoing degenerative changes, even in those stupendous days of record making. Like the factories, mechanization was changing the character of the game. In 1820 the crews had been Yankee from top to bottom, and every lad who worked hard and studied in intervals ashore at the little navigation schools might work his way up to mate and master. Every man owned a share in the voyages. But the great racing machines of 1855 were almost wholly manned by men of alien birth. The familiar personal relation of the small close-knit crew of the schooner was lost, and instead a huge disciplined organization of muscle-men was the needed element to haul up these acres of sail, fend off, haul cargo, and wear ship. Mates and masters worked isolated, aft on the quarter-deck. Able seamen were now handled by the bosun, a dozen to a halliard or a capstan, a hundred aloft on the yards to shorten sail. No longer did you put to sea with your neighbors from the same town. The man next to you might be a Kanaka picked up in Calcutta or some riffraff shanghaied out of a bordello in Liverpool.

Worse still, sail often made no profit. To be sure, a gold rush in California or Australia was enormously profitable. But more and more the trade routes were becoming systematized. Individualistic deals by merchant masters in new ports were hard to find. Regular packet ships were plying between all the important seaports, in the fiercest of competitive routine. Freight rates were becoming standardized. Year by year the certainty of steam navigation was driving out the vicissitudes of wind and sail. Over the Atlantic cable after 1856 purchases and sales could be consummated by a merchant sitting in his countinghouse, listening to his telegraphed market reports. Men stopped building clipper ships after 1856 simply because they didn't pay. The long gamble, the thrill of the chase, the risk taking, and the climb up the ladder were no longer the way to the top. Let the stevedores and roustabouts do the hard work—business is now the way to success. Use machines to save your muscles.

The same thing was happening in the towns. Volume production was the thing. Brockton and Bridgewater and Lynn employed thousands in their shoe factories. Tremendous cotton textile mills were already operating in New Bedford, Fall River, Lowell, and Lawrence, for which Worcester and Hopedale and Whitinsville were turning out the looms and spindles. Oliver Ames in North Easton had already made thousands of shovels for the California and Australia gold rushes and was providing more thousands for building the Union Pacific Railroad, of which he became president. It seems amazing to learn that this industry was built up with ox teams delivering shovels to Boston and bringing back iron to Easton, using several days for the round trip. Only in 1855 was the Easton branch railroad completed. Railroads to Bridgewater and Taunton in the mid-forties had enabled them to go into heavy industry, and they promptly began producing railroad locomotives and heavy machinery for steamships. Fitchburg soon had control of the circular saw industry, Athol of machine tools, especially planing machines, and Worcester of envelope making. Spencer manufactured wire, and Gardner, chairs. By mid-century $10 million worth of whale oil and whalebone annually made New Bedford the whaling capital of the world, owning 329 ships and making of her port the fourth largest tonnage district in the United States, twice as large as Philadelphia and surpassed only by New York, Boston and New Orleans. Her Wamsutta Mills soon placed her high among the Bay State's textile cities also.

Walpole and Norwood were hard at work in a variety of textile and paper industries, laying foundations for a long reign in floor covering and roofing materials which still goes on after a century and a half. Danvers and Peabody were one great tannery supplying the shoe factories of Salem, Lynn and Beverly. Lowell, the new brick city sprung Aladdin-like from the wilderness beside the falls of the Merrimack, was a source of wonder to a British observer in 1827. He marveled at the nicely dressed girls, in bright shawls and gay bonnets, who worked from dawn to dusk at the new machines, wearing tortoise-shell combs at the back of their heads. He admired the good ventilation and excellent discipline, so different from conditions in the English factories of Manchester. Founded by the genius of Nathan Appleton and Patrick Tracy Jackson, after Francis Cabot Lowell's death, this great textile center had grown to 33,000 by 1850.

So the world began to change. Except for cowboys and Indians in the opening West, the frontiers of adventure fast were disappearing. Romanticism began to merge with Victorianism. Soft coal was replacing muscle and sail. Men began to have to invent sports to take the place of adventure. The glamorous undertakings were mostly now in the mind—invention, science, the fine arts, new machines. Steam Cunarders surpassed the Atlantic records of sailing ships. Boys no longer ran away to sea. Railroads took the place of coasting schooners. Neglected water wheels rotted away and fell to pieces by quiet millponds. Black smoke belched from steam boilers all over the place. Nobody sang sea chanteys any more. Success would soon be measured in terms of Horatio Alger stories. The countinghouse and the typewriter were displacing the quarter-deck and the quill pen. Potential Cressys and Colliers must sit by small tillers in little yachts and dream that a Genoa jib is a skysail and that Massachusetts Bay is

Malacca Straits or the Spanish Main. Indian fighting would soon turn into cops and robbers. Even the wild West show would become a legend. In the Gilded Age, baseball would replace the Oregon Trail. In the world of imagination, this is what railroads, steamships and the telegraph did to the venturous young Republic. Fresh wind and sparkling water power slowly turned to sooty steam.

CHAPTER FIFTEEN

The Periphery of Massachusetts

By the middle of the nineteenth century little remained of the old dominating Puritan hierarchy that had played the tyrant to Massachusetts during its first century. In its place Greater Boston had drawn to itself through commercial bonds a growing industrial complex of factory towns that now extended in a widening circle to Brockton and Taunton to the south, beyond Worcester to the west, and northward to the Merrimack. Accidents of topography bound both the industrial economy of central Massachusetts and the coastwise schooner commerce of Massachusetts Bay to the world-ranging ocean shipping of Boston's deep-water port. Failure of good railroad linkage to the West only accentuated this centripetal dependence of the eastern mainland of Massachusetts on its great seaport. The turnpikes and railroads, instead of serving, as in the Middle Atlantic states, to provide egress to newly developing states beyond the borders, functioned in Massachusetts rather to link a larger rim of industrial towns to the Boston hub. Even the Middlesex Canal served this function. In a larger sense Boston had long since become the commercial capital of the New England coast from Nova Scotia to Cape Cod. Even after Maine's acquisition of independent statehood in 1820, its shipping still orbited around Boston by a kind of economic necessity. Indeed the Canadian shipping of Nova Scotia and New Brunswick was still oriented toward Boston by descendants of Boston loyalists who had settled there during the American Revolution.

Economic orbits almost by necessity direct and contain whole intellectual and social cultures. The cult of proper Bostonianism, with which the later nineteenth century branded certain aspects of New England society, was an inevitable corollary of the industrial and commercial imperialism of Boston as the hub of a New England economy. The regional orbit of Harvard intellectualism and of the influence of Concord and Cambridge authors was to some extent defined by the limits of the Bostonian area of economic colonialism. This was a special kind of Yankeeism, to which people in Rhode Island, Connecticut, Vermont and New Hampshire reacted with a certain emotional resentment, just as they had done years before toward the outrageous arrogance of the Massachusetts Bay Puritans. Proper Bostonianism has become a national legend and is sometimes confused by Westerners with the New England character in general. Nothing is more amusing than to see an indignant Connecticut Yankee setting the record straight to some innocent Minnesotan who has unthinkingly called him a Bostonian.

People from other regions of the United States similarly fail to understand that certain peripheral areas of Massachusetts itself likewise share strong resistance to Bostonian domination, and in this sense are centrifugal in culture and traditions. To some of these areas it is important to give attention in this book, since their independence of background has often enriched the Massachusetts scene. These areas include Massachusetts' south coast, western Massachusetts, and the Connecticut valley.

Already we have noted the differences in liberality of conscience and relative poverty of economy that from the beginning set apart the Old Colony of Plymouth from the substantial culture of Massachusetts Bay. After the fusion of the two colonies, southeastern Massachusetts, including Cape Cod and the islands of Nantucket and Martha's Vineyard, and also the southward-facing towns along Buzzards Bay, continued to develop as extensions of a distinct and proudly independent society never really a part of the Greater Boston commercial system. While other shipowners than Duxbury's Ezra Westons had close affiliations with Boston merchants, the seagoing traditions of Wellfleet, Nantucket and New Bedford ran to whaling as a huge independent enterprise little connected with Boston. The Quakers of Nantucket and New Bedford felt more closely allied to their colleagues in Rhode Island than to Boston's Puritans. The bold barrier of Cape Cod by its very geography directed southeastern Massachusetts' coastwise commerce to harbors along Rhode Island and Connecticut shores, where Boston traffic was scarcely seen. For similar reasons Martha's Vineyard and Hyannis became ports of call for New York and Philadelphia shipping on its way to Canada, and thus brought southern Massachusetts harbors into natural contact with merchants of those ports, at first as provisioners and eventually as participants in coastwise trade. New Yorkers early began to use Nantucket and Cape Cod for summer residence, just as they did Newport. This brought to these areas a cosmopolitan flavor still further differentiating them from the rest of Massachusetts. Since whaling took southern Massachusetts' world commerce to the North and South Atlantic, to the Pacific, and eventually to the arctic, whalers' contacts with Boston shipmasters were quite as likely to be at sea or in exotic ports in the South Seas as in Boston itself.

Not many years ago a grizzled Cape Cod retired sea captain was confronted by the occupant of a chauffeured automobile in a Chatham street and asked how far it was to Harwich and whether there was a hotel there. The old man said it was seven miles to Harwich, and he didn't know whether there was a hotel there or not. "Isn't that like these old codgers," remarked the motorist to his chauffeur. "They've lived here all their lives, and don't know whether there's a hotel in a town seven miles away!"

The old man's hearing was better than the tourist counted on. "I've been around the world sixteen times," he bristled, "and I don't give a damn whether there's a hotel in Harwich!"

Mackerel fishing and shipbuilding suffered the same fate at Wellfleet, Brewster, Chatham and Hyannis as they did in Scituate and Duxbury after 1840. Shoal-water harbors could no longer accommodate the larger vessels required to be competitive. Even Nantucket's whaling could not long exist on the basis of floating large whalers over the sand bar of Nantucket harbor with pontooned "camels," and these vessels inevitably migrated to New Bedford, which remained the world capital of whaling until after the War Between the States. Cape Cod, particularly at Dennis, maintained an ingenious and astonishingly extensive industry in the production of salt evaporated from sea water during the early and middle years of the nineteenth century. First initiated by British restrictions on importation in the War of 1812, and subsequently encouraged by American subsidies, hundreds of evaporating vats fed by windmill-powered pumps were constructed on almost every beach and salt marsh on the upper Cape. This thriving industry vanished only when the subsidies were withdrawn. In the same period the town of Sandwich distinguished itself by its meteoric, but brief enterprise in the manufacture of Sandwich glass, which in recent times has become the basis of a collector's hobby. But the economy of the whole region lost impetus with the abandonment of sailing ships, reverting to cranberry raising, lobstering, "pogy boat" fishing, and a few handicraft industries by 1900. On the Buzzards Bay mainland, textile and ironworkers' industries thrived in New Bedford and Fall River for a generation longer. Increasingly the whole area in modern days has become primarily a tourist paradise, attracting summer visitors, especially from New York, and yachtsmen and retired people who love its special flavor. Sand dunes, miles of beaches, quaint villages, and warm water for swimming are the new assets of the region, which once was alive with saltworks, windmills, commercial wharves and sailing ships.

The Connecticut valley and the Berkshires shared a historical background quite different from that of eastern Massachusetts. Their first pioneer towns were founded by religious liberals who for one reason or another had rebelled against the rigidity of Puritan doctrine. These doughty pioneers saw their towns repeatedly burned and abandoned in successive Indian wars. In all of Berkshire, Hampden and Franklin counties only Springfield, Westfield, Northfield and Sunderland managed to persist as active towns up to 1715. Thus almost the first two centuries of Massachusetts in these western areas were a battle for survival, during which they felt a much closer liaison to the Connecticut towns down the river than to Massachusetts Bay. After Plymouth Colony had set up its Connecticut trading post at Windsor in 1633, its settlers were soon rapidly outnumbered by the arrival of Thomas Hooker's dissenting congregation from Dorchester. Similar Hooker-led migrations from Watertown and Cambridge soon founded Wethersfield and Hartford. Roxbury's congregation that founded Springfield sent its leader, William Pynchon, as its representative to the General Court of Connecticut at Hartford for two years before its location within Massachusetts forced separation from the Connecticut towns.

Only in the relatively peaceful period from 1715 to 1750 did the Massachusetts settlers finally get a chance to expand and firmly establish multiplying towns along the fertile flood plains of their beautiful valley. During the same period settlements at Stockbridge and Great Barrington beyond the Berkshire Hills for the first time produced firm outposts for Massachusetts within striking distance of its flourishing New York neighbors along the Hudson. Even these towns, established as Indian missions during Jonathan Edwards' "Great Awakening" revival movement, looked to Yale College and the Housatonic and Connecticut valleys for their chief motivation.

Again in the Seven Years' War and the Revolution western Massachusetts was subjected to a generation of recurrent warfare requiring successive drafts of the militia for the campaigns that repeatedly swirled up and down the Champlain valley. Through their towns marched armies, prisoners, camp followers, and all the ragged wounded and defeated rabble that these battles spawned, making levies of food and cattle and horses which pioneer farmers could ill spare even in normal times. Their individualistic sons were sent to serve under British redcoats, whom they detested, and later under aristocratic New York Dutch patroon commanders, from whom they sometimes deserted. They then came home to find a postwar depression and inflation out of which, in desperate indebtedness, the only thing some of them could think of to do was to join Daniel Shays' rebellion to keep the law courts from confiscating their farms.

This was the kind of background from which western Massachusetts emerged into the newly won United States. Small farmers, particularly in the thinly settled hill towns, often decided they had had enough of Massachusetts. The soon-recovered prosperity of the seacoast scarcely benefited them at all. Many of them emigrated to the opening West in whole families. More often, the young men left, leaving parents to subsist as best they could on the old homestead, which was abandoned on the death of the old folks. This process went on for a century. Even today there are ghost towns in the western Massachusetts hills whose small remnant of population has left only one distinction: in presidential elections every four years they all vote at six o'clock in the morning and make the headlines for having the earliest results counted in the nation.

Until 1810 no town in western Massachusetts had attained a population above 3,000 and only Northampton and Springfield approached this number. North-and-south highways connected the Connecticut valley towns from Greenfield to Springfield on both sides of the river and continued southward to Hartford and New Haven, but aside from the eastward ferry and road from Northampton to Worcester there were few communications to Boston. Until 1820, Hartford's roads into eastern Massachusetts were much better than Springfield's. To the west only horseback trails led from any of the Connecticut valley towns across the Berkshires, though another north-south highway following the Housatonic River joined Williamstown and Pittsfield to Stockbridge, Great Barrington, and eventually New Haven. Massachusetts' first Connecticut River bridge, at Springfield, was not built until 1805. Canals around the falls of the river at South Hadley had already made barge traffic downriver possible before there were any bridges. Thus until 1810 the economy of western Massachusetts was inevitably limited to such agriculture, sheep raising and small industry as could find its outlets southward into Connecticut by ox team or river boat. It was a separate economy, divorced from eastern Massachusetts by the limitations of its transportation system.

Certain events were occurring which were to forecast a

better future for western Massachusetts. Establishment of the United States Armory at Springfield in 1777 set in motion a beginning of industry. Pittsfield had a woolen mill by 1801. The establishment of Williams College in 1793 and Amherst College in 1821 began to provide trained leadership for a new generation. Stimulated in the beginning by the British blockade, by 1825 more than twenty turnpike corporations and an equal number of bridge-building companies were hard at work surveying and building east-west highways to carry regular stagecoach service from Boston to Albany. In 1839 a new steam railroad began to provide service between Worcester and Springfield, and by 1855 western Massachusetts was covered by a network of fifteen railroads, letting inhabitants out from behind their mountain barriers and letting summer visitors in. Still more important, freight traffic now made possible a full participation of these western counties in the burgeoning industrial revolution, that rapidly made of the Springfield-Westfield-Holyoke-Chicopee area an industrial complex rivaling those of Fall River-New Bedford, Lawrence-Haverhill, and the Greater Boston region. Springfield's population grew to 10,000 by 1840, and its textile, paper and machinery factories soon mushroomed into the expanding cities of Westfield, Chicopee and Holyoke, to produce an industrial region today populated by almost 300,000 people. Pittsfield and Greenfield, North Adams and Northampton underwent similar industrial growth. Mount Holyoke College, founded at South Hadley by Mary Lyon in 1837, inaugurated the higher education of women, furthered by Smith College in Northampton in 1875. Westfield's State Teachers' College had already been established in 1844. At Amherst a second college, the Massachusetts Agricultural College, was set up as a land-grant institution in 1867 and became the nucleus for the modern University of Massachusetts. These were followed by Dwight L. Moody's Northfield and Mount Hermon seminaries and later by Springfield's American International and Springfield colleges to round out a group of scholarly centers that participated fully in Massachusetts' cultural renaissance. The splendid libraries and museums at Springfield and Amherst and the modern music festival, theater and schools at Stockbridge can be looked upon as an outgrowth of this very rapid cultural growth of western Massachusetts in the nineteenth century. Lenox provided inspiration to Nathaniel Hawthorne and Henry Ward Beecher. Herman Melville, Oliver Wendell Holmes and Henry Wadsworth Longfellow found recreation and creativeness in their homes at Pittsfield. Noah Webster wrote part of his dictionary at Amherst, as did Emily Dickinson her poems. The Springfield *Republican* under Samuel Bowles was a nationally famous journal of opinion.

The historical flavor of western Massachusetts seems necessarily of more modern vintage than that of the colonial east. Little remains to remind one of the shrewd business deals of William Pynchon and his capable sons, whose control of trade in beaver skins, pipe staves and provisions extended from land deals in the founding of Northfield, Northampton and Hadley to the building of the first warehouse on Warehouse Point in Connecticut, from which cargoes were shipped to the West Indies and to England. It seems today almost an anachronism to realize that two of the English regicides, Generals Whalley and Goffe, who condemned King Charles I to death, lived in hiding for probably ten years or more after 1660 in Hadley at the house of Parson Russell. Whalley was a first cousin of Oliver Cromwell. The successive Indian massacres at Deerfield, the "Northwest Frontier of New England," in 1675 and 1704 have been referred to in previous chapters. Little of the original Deerfield survives as a monument. But thin as these reminders of the seventeenth century are, the antiquarian or the tourist searches with even more frustration for physical memorials of the eighteenth century. At Stockbridge there is the Mission House, at Williams, West College, and here and there are to be seen a few surviving buildings, at Hadley and Northampton and Pittsfield. Elsewhere a few old taverns survive. But apart from these, western Massachusetts is in its physical appearances a nineteenth-century culture. It grew to maturity suddenly, in the period of the steamboat and the railroad.

The river traffic consisted mostly of flatboats, occasionally with sails and poling devices to get them back upstream, but more commonly the flatboats were broken up for their timber when they arrived at Hartford. A few small steamboats managed to cope with the rapids above Springfield, the earliest one on the Connecticut River invented and built by Samuel Morey in 1793, six years after John Fitch's original invention, of which Morey was unaware, and fourteen years before Robert Fulton's. Stern-wheelers built by Thomas Blanchard thrived briefly on the Connecticut after 1826. Charles Dickens wrote a deprecatory account of riding a small steamboat downriver among February ice-cakes from Springfield to Hartford during his American tour. But the most active steamboating on the Connecticut River was not in Massachusetts, but rather below Hartford, where service to New York by the Connecticut Steamboat Company persisted long after the railroads arrived. In Massachusetts most Connecticut River traffic was of the canalboat type. Tobacco, potatoes, celery and onions were the agricultural products, especially leaf tobacco for cigar wrappers, on which Connecticut valley farmers grew wealthy from 1830 on. The red tobacco fields of the lower valley are as indelible in the visitor's memory as the abrupt traprock cliffs of Mount Tom and Mount Holyoke.

The nineteenth-century flavor of the valley also included

some problems. Like Lawrence and Fall River, the explosive growth of factories in Holyoke and Chicopee produced too rapid immigration without adequate community facilities to digest the influx of immigrant population of many origins. When the small hamlet of Ireland Parish, a part of West Springfield, was rapidly transformed from a farming hamlet into the mill city of Holyoke, the influx of Belgian, Scotch, Irish, German and French-Canadian people produced social problems that threatened the very life of the community. Since the entire development was a private exploitation of new power from the building of dams, there was no community organization or "civic religion" available to lead in such voluntary social agencies as distinguished the Americanization efforts in the older communities in eastern Massachusetts. For many years the result was almost disastrous. Only after a long struggle, aided by the Roman Catholic Church, have the lessons of community planning been learned, and a better equilibrium of living attained in these cities. That these efforts have been successful is a tribute to many self-taught leaders whom these cities themselves produced.

This self-taught characteristic of the western counties is perhaps the most notable human trait in western Massachusetts' history. The independence of thinking that was the hallmark of these Massachusetts Victorian frontiersmen produced everywhere people of strikingly original character. William Cullen Bryant at Cummington, Edward Bellamy at Chicopee, and Robert Frost, Eugene Field, Helen Hunt Jackson, Emily Dickinson and Noah Webster at Amherst—all were of this breed. Northampton's mayor Calvin Coolidge, who became Massachusetts' only upstate President of the United States, is a case in point. Dwight L. Moody, of the Northfield schools, and particularly Mary Lyon, whose whole career was one long crusade for the higher education of women, were typical of this unflagging devotion to an idea regardless of obstacles. Every city in the western counties owes its industries, its colleges, its special flavor as a community, to largely self-taught leaders, or to leaders taught in the distinctive western Massachusetts schools, who then often attained national recognition without the advantages of the traditional background of the old culture along the seaboard. Like the men of the Virginia piedmont, they made their own way, often in opposition to the aristocratic leaders of the tidewater, but eventually winning the respect even of Boston's old guard. In Massachusetts this was the pinnacle of success.

From every aspect, the rapid industrialization and culturalization of western Massachusetts, after nearly two centuries of stubborn, frustrating isolation from the main currents of Massachusetts' growth, constitutes one of the most amazing turnabouts in the commonwealth's history. The western counties need now bow to no one. Hard work, enterprise and resourcefulness have brought their society abreast of the rest of the state, in scarcely half as long a time as it look the east to reach the same objectives.

CHAPTER SIXTEEN

Slavery and the Union

The history of any subdivision, be it city or state, in an expanding nation necessarily proceeds from the particular to the general. Small parochial episodes in the early days of Plymouth Plantation or Massachusetts Bay assumed vast significance for the future of the United States, although only a few hundred people were involved. Those episodes became symbols or precedents, which whole generations have since studied for the portents to be found in them of what was to come. The portrayal of such episodes presents no problem, but rather a golden opportunity, to the historian. But when the nation's population grows to twenty million, and its subdivisions multiply, the significance of single episodes in any one of them pales alongside the protean changes taking place throughout the great Republic as a whole. In a period like the nineteenth century, it would be stupid and pompous to claim that Massachusetts, or any other state, had dominant influence or power over national affairs. Each made contributions, usually in the form of enlightened leadership by men whose convictions were vehement enough to make them spokesmen for great national issues. The regional historian, dedicated to the task of portraying the history of his state in the nation, is in the dilemma of choosing either how to represent, in some necessarily oversimplified form, the role that his state played in certain continental convulsions of such scope that no regional viewpoint can hope to be undistorted, or of omitting them entirely, which is a greater distortion.

Such a national convulsion was the slavery controversy, from 1830 until the end of the Civil War. The role that Massachusetts played was a very complicated one, possessed as she was of a maritime and industrial economy dependent on cotton and also of a growing intellectual elite demanding the abolition of slavery. In order merely to illustrate the ramifications of these opposing factions, this chapter will utilize the frankly symbolic device, and consequent distortion, of presenting the slavery controversy in terms of the careers of Massachusetts' two great leaders in the struggle, William Lloyd Garrison and Daniel Webster. Similarly the crisis of the Civil War will be represented by an account of the positive contributions toward preserving the Union of Massachusetts' patriotic governor, John A. Andrew, without attempting any further analysis of the many other involved issues that clouded the North's prosecution of the war. There is not space in a book of this sort for a truly balanced historical discussion of the national problems in these prodigious quarrels. What follows is therefore offered as an admittedly partial but unprejudiced essay.

Already in the 1830's Webster and Garrison were beginning to define issues fundamental to the causes of the coming War Between the States. In his reply to Hayne in January, 1830, Webster climaxed his speech with the marvelous exclamation: "Liberty and Union, now and forever, one and inseparable." Only a year later Garrison opened his first issue of the *Liberator* with: "On this subject I do not wish to think, or speak, or write with moderation. I am in earnest—I will not equivocate—I will not excuse—I will not retreat a single inch—*and I will be heard*." In the United States Senate and before the Supreme Court Daniel Webster was reiterating in

speech after speech a profound conviction that the preservation of the Union was the great issue in the approaching storm.
Barely out of jail for libel (he had, in print, denounced two
of his Newburyport fellow citizens for participating in the
slave trade), William Lloyd Garrison was using his abolitionist
newspaper as an antislavery weapon. Webster had constructed
his legal career on a series of major victories before the Supreme Court, many of them won on the issue of consolidating
the federal Union against the individual claims of the separate
states. The "godlike Daniel" would have completed his contributions to thus strengthening the national structure and
been already in his simple grave in the Winslow cemetery on
his Marshfield estate eight years before the tempest broke. By
contrast the fulminating young Garrison would be climaxing
his rabble-rousing reforms only with the firing at Fort Sumter,
whose guns seemed to be destroying everything that Daniel
Webster had lived for. Curiously enough, the Union scarcely
could have been saved without the prodigious combativeness
of either of these men.

The fundamental national struggle that was going on,
which eventually erupted into the Civil War, was clearly also
a warfare between elements in Massachusetts society well exemplified by Webster and Garrison. Webster started as a
Federalist, fought for the sanctity of contracts in the Dartmouth College case, supported in suit after suit before the
courts the federal control over waterways, over its bank, over
bankruptcy proceedings, and then became for many years
Massachusetts' leading advocate in Washington of protection
of industry by high tariffs. When forced into compromise he
always sacrificed other purposes to support the Union, even
momentarily aligning himself with Andrew Jackson to do
this. His love of the Union persuaded him to accept the
Missouri Compromise in 1850 in opposition to the liberals in

Massachusetts itself, thus provoking from abolitionist John Greenleaf Whittier the bitter verse:

> From those great eyes
> The soul has fled.
> When faith is lost, when honor dies,
> The man is dead.

Yet Boston was with Webster. Bostonians liked that majestic, leonine figure fighting with gorgeous oratory all opponents of Boston's aristocracy of manufacturers and businessmen. These men had built in Webster's generation a new prosperity for Massachusetts and New England.

But Massachusetts also had a growing faction struggling for the rights of man. There was, as we have seen, an enlightened new generation of people who felt that the work of the American Revolution was as yet unfinished, and that within the industrial revolution social changes were needed to increase public education and hospitals and improve the lot of the industrial worker. These were the people who, out of what we have called civic religion, were supporting community organizations, liberalizing the franchise, and favoring more democratic institutions. These reformers were gradually developing a concerted opposition to the domination of Massachusetts by conservative merchants and industrialists of the Whig party. Some of these were what we would call nowadays the intellectual fringe—the Brook Farm extremists and some of the transcendentalist Unitarians. But there was also a solid core of able crusading reformers—the Horace Manns, the Lemuel Shattucks, the Dorothea Dixes, who began to command a ground swell of popular support from humbler sources in the electorate. While the panic of 1837 decisively stifled early trade unions, it did not destroy increasing resentment at the growing exploitation of factory workers in large cities by owners. Although cotton manufacturers' profits were increasing to 20 per cent annually, wages were often forced down and volume of work increased. There was discrimination in wages and privileges between native Yankees and Irish Catholic immigrants. Thus cruelly antagonized, the latter were naturally converted into a special discontented class. Furthermore, there was extensive exploitation of female and child labor by factory owners, on the lame excuse that the discipline was good for their morals. Often they were packed into dormitories a dozen to a room. Here again another discontented group was hungry for reform.

Among such people as these William Lloyd Garrison's fanatic abolitionist movement began to find converts. In the beginning most of them were inconspicuous people. The conservative Congregational and Unitarian clergy were almost solidly opposed. Even cotton factory workers were usually as reluctant as their employers to interfere with the slavery system since it provided the raw material on which their livelihood depended. But here and there individuals began to see that the issue of slavery must be faced, else American claims of liberty must become hollow pretenses. Growing numbers of thoughtful people were concerned with slavery's threatened spread into Texas and the Southwest, even though they disagreed with Garrison's violent methods.

Garrison's New England Antislavery Society was founded in Boston in 1832, and a National Society in Philadelphia the following year. Garrison promptly brought these societies into association with the English antislavery groups of Wilberforce and Clarkson, who secured in 1834 the emancipation of Negroes in the West Indies. By 1837 an obviously rabid crowd of cranks and fanatics had organized more than two hundred abolition societies. "Respectable" people usually avoided the issue, but were universally afraid of it. Still Garrison insisted on being heard. His scathing editorials attacking the hypocrisy of the majority mounted in vehemence. The anger of his conservative opponents grew proportionately. It began to become obvious in both the North and the South that neither hush-hush avoidance of the controversy nor compromises like that of the American Colonization Society bent on recolonizing Negroes in Africa would work. Garrison's stinging speech sometimes drove angry conservatives into mob violence, but each riot only steered more converts into his crusade.

Successively at Lynn and Abington and Concord, the English abolitionist George Thompson was mobbed. The poet Whittier and Samuel J. May were pelted with mud and stones at antislavery rallies at Concord and Haverhill. Other abolitionists were mobbed in Worcester County. A double gallows was erected in 1835 before Garrison's Boston home, intended for him and George Thompson. Just previous to this, a protest meeting in Faneuil Hall had assembled Boston's first citizens to hear ex-Senator Peleg Sprague and Harrison Gray Otis denounce the abolitionists. In October, when Garrison arrived to address a little meeting of the Boston Female Antislavery Society at 46 Washington Street next to the *Liberator* office, a mob of several thousand, brought together by a scurrilous handbill distributed by two prominent merchants, broke up the meeting and dragged Garrison with a rope along Washington Street to the City Hall, then in the Old State House. There Mayor Lyman rescued him, hid him for a while in his office, and finally incarcerated him in the city jail for disturbing the peace. How addressing a meeting in the privacy of the society's own quarters became a disturbance of the peace was left unanswered, but jail was the safest refuge, obviously, for Garrison at that moment. Maria Weston Chapman, who was present at the meeting, described the mob: "As far as we could look either way the crowd extended— evidently of the so-called 'wealthy and respectable' . . . We saw the faces of those we had, till now, thought friends."

This disgraceful episode made friends for the abolitionists. Dr. Henry I. Bowditch, who witnessed the mob, "from that moment became an abolitionist." So also did Charles Sumner. Soon also Wendell Phillips, a matchless orator, threw over- board his fine social position and assured career as a brilliant young lawyer and became an aristocratic traitor to his social group, by joining Garrison as a result of the mob episode. Phillips repeatedly imperiled his life by applying all his talents, his ample fortune, and the gift of his magnificent oratory to the crusade for abolition. From here on, with the help of such able journalists as Horace Greely, and with the redoubtable John Quincy Adams repeatedly rising in the House of Repre- sentatives in Washington to offer antislavery petitions, which were angrily and repeatedly voted down, the abolitionist cause came of age as a national issue. In the 1840's many prom- inent Massachusetts people joined the crusade. Edmund Quincy, Ellis Gray Loring, and Francis Jackson spoke to a crowded Faneuil Hall protesting the Lovejoy murder. Ralph Waldo Emerson, Longfellow, and James Russell Lowell lent their talents to the movement. Even such brilliant clergymen as John G. Palfrey, Theodore Parker and William Ellery Channing fell in line. By 1838 Massachusetts had 222 local antislavery societies, and over the nation there were 2,000 by 1840. Local chapters seemed almost comparable in their mobili- zation to the Revolutionary Committees of Correspondence except that Garrison steadfastly refused to join his crusade to any political party and repudiated the short-lived Liberty and Free Soil parties.

There was natural dissension about Garrison's nonpolitical

methods. Rival abolitionist societies using political action fought the annexation of Texas and the Mexican War. Massachusetts officially protested both the war and the annexation, so strong had antislavery sentiment now grown. But Garrison clearly saw that the Texas annexation was inevitable, as was the further annexation of Arizona, New Mexico and California after the war. He believed that political loyalties would necessarily undermine the single-minded nature of his crusade. He believed that sooner or later, if the pressure was kept on, by constant agitation, the slavery system must fall through its own internal weaknesses, excesses, and its denial of freedom. He and his supporters calmly accepted the possibility that the Union would be brought in jeopardy in the process.

James Truslow Adams well summarizes Garrison's conviction: "that the roots of slavery were so deep and the possibility of a peaceful settlement of the matter so slight, that the question of slavery was at bottom the question of the Union. It was not that slaves were held in the South and not in the North. Large classes in the North were committed to the defense of slavery. The responsibility for its continuance lay as much upon them as upon the actual slave owners, and if the Union continued, not only could that responsibility not be avoided but the influence of slavery would be forced more and more by the South on the Northern states. Believing this issue paramount to all others, Garrison finally came out in fiery denunciation of both the Union and the Constitution." He influenced the New England Antislavery Society to pass, in June, 1843, a resolution "that it was the first duty of every Abolitionist to agitate for the immediate dissolution of the Union, and that they could not consistently support the Constitution, even to the extent of voting for any candidate for Federal office." Garrison, Edmund Quincy and Wendell Phillips supported this resolution, which passed by 250 to 24.

In making this final conclusion of the abolitionist creed, William Lloyd Garrison was forecasting the inevitable Civil War as clearly as did the nullification and secession arguments of South Carolina. For of course this was treason. It brought the abolition movement squarely in opposition to all those millions of sincere citizens whose first loyalties were devoted to the maintenance, intact, of the American Republic. Chief among the defenders of that faith, of course, was the indomitable Daniel Webster, Garrison's fellow citizen in Massachusetts. Though they worked in different arenas, these two men were obviously pitted against each other in sharp conflict on the matter of defense of the Union. Webster might be Garrison's most effective antagonist. It is therefore of crucial interest to learn what Webster thought of Garrison and the abolitionists.

Daniel Webster disapproved of slavery as thoroughly as did Garrison. In his Plymouth oration in 1820 he had denounced the African slave trade. In the reply to Hayne in 1830 he declared that slavery was "one of the greatest evils, both moral and political," but that it "has always been regarded as a matter of domestic policy left with the States themselves, and with which the Federal Government has nothing to do." In 1837 he said that he should do nothing "to favor or encourage its further extension." But at that time and in 1840 he argued: "Slavery as it exists in the States is beyond the reach of Congress. It is a concern of the States themselves." Like John Quincy Adams in the House, he supported "free petition" by presentation of antislavery petitions in the Senate. Webster did everything in his power to block the annexation of Texas. He was unsympathetic with the Mexican War, though ironically his second son, Edward, enlisted and died in that war. Claude M. Fuess in his *Daniel Webster, Statesman* well summarizes Webster's attitude toward slavery: "He deplored the existence of slavery; but he had no intention of wrecking the Union in order to eradicate it from American soil; and he did not foresee the disruptive force of an institution opposed to the great American principles of equality before the law and personal freedom." He disliked fanatical abolitionists. "He listened to their political creed and realized that they were quite willing to let the Union be destroyed if only slavery could be eliminated. He was horrified. How could he sympathize with a man like Garrison, who wrote: 'I am for the abolition of slavery, therefore for the dissolution of the Union'?"

In 1850 a critical situation arose. The annexation of additional territory in the Southwest, by the Treaty of Guadelupe Hidalgo, and the subsequent gold rush to California produced an immediate question of further extension of slavery beyond the Mississippi. Threats of civil war were already in the air. Webster pondered the compromise proposal made by his old friend Henry Clay: admit California as a free state; take no action on slavery in the new territorial governments; abolish the slave trade in the District of Columbia; and tighten enforcement of the Fugitive Slave Act. These were balanced concessions to North and South. Webster agreed, and offered his support on the Senate floor. In his "Seventh of March Speech" Webster impartially defended the obvious compromise. His speech was not of the ringing quality that had brought people to their feet cheering his defense of the federal Union in the reply to Hayne twenty years before. But the substance of the speech was thoroughly consistent with the whole theme of Webster's career, which was one long battle for the preservation of the Union, at any cost. Most historians agree, despite Whittier's bitter verse quoted above, that in the compromise of 1850 both Henry Clay and Daniel Webster were motivated by "unselfish devotion to what they believed to be the good of their country," as Rhodes expressed it. The measure won, thanks to Webster, and for yet another ten years the Civil War was delayed. Time seemed on the side of those who opposed the extension of slavery. Every possible concession had been made, and when war did come it was won by those who, like Daniel Webster, were ready to lay down their lives for the preservation of the Union.

After this last of the many heroic debates in which Webster participated with such epic distinction he lived only two years. He once wrote to his son Fletcher: "The giants grow strong again by touching the earth: the same effect is produced on me in touching the salt seashore." But when he returned to Marshfield in 1852, sick and worn from the combined symptoms of cirrhosis and being thrown from his carriage, the "place of places," as he called his beloved farm, could not revive him. He was also disappointed that the eloquence of his good friend Rufus Choate had not succeeded in persuading the Whig convention to nominate him for the Presidency instead, for the second time, of another military hero. Webster had spent nineteen years in the Senate, and six years as secretary of state under Tyler and Fillmore, still holding that office when he died in October, at Marshfield. Ralph Waldo Emerson, who was at Plymouth when he died, wrote in his *Journal:* "The sea, the rocks, the woods, gave no sign that America and the world had lost the completest man."

No Massachusetts historian can forbear, at this point, to insert what might seem in other states a digression, on the personal characteristics of Daniel Webster. Four paragraphs from Claude M. Fuess will serve the purpose admirably:

Almost from his infancy Webster was a lover of the outdoors; and he spent as many hours as possible in the open air. He climbed Mount Washington, not far from

The Old Man of the Mountain, whom he was thought to resemble. He liked to hunt and sail a boat; and he cast a fly into such widely different waters as the trout brooks of Cape Cod and the Great Falls of the Potomac. He enjoyed nature, and had a scientific knowledge of various species of flora and fauna. In 1824, after he was well established in Boston, he commenced spending his summers at an estate in the town of Marshfield, owned by Captain Thomas, from whom, in 1831, he bought the farmhouse and land. Gradually he acquired adjoining property until he owned more than two thousand acres and created a fruit and stock farm which was the envy of his neighbors. Into its maintenance and improvement Webster poured the fees from his law cases, attending personally to many of the details of management. When his duties at Washington were over each spring, Webster, usually racked by his chronic hay fever, would return to the peace of Marshfield, with its pure air and aromatic pine forests.

Webster reveled in the life of a gentleman farmer. He was up early, before five o'clock, "to test the freshness of the early dawn," feeding his prize cattle with ears of corn from his own hand and going out often with the laborers into the fields. Until a year or two before his death he was a crack shot, supplying his friends frequently with duck and woodcock. He kept a well-equipped fishing boat in a harbor only a few hundred yards from his house. Like Walter Scott, whom he resembled in other respects, Webster was most hospitable, and there were always guests under his roof. He took pride in playing the role of lord of the manor, and no one could have assumed it more gracefully. Part of the day he spent in his library; but in the evening he gave himself up to his visitors, telling stories and occasionally making a fourth in a rubber of whist. He had a keen sense of humor which was shown in impromptu verses; and in his more exuberant moods he could be heard singing and shouting about the house.

Webster had an adequate appreciation of his own picturesqueness and rather enjoyed the impression which he created. In his later days he was often followed in the street by an admiring throng, and at the inauguration in 1848 of Edward Everett as President of Harvard College it was Webster who drew the attention of the spectators. When offended, he could be very haughty, and some dramatic stories are told of his arrogance to lesser men who had been so unfortunate as to offend him. On state occasions he liked to appear in a court dress, with gigantic brass buttons and a beautifully starched neck cloth.

Webster did not need gorgeous attire to make him the center of interest. He walked this earth, as some one has said, "clad in the panoply of an imperial manhood." Carlyle described his eyes as "dull anthracite furnaces, needing only to be blown." He was called by Sydney Smith "a small cathedral all by himself." Even Emerson who never quite trusted Webster, spoke of him as "the old Titanic Earth-Son." By sheer magnificence of personality he dominated every gathering which he attended; and the adjective "godlike" sometimes used with regard to him did not seem extravagant or ridiculous. "In all the attributes of a mighty and splendid manhood," said Senator Hoar, "he never had a superior on earth."

Austere granite tombs in the old Church of the Presidents at Quincy and an inconspicuous marble pedestal in the old

Winslow family cemetery at Marshfield shelter the remains of three great American statesmen: John Adams, John Quincy Adams, and Daniel Webster. The death of Webster, and of John Quincy Adams, whose collapse, in harness, on the floor of the House of Representatives preceded by four years Webster's passing, brought to an end the era of builders of the Republic. Both were born before the Revolution's end, though Adams was already serving in Europe as a boy secretary to his father when Webster was born. But Webster's father had served as a captain under George Washington in the New England campaigns of the Revolution, and Daniel's early years were profoundly influenced by his father's admiration of the first president. Both Adams and Webster, as secretaries of state, added to the luster of the United States in international diplomacy, the one through the Monroe Doctrine and the other in the negotiation of the Webster-Ashburton Treaty. Both contributed to the stability of the federal constitutional system: here Webster was unsurpassed. Wholly different in temperament, tasks and background, they provided perfect illustrations of the possibility that in America a rough-diamond sort of man can become a champion of economic and federal power, whereas a man nurtured in aristocracy may develop into a scholar of democracy and a defender of freedom.

But the world still revolved, even though giants passed on. Garrison was still very much alive, and so were Harriet Beecher Stowe and Whittier and Wendell Phillips, and countless new agitators in Massachusetts and in Ohio and Illinois. Fugitive slave cases rocked Boston courtrooms under the able defense of Richard Henry Dana, Jr. While the Ohio valley was its most important route, the Underground Railroad also had many quiet stations in Massachusetts, especially in the Connecticut valley towns, through which escaped Negroes were smuggled into Canada. On the other hand, Stephen A.

Douglas secured the repeal of the old Missouri Compromise and opened up Kansas and Nebraska to the possibility of slavery. Successive Democratic victories in 1852 and 1856 emboldened the Supreme Court to declare in the Dred Scott decision that Congress lacked the power to exclude slavery from the territories. Such issues, cutting across party lines, set up threats to old political parties and demanded new loyalties and alignments. The old party system was going to pieces. Antislavery forces in Massachusetts elected Charles Sumner to the Senate, Nathaniel P. Banks to the House. A new Republican party was being constructed out of remnants of Whigs, Democrats and Free-Soilers. For this new party there appeared out of the West a new champion, tall and rawboned, but able to debate Stephen Douglas to a standstill. Newspaper reports of Abraham Lincoln's speeches propelled him so rapidly into national prominence that as the Republican candidate in the campaign of 1860 he split the Democratic party and won the Presidency. His platform of opposition to extension of slavery in the territories, protection for American industries, and free homesteads in the West for discontented Easterners, welded together elements of the economic and antislavery philosophies of the North with a popular issue for the West. But it seemed a mortal blow to the South.

Before Lincoln could be inaugurated the whirlwind had begun. Six southern states seceded. What the border states would do remained in doubt. The safeguarding of the government in Washington was already in jeopardy.

The behavior of Massachusetts in this crisis was heroic. When John A. Andrew of Hingham was swept into the governorship in the Lincoln victory, he was one of the few who, from personal investigation in Washington, was convinced that war was inevitable and that his own duty was to prepare Massachusetts for it with unflinching energy. Kept informed of national developments by Charles Francis Adams, he set to work promptly after his inauguration in January to revitalize and equip the Massachusetts militia. Convinced that the danger to Washington was real, he played his role in such a way as not to interfere with Lincoln's efforts to make peace with the South by negotiation. But when the negotiations collapsed and Fort Sumter was fired on, Andrew was one of the first who was ready.

Lincoln's call for 75,000 troops on April 15, to defend Washington, was therefore met instantly by Massachusetts. Andrew sent three regiments on April 17, the first movement of armed forces anywhere in the North. The 6th Massachusetts Regiment was fired on while marching through the streets of Baltimore two days later, which was the anniversary of the Battle of Lexington. They reached Washington with few casualties, and for the next week were the only troops available to protect Lincoln's government. At the end of that week reinforcements began to arrive, still from Massachusetts. Andrew's efficient organization, helped by the merchant John M. Forbes, who furnished ships and provisions, tided over the crisis until a wave of patriotic fervor began to unite many groups in the North who had been till then irresolute. By then the jittery period which could have produced collapse and disaster was over.

Who would have thought that Daniel Webster's son Fletcher would ever be leading a regiment down Boston's State Street singing "John Brown's Body" or that two years later he would be dead, on the field at Manassas? Already men from Quincy and New Bedford were reinforcing the few regulars in the garrison of Fortress Monroe, thereby supporting the flank of the Lynn and Pepperell regiments in Washington. Regiments from Cambridge, Roxbury, Boston, Taunton, and Springfield soon followed, along with a regiment of

Irish volunteers from widely distributed areas in the common-wealth. By the end of 1861 Governor Andrew's extraordinary diligence and the prompt rally of all factions to the support of the war effort succeeded in recruiting, training and sending to the front 29 Massachusetts infantry regiments, totaling more than 33,000 men. This number was doubled in 1862. Similarly one fifth of the officers and men of the Union Navy were from Massachusetts, totaling 17,000 men by the end of 1863. By that date the Bay State had provided 83,000 men for the Union Army, the vast majority of them volunteers. Among Governor Andrew's unusual achievements was the mobilization of two regiments of Negro volunteers. Compulsory drafting of troops became necessary in Massachusetts only after the middle of 1863. By the end of the war the state had sent 146,730 men into the armed forces. Of these 13,942 died during the war.

At such a cost, in lives and misery, Massachusetts paid her share in the convulsive struggle to preserve the Republic undivided. The warfare was as much one to resolve the irre-concilable positions of men like Webster and Garrison as it was between the North and the South. Both had been forecast by the classic statements of Massachusetts' two great leaders in the 1830's. A war between the states eventually achieved the ultimate ideals of both men. The Union was saved; slavery was abolished. Many of the economic and social wounds in-flicted on the South still remain as blights which only a less doctrinaire and more quietly constructive generation is grad-ually healing. As to the North, no one has ever better expressed the common objective for the reunited Republic than did Abraham Lincoln in his resolve at Gettysburg "that this nation, under God, shall have a new birth of freedom, and that government of the people, by the people, for the people, shall not perish from the earth."

CHAPTER SEVENTEEN

Woodenware to Aluminum

The genesis and development of any Massachusetts industry can best be understood, as in the already described shipping empire of the Ezra Westons of Duxbury, by choosing a family dynasty, in any one of hundreds of available towns, and following it through three or four generations of its growth from humble beginnings. Against such a background the changes in way of life, in physical conveniences, and in the general economy become more easily apparent. Classical instances of this process are legion: the textile empires of the Lowells, the Durfees, and the Slaters; the Taunton ironworks of the Leonards; the eventual monopoly in shovels won by the Ameses of North Easton; and the boot and shoe dynasties of Lynn and Brockton. It is human to take pride in one's own, and since it serves the purpose equally well, so long as one does not entangle the reader in a maze of genealogy, the author will utilize the career of his paternal grandmother's family, the Hunts of East Douglas, as an illustration of the type of success story that established Massachusetts as an industrial commonwealth. This time it was axes and hatchets. Inasmuch as this industry never became one of the enormous giants, like American Woolen or Wamsutta Mills, its use in this context is perhaps more typical. Its emigration to another state occurred sooner and with less fanfare.

Ezekiel Hunt, of the fifth generation of a Concord family that had moved to Ipswich, himself migrated about 1760 to Douglas, then a small frontier Massachusetts town on the Rhode Island border, settled a generation before in the New Grant of the town of Sherborn. He was a blacksmith, and presumably carried on that trade in Douglas, though he also served, in his forties, as a soldier in the Revolution. In 1798 his two young sons, Oliver and Joseph Hunt, built a new blacksmith shop in the briskly thriving community of East Douglas. There the Hill and Dudley families both maintained inns on Main Street, which was then a part of the principal Colony Road, or turnpike, between Boston and New York. Situated 46 miles from Boston, this was obviously a strategic point for a shop that could replace lost or loose horseshoes for stagecoach or horseback rider. Water power at the falls of the Mumford River, in the middle of East Douglas, had already been used for many years for a sawmill and a grain mill, and the principal industry of the area had become the production of cedar shingles, lumber, hoops and barrel staves for the Boston market. Abundant power to run a triphammer and a forge bellows was therefore available for the Hunt brothers at the site they had chosen. Because of the woodworking industries adjacent to them, they found themselves frequently called on to repair broken axes and other edged tools or to remodel them for specialized purposes. So adept did they become at this phase of their blacksmithing that they soon began to design axes of their own make, marked by a cold chisel with the initials "I O H," for Joseph and Oliver Hunt. They therefore built a second shop at Douglas, on a tributary brook, where Oliver devoted himself wholly to the production of axes. During the embargo and the War of 1812 there were financial difficulties and reorganizations, but manufacturing continued and the reputation of the axes grew. Broad hatchets, shingling hatchets, lathing hatchets, and claw hatchets were added to the line. As early as 1816 Oliver's 17-year-old son, Warren, was driving a span of horses to Boston, often at night, and peddling hatchets along Beacon Street the next day, selling the balance of the load to a merchant in Dock Square, and returning to East Douglas with a load of steel and iron. Soon a sales agent was employed, who found ready outlets for all the Hunt axes and hatchets the young company could produce. A third shop, for forging and grinding, was built in East Douglas. Before long rolling mills and other heavy machinery were installed to replace some of the handwork. A new brick shop was built for drawing patterns, polishing and finishing, and later a stone building for forging and grinding, including drilling machines newly invented to drill out the "eyes" of the axes. Young Warren Hunt had become general manager at the age of eighteen. The Hunts became highly skilled in the tempering of steel. A sea captain brother of Charles Scudder, the Boston hardware merchant, joined the firm.

The distinctive feature of the Douglas axes was that the edged steel blade was embedded deep into the softer iron bitt instead of being applied or "overcoated" around it. Thus the axe stood up for years of hard usage and grinding so long as there was enough of the implement left to be called an axe. "Overcoated" axes were soon worn out when the surface was ground away. By 1831 the Hunt brothers were manufacturing at Douglas "5000 dozen axes and 3000 dozen hatchets" annually.

Fulling mills, satinet and cassimere factories, and cotton spinning and weaving mills were soon added to the industrial fabric of East Douglas, although they were more extensive in neighboring Webster, where Samuel Slater's family had a chain of mills. Some of the Douglas textile factories thrived, but the buildings of those that failed were often taken over for further enlargement of the Axe Company, which in 1835 was incorporated as the Douglas Axe Manufacturing Company. Soon scythes, Spanish machetes, sugar-cane knives, and other exotic edged tools began to flow out of the Douglas Axe mills. The firm was now the leading American axe manufacturer. Sources of New England iron, which had sometimes been processed as far away as Pembroke, Maine, before 1860, were exhausted, and even Pennsylvania iron had to be supplemented by English steel by the outbreak of the Civil War. That was why the author's great-grandfather, Oliver Hunt, Jr., went to Sheffield in 1860 in tall hat and brass-buttoned waistcoat on the double mission of consultations on tempering techniques with English steelmasters, and arrangements for the purchase of steel. No doubt these negotiations were greatly appreciated a year later when the firm began to be an important source of swords and bayonets for the armies of the North in the Civil War. The English source of fine steel was also the reason that the company's officers agitated in 1874 for removal or reduction of tariff duties on English steel.

Picks, mattocks, bench axes and adzes were also being produced. Douglas tools were winning medals at the World's Fair in London and at the Vienna and Paris Expositions. American tools and cutlery not only were in control of the domestic market but secured also a world-wide reputation in most countries. While American tool factories still employed more manual labor relative to output than did most branches of the iron and steel industry, a condition that favored foreign competitors with lower wage rates, they still gained in competition because of fine craftsmanship. Their mills excelled in labor-saving techniques and skills even while their New England firms were transporting raw materials from Pennsylvania and England. By the 1870's the Douglas Axe Manufacturing Com-

pany's plants extended for nearly a mile along the Mumford River. Scarcely could Ezekiel Hunt, the blacksmith who had died in 1803, have dreamed what his sons and grandsons would build in Douglas, and the world, during seventy-five years.

Alas, the epilogue is distressing. In the long run Pittsburgh could not be denied. Massachusetts designs, skills and enterprise were not unique. It was not necessary to transport Pennsylvania steel and iron to Massachusetts for manufacture. The Douglas Axe Manufacturing Company could be purchased. It could be moved. Victor S. Clark writes in his *History of Manufactures in the United States:* "The American Axe and Tool Co. had been incorporated as early as 1889 to combine 12 axe works, including eventually the famous establishment at East Douglas, Massachusetts." And further: "This corporation, which purchased outright the plants of its constituent works, and operated them under the management of their former owners . . . declared its object to be not to advance prices, but to economize production by being able to purchase raw materials cheaper." How hard local enterprise died can be judged by the fact that eleven years later, in 1900, the *Commercial and Financial Chronicle* could still report that the American Axe and Tool Company "has bought 38 acres at Glassport and *will erect* there its *proposed* plant to take in all the scattered establishments *now operated.*—The plants are *now* at Beaver Falls, Pa., Mulkall, Pa., Lewistown, Pa., Ballston Spa, N.Y., East Douglas, Mass., and Oakland, Me." (italics the author's.) But R. M. Smythe's 1904 edition of *Obsolete American Securities* records the actual fact: "Douglas Axe Manufacturing Co., Inc., Mass. Dissolved 1892."

Gradually all the Douglas activities were absorbed. Today no axes have been made in Douglas for fifty years. One searches now almost in vain to find physical remnants of the shops. Two stone buildings, one of them a ruin, the other used for differnt purposes, remain of all the Hunt empire. On two of the millsites there are modern woolen mills. Oliver Hunt's fine Greek revival mansion, with the paint scaling from its noble Doric columns, is now cut up into apartments. None of the Hunt family lives in Douglas any more. One must read the published history of the town to find some glimmering of that former glory.

This Douglas axe story is just one example among thousands of what happened to New England industries that were built fundamentally on superb handicrafts. The nineteenth century was a century of mechanized handicrafts. The twentieth century is a century of automated machines making identical products without handicrafts.

As a matter of history, therefore, it is of interest to trace the flow of change in the type of products that an industrial area like Massachusetts manufactured as the nineteenth century went on. For the physical manifestations of its culture were greatly influenced by the household equipment, the farm tools, the means of transportation, and the laborsaving devices which the industrial revolution supplied. Part of the tragedy of East Douglas is that there are not as many axes and hatchets and scythes used today as there were in 1875, and practically no horseshoes. The age of woodcraft was dying. In modern terms, the Axe Company was caught with its diversification down. It should have turned to the making of those new machine lathes, or twist drills or hack saws, or textile machinery. Some similar firms did so, and survived. Those that survived rolled with the punch. The one-crop industry usually went under.

Woodcutting hand tools were still the basis of fashioning most useful devices until 1860. Wooden spinning wheels had been replaced by wooden jennies and water frames still using wooden spindles. The cobbler sat on his wooden bench lighted by a whale-oil lamp on a wooden bracket, using wooden-handled shoemakers' tools to drive wooden pegs over a wooden last. Many clocks still used wooden works, and larger oak gears transmitted much of the power from wooden belt pulleys in factories. Even the lathe was usually a cluster of steel chucks, knives and worm gears set into a wooden frame. Wooden brace bits, bucksaws, block planes, "Yankee drills," carpenters' clamps, vises and band saws all used a minimum of metal parts or cutting blades. Buckets, ladles, scoops, butter churns, washboards, meat grinders, coffee mills and flour sifters, sausage stuffers, and even the early washing machines were made of wood through the first half of the nineteenth century. Steel or cast or wrought iron was reserved for the cutting edges, the baking and cooking and fireplace implements, the nails, hinges, latches, scales and steelyards, the guns, the stoves, the betty lamps and plow blades where softer materials would not serve. Sheet iron was indeed beginning to be adapted to dust pans, cheese graters, reflecting ovens, tinder boxes, cooky cutters, tea and coffee pots, kitchen canisters, sconces and milk containers mostly where the older copper and pewter or cast iron were unwieldy or more expensive. But even on the farm the rakes, cultivators, shovels, oxbows, hay wagons, fences, corncribs and covered bridges were still made of stout hickory or oak or pine. Forests were still abundant and cheap, and unless unusual wealth made the owner covet the more expensive metals, a little extra labor in fashioning wooden utensils was preferable in most households, so long as handicraft was the essential ingredient in their production. Hatchets, axes, saws and drawshaves were the production tools of the nineteenth century.

But the development of machine production brought prices down and steadily killed off the handicrafts. When glass could be pressed by a machine in a mold instead of b boriously blown; when sheet iron could be rolled thin and stamped or molded into coal hods, buckets, washbasins, and frying pans; when cast-iron pumps could replace the wooden well sweep and bucket; and when coal stoves and the tinsmith's stovepipe eliminated the fireplace and its endless woodchopping, the era of dependence on both wood and handicraft labor was beginning to slip.

The decreasing dependence of America's rapidly growing population on supplies of wood, for both fuel and building materials, was probably a godsend to the American landscape. Before the invention of solar evaporation in Cape Cod's saltworks, sea water was laboriously boiled down in iron kettles to make salt. Nearly four hundred gallons of sea water, boiled by burning a cord and a half of wood, was needed to produce a bushel of salt. In the year 1770, at the peak of this method of salt production, nearly 100,000 cords of wood were burned to produce the 70,000 bushels of salt used by New England's fishing fleets. The smelting of bog iron ore, the production of Sandwich glass and lime and turpentine, and the stoking of kilns in brickyards all required similarly unbelievable quantities of firewood or charcoal in the period before Pennsylvania's coal became available. And the ordinary needs of the Massachusetts population for heating their houses, even though parts of the houses were shut off and not heated in winter, used such quantities of hardwoods as to be a continuing threat to forests until coal and oil came into general use. Not only Cape Cod but many very large areas of southern New England were almost completely denuded of their trees before the Civil War for these purposes. Only the advent of coal permitted some of these areas to grow new forests. Others can never be reforested, and remain scrubby moorlands to this day. Nantucket, much of Cape Cod and southeastern Massachusetts, which once were adorned with magnificent pine forests, will always bear the scars of the age of wood for fuel.

A somewhat similar denuding began to occur to Massachusetts' handicraft skills. The passing of the wooden ship destroyed a whole shipbuilding industry in coastal areas. As the fisheries declined, and the railroads took over the schooner trade, large segments of the seagoing Portuguese turned to gardening, house painting and carpentering, or working in factories. The specialized artisans in silversmithing, clockmaking, and cabinetmaking, whose skills had so adorned the Federalist period, gradually succumbed to the competition of cheap machine-made imitations of their wares. In architecture, after the brief Greek revival period of the 1830's, when Americans perceived the analogy of their young Republic to the classic era and decorated their houses and churches with imposing pediments and Doric columns to celebrate their prosperity, the styles degenerated into wooden Gothic and the gingerbread of Victorianism. It was difficult to pull out of the awful degredation of the Civil War. Cast-iron fences replaced the clean white pickets of the woodenware period. Textile millionaires actually fronted some of their mansions with ornate cast-iron Corinthian columns and replaced carefully hand-wrought iron balustrades with machine-made cast iron in pompous designs. The only circumstances that saved our beautiful maritime architecture in the seaport towns was the fact that their prosperity faded in the machine age and their people could not afford to rebuild in the styles of the 1870's. But elsewhere, cupolas and bay windows, wooden castle towers and imitation French roofs and mansards were in their glory, adorned with slate or tin roofs and machine-designed gingerbread that was the despair of honest carpenters.

Hand-wrought metal and wood just disappeared. Doorknobs, locks and latches were all machine made, though sometimes beautifully adorned with molded glass or porcelain. Brasswork in drawer knobs was now stamped in floral designs. Machines turned out identical kerosene lamps, chafing dishes, coffee grinders, teapots and washboards for the tremendously enlarged market. Unskilled labor at the machines could provide dozens of serviceable objects for the price of one of the old handicrafted pieces. Thus almost any citizen could now afford utensils and household devices that had been the exclusive treasures of the wealthy in former days. As the manufacturers prospered, their machines changed. No longer need the framework of looms, lathes, shoe machinery or band saws be made of wood. Cast iron was everywhere. Even the carpenter's own bitstock, plane and mallet could be made of it. Floors of the old mills had to be shored up, sometimes collapsed, because of the weight of iron in the new machinery. Massachusetts' bog iron was long ago exhausted, but Pittsburgh could supply all needs. Farmers had horse-drawn hay rakes with iron wheels and set up iron windmills to draw their water from the well. They even piped it into steel tanks and had running water in the new soapstone sink in the kitchen. Flush toilets took the place of the old wooden outhouse. Some houses were even installing central furnaces for heating, with iron pipes and hot-water radiators piercing the old partitions. Life was shot through with exciting new devices.

So the plumber slowly gained on the cabinetmaker. Gaslighting was installed in Boston. Bridges were being built of steel. Cast-iron horse fountains, sometimes even containing a little low drinking spout for dogs, appeared in the town squares. The cities were building horsecar rapid transit systems on iron rails in the public streets. Iron turbines were replacing wooden water wheels, and often steam donkey engines took the place of the turbines. Public water supplies with reservoirs and steam pumps tore up the streets of the towns with their networks of piping. Iron was king, and the wrench took the place of the axe.

It was not therefore surprising that the Douglas Axe Manufacturing Company was moved to Pittsburgh, where it became a subsidiary of the larger industry of iron and steel. The deeper significance of the story is of course that New England could not compete successfully in heavy industry with Pittsburgh when transportation of large quantities of iron and coal from Pennsylvania was needed. Such heavy industry could always be more economically conducted near to its raw material supply, especially if its markets were also moving westward. As the lumber camps progressively left Massachusetts and moved into such areas as Canada and Michigan, the axe moved with them. Pittsburgh was thereafter in a much more favorable position to compete than any Massachusetts region in this industry.

An interesting commentary to this chapter is that the author's grandfather, Elijah Howe, Jr., of Dedham, taught school in the East Douglas High School for two years after his graduation from Amherst College. He was a bookkeeper in a Boston bank when he was married in 1857 to the daughter of Oliver Hunt, Jr. But in 1864 he resigned from the bank and became New England agent for the Black Diamond Steel Works of Pittsburgh. For the next twelve years he traveled throughout New England, visiting every machine shop and factory where steel was used. Among others, he provided the steel used for the drills that bored the Hoosac Tunnel when railroads finally penetrated that barrier in the Berkshire Hills. Already in the 1860's a son-in-law of Oliver Hunt had come to the conclusion that Pennsylvania offered a safer berth in steel than East Douglas.

A final, fiction-like commentary exists in the fact that

Captain Alfred E. Hunt, a nephew of Oliver Hunt, Jr., and an M.I.T.-trained metallurgist previously with the Black Diamond Steel Works became in 1888 president of the Pittsburgh Reduction Company, of which the vice-president, Charles Martin Hall, was inventor of the modern process of producing aluminum. The Pittsburgh Reduction Company soon became the Aluminum Company of America, of which Roy Arthur Hunt, Alfred's son, was president from 1928 to 1951. He was still chairman of its Executive Committee in 1958. Thus did three generations of woodworking steel toolmakers breed a race of aluminum men. It is a neat trick to jump from horseshoes to hatchets to airplanes in five generations, but is this not what we have all done, in our own fashion?

By the way, the American Axe and Tool Company, of Glassport and Pittsburgh, was reported in 1922 as being no longer in business.

CHAPTER EIGHTEEN

Immigrants and Proper Bostonians

Only the earlier half of Massachusetts' industrial revolution is exemplified by such handicraft-based industries as the Douglas Axe Manufacturing Company. They belonged to the same type of community and social organization, Yankee from top to bottom, that had developed the China trade and the fisheries. The huge accretions of mass production factories in the rapidly growing cities of the commonwealth during and after the Civil War were built on an entirely different principle, like the clipper ships, in that they depended on huge numbers of low-paid, unskilled labor for the operation of their machinery. This production phenomenon, which developed Massachusetts' enormous textile, shoe, paper and machinery industries, came about not only because of Yankee skills but also as a result of the availability of a long-standing surplus of immigrant laborers. The only other requirement was capital for building machines and factories. The Bay State's maritime families could provide plenty of capital. But without immigrant labor the great manufacturing centers of Holyoke, Worcester, Lawrence, Lynn and Fall River could never have functioned as they did in the commonwealth's economy.

In order to understand this injection of industrial gigantism into the life of Massachusetts, and the profound social changes it produced, we need to mention the European conditions that brought it about. For the motivation of these immigrants was not simply a desire for change, a search for liberty, or an escape from tyranny. Such motives did indeed influence the character of immigration among certain of the German groups who settled in the Ohio valley. But the peasant Irish who came and settled in Massachusetts in the 1840's and 1850's came primarily for one reason. They came because their share-cropper status in Ireland under changing agricultural systems had reduced them almost to starvation. After Ireland's potato famine they swarmed into Boston in such abject poverty that they could not afford to move westward. They had to settle down in slum areas in Boston and neighboring cities and make what living they could in the most menial work available at the bottom of the economic ladder since they had no training for better occupations. By 1855, according to Oscar Handlin, a definitive researcher in this field, more than 50,000 Irish fugitives from the potato famine were domiciled in Boston, almost all having arrived since 1840. They already constituted more than a third of Boston's population. Handlin says: "Thousands of poverty-stricken peasants, rudely transposed to an urban commercial center, could not readily become merchants or clerks; they had neither the training nor the capital to set up as shopkeepers or artisans. The absence of other opportunities forced the vast majority into the ranks of an unemployed resourceless proletariat, whose cheap labor and abundant numbers ultimately created a new industrialism in Boston. But for a long time they were fated to remain a massive lump in the community, undigested, undigestible." The emigrant aid societies and the parish priests could care for few of them. In 1850 six thousand of them were transient day laborers. Thousands of the women eked out the family income by domestic service in Boston homes. Many found refuge caring for horses in livery stables, or as waiters in restaurants, or peddlers, or janitors, or bartenders. These Irish were a step below the Negro barbers, chimney sweeps and seamen in the economic scale. Handlin writes: "From every part of the United States construction bosses in embankments and water projects, tunnels, canals and railroads called on Boston for the cheap manpower they knew was always available there." Yet the pay was so low that Irishmen returned home to Boston with no more money than they had started with. "Unscrupulous exploitation was the theme of the construction camp; and dirt, disorder and unremitting toil were its invariable accompaniments. . . . Ferried over the Atlantic, and carted over America, despised and robbed, downtrodden and poor, they made the railroads grow."

Along Boston's wharves, in disused warehouses, cheap boardinghouses, and run-down tenements the Irish crowded, constantly increasing as the Cunarders and sailing packets brought new hundreds of them. They lived in sheds and shanties, a whole family to a room, one privy and one sink to a whole tenement, amid decaying rubbish, dilapidated stairways and leaking roofs. So bad were the sanitary facilities that tuberculosis and intestinal diseases thrived in these hovels: it was said that the Irish lived an average of only fourteen years after reaching Boston. Boston's death rate became twice as high as that of the rest of Massachusetts in 1850. Inevitably alcoholism, prostitution, illegitimacy and insanity grew among them as the wretched conditions under which they lived degraded some of these simple farming people into pallid, hopeless riffraff, without self-respect or decency. The problem was so intense from the social standpoint that conservative Boston employers, fed up with thievery, drunkenness and laziness, repeatedly headed their employment advertisements with the letters "N.I.N.A.," which was universally understood to mean "No Irish need apply."

Yet these same Irish gave a tremendous boost to industry by "holding out to investors magnificent opportunities for profits from cheap labor costs." Boston itself, which had been previously a commercial and distributing center, quadrupled its number of industrial employees between 1845 and 1865, from 10,000 to 40,000. During these years it became the nation's fourth manufacturing city. Ironworks, glass manufactories, copper and brass foundries, and the production of ready-made clothing, sewing machines, locomotives, sugar, organs, pianos, dredging machinery, kerosene, and furniture were either established or greatly expanded during these years when Boston had a labor surplus. Thousands of the "cheap labor" workers in these new factories were the despised Irish, men and women, who could be taught the monotonous machine-paced tasks that industry needed for the mass production of all kinds of products. Employees might move out of Boston to the new factories in Lynn, Salem, or Brockton, or migrate to New Bedford, Taunton, Worcester, Lowell or Lawrence, but their places were promptly taken by new arrivals from the Enoch Train or Harnden or Cunard Atlantic packets. The supply was inexhaustible. And so long as this was true Massachusetts' low-cost industry could compete in many markets.

The Irish immigration slowed down after the Civil War, but the flow of immigrants did not stop. First French Canadians, then Portuguese, Italians, Greeks, Poles, Czechoslovakians, Russians, Finns, Letts, Lithuanians and Syrians joined the procession, keeping the labor market overflowing past the end of the century. Many new elements were added to the old Anglo-Saxon culture. Slavic, Mediterranean, Semitic and Celtic influences served eventually to enrich Massachusetts' thinking, permeate its folkways, enliven its speech, and add new perspectives to its graphic arts, music, and literature.

But the immediate effect was its stimulation of Massachusetts industry. In the latter half of the century more than a third of the nation's woolens were produced in Massachusetts. Fall River, Lawrence, Lowell, and New Bedford led all other cities in cotton manufacture. By 1890 Lawrence was third and Lowell fourth among American cities in the manufacture of woolens. By 1900 Massachusetts produced almost half the shoes in the United States, a quarter of these coming from Lynn, and large fractions from Brockton, Haverhill, Marlborough and Worcester. Shoe machinery from Beverly, Boston and Waltham and paper-mill machinery from Lowell, Pittsfield, Lawrence and Worcester were world-famous. All this prodigious and bustling prosperity rested, once the machines had been built and paid for, on the shifting base of a labor surplus provided by unceasing immigration through Boston's port, which remained a good immigrant port because it also furnished the shortest commercially practical route for sending the British mails to Canada.

Meanwhile, from 1870 to 1900, the United States population doubled, from 38 million to 76 million. Of the new people 11 million were immigrants. As the cities grew, urban residents became a third of the total population, as opposed to a fifth previously. In the Northeast half the people lived in cities. West of the Alleghenies mechanized farming and new industrial cities followed the railroads across the plains. New England, like all the other eastern areas, steadily lost its relative importance in the national scheme. Financial and maritime leadership began to leave Boston and set itself up in New York. Each region began to learn what it could do best and what it must relinquish to some other region that could do it better. Boston continued to be a mecca of education, engineering science, and medicine, but influences were already stirring that would eventually move shoe and cotton industries nearer the sources of raw materials in the West and South. The regional differences were becoming qualitative and specialized, which must inevitably change the relationship of Massachusetts to the nation. This is always a remorseless accompaniment of national growth. Explosive physical expansion of the United States was the dominant feature of the last third of the century, and regional interests no longer could dictate their role in the over-all economy.

The usual legendary image of Boston in the Victorian period scarcely suggests that Bostonians were aware of immigration problems or changes elsewhere in the nation. For several generations the name of Boston has borne a reputation for exclusive aristocracy and social prestige as provincial and pompous as that of its Puritan forebears. Since this allegation of Back Bay patricianism is a part of Massachusetts history, it may be well to examine it with some critical good humor. As has already been suggested, people of Irish extraction already had had some acquaintance with the Cold Roast Boston tradition.

Late nineteenth-century Boston society began to migrate westward from the slopes of Beacon Hill into the new brownstone mansions along the spacious avenues of the Back Bay soon after the Civil War. "These broad and handsome streets," says an 1879 Boston handbook, "are lined with imposing and stately private and public edifices, the architectural designs of which, in many cases, are most ambitious and elaborate, rendering this part of the city justly famous. Indeed, its refined elegance is always remarked with genuine enthusiasm by visitors, for no other city in this country, nor possibly in any other, displays, in a like space of territory, so much solid wealth, and so many superb structures, public and private, as are here spread before the eye. . . . Bostonians are proud of this section of their city, and their pride is surely pardonable."

The "refined elegance" of this new aristocracy was indeed a far cry from the original sternly Puritan society set up by the brilliant minds that clustered about John Winthrop and his gifted son. Only through marriage, for the most part, did such old Puritan families as the Bradstreets, Dudleys, Wards and Nortons participate in this new, glittering Bostonianism. Occasional Bradfords, Winslows, and Saltonstalls briefly decorated the Victorian aristocracy, but for the most part it was not founded on either Puritan or Pilgrim ancestry as the source of its social prestige. *Mayflower* descent is considered of much more importance in states west of the Hudson than it is anywhere in New England. And families firmly rooted in the maritime life of New Bedford, or the industries of Fall River, Worcester or Springfield, rated as little prestige in the Back Bay as a Pittsburgh steelmaster. Many descendants of the brilliant China trade mariners of Salem, like the Derbys, the Crowninshields, Pickerings, Peabodys, Searses and Cabots, had to move or marry into the commercial life of Boston if they were to maintain their place in the social orbit of Back Bay society. Commercial wealth, of one origin or another, was an outstanding requisite of this new aristocracy, even though it often carried with it a remarkable consistency in its pursuit of learning and the fine arts.

Literary historians have rightly revered the Golden Age of New England literature in the first half of the nineteenth century, but have frequently castigated the "Gilded Age" that followed the Civil War, of which the Back Bay was Boston's symbol. There is no question that the Concord and Cambridge groups of philosophers and poets were the high point of New England culture and that the falling off in genius that characterized the postbellum society was, by contrast, a lesser grade of cultural achievement. The commercialism of late nineteenth-century Boston, with its dominant merchant and industrial class administering world-wide business in textile mills and countinghouses, railroad offices and insurance companies, has seemed to men like Lewis Mumford and Van Wyck Brooks as a money-mad "pragmatic acquiescence," from the cultural standpoint. Even the vigorous innovations in scientific invention and research represented by Harvard's natural science achievements and the founding of the Massachusetts Institute of Technology have failed to impress such historians as creditable or constructive. They look down their noses at the whole Victorian period.

I believe, as applied to Massachusetts, that this is a warped and unrealistic viewpoint. Every historical period has its economic phase. Wealth sometimes serves to nourish creative ferments, whether in Rome, in Renaissance Italy, or in Victorian Boston. Culture is no monopoly of the half-starved poet or of the literary critic. And no better example of the combined assets of wealth and creative intellectual originality can be cited than in the instance of Boston's Back Bay aristocracy in this period which created the Cold Roast Boston legend. The fact that it has at times become a target for poking fun, for the creation of a traditional joke about Boston, is of course testimony to the fact that Bostonians took it too seriously, but also it is a tribute to its vigor and virility. If it had collapsed under criticism, the joke would be no longer a joke.

The sturdiest among the leading families in the Back Bay's society were of course founded on the materialist bedrock of success in commerce and industry. Cleveland Amory in his *Proper Bostonians* quite accurately emphasized that every such family had its "nineteenth century merchant prince. Whether in shipping, in railroading, in textiles, in mining or in banking, he is the stout trunk of almost every First Family tree. . . . There is scarcely a Family that does not owe its position in the city's Society to the money he made and saved and left in the spendthrift-proof trusts for them." Some, like the Adamses, acquired their money partly by marriage. But whether by the male or the female line, Lowells, Cabots, Forbeses, Lodges, Coolidges and Parkmans arose to leadership through their competence in a commercial society. Yet the amazing phenomenon in Boston was not that it was commercial but rather that its materialism in no way destroyed its cultural achievements. A family deeply rooted in industry by a textile king, Francis Cabot Lowell, and a great merchant, John Amory Lowell, proceeded to sire two poets, James Russell Lowell and Amy Lowell, an astronomer and an architect, Percival and Guy Lowell, and a college president. A. Lawrence Lowell, and then left, in the Lowell Institute, a scientific and cultural foundation of enormous significance in adult education. Similar observations could be made in the Forbes and Holmes families, the Coolidges, the Lawrences, and other striking examples among the Back Bay patricians. In Boston the materialism of the Gilded Age wiped out neither the public spirit of the Puritan founders nor the culture of the Golden Age, but actually advanced these objectives. A society that could produce an Oliver Wendell Holmes, a Charles W. Eliot, a Lemuel Shattuck, a Henry I. Bowditch, an Elizabeth Peabody and a Henry Lee Higginson was not fundamentally a materialistic society. Its recognition of the merits of people like Agassiz, William James, William Dean Howells, Nathaniel Shaler, John Singer Sargent, Alice Freeman Palmer and G. Stanley Hall further emphasized its devotion to progressive ideas and new educational and scientific principles. Even if it could not solve immediately such awful social problems as its slums and its immigration problems, it still worked hard at its civic and cultural tasks, and produced the community tools with which solutions might be found.

Bernard Berenson
Louis Brandeis

Nationally, the critics' evaluation of the Gilded Age had more validity. Postwar scandals, both in the federal government and in business, have left us a rather seamy picture of the last third of the century. While Boston had its slums and underpaid labor, the South had reconstruction; the West, railroads and homesteads; and the whole East, too rapid industrialization and immigration to absorb easily. A social and economic revolution was going on in the United States which still is not finished seventy-five years later. In the early stages of so universal an upheaval it was not surprising that the era was studded with the names of *nouveau riche* millionaires of a breed that carried in their heritage none of the restraining philosophy of the Puritan and the patriot. The disreputable stock manipulations of the Jay Goulds and Jim Fisks in railroads and western lands, often abetted by shady members of Congress who personally profited from the deals, have fixed a jaundiced color and a fecal odor on the whole period. Such colors and odors unfortunately pervaded the careers of Rockefellers, Carnegies, Fricks and Schwabs, Vanderbilts, Garys, Morgans and McCormicks despite their great administrative capacities for constructing and financing our twentieth-century industrial empire. By present-day standards the nation was tainted by political corruption, oppressive tyranny over labor, and utter disregard of the small investor. These men were no more immoral than the system that produced them, but it took a good deal of philanthropy in their later lives to deodorize the wild oats of their youth. It is the good fortune of the Republic that both their industrial contributions and their philanthropies have continued to serve well the nation's growth long after the effects of their earlier excesses have been dissipated.

In the Gilded Age, nationally, Massachusetts' role was less dramatic and more constructive than that of most states.

In business she was conservative, her financial oligarchy tightly controlling her rapidly growing industrial, insurance, railroad and banking interests. In the pursuit of improvements in education, libraries, museums and health activities, and in the Americanization of new waves of immigrants, she often led the way. She made many contributions to liberalism in government, such as the Australian ballot, civil service reform, the Employers' Liability Law, and her pioneer State Department of Health. These were the beginnings of a liberal revolution against the excesses of capitalism and demonstrated the continued vigor of the Yankee conscience as a counterpoise to the weight of corruption elsewhere.

When Massachusetts men were captains of industry, most of them kept their skirts cleaner than the average. The Ameses of North Easton, who had grown rich on shovel manufacturing, were necessarily involved in the Crédit Mobilier scandal in connection with the building of the Union Pacific Railroad, of which Oliver Ames was president. Yet Oliver served four terms as lieutenant governor and three as a capable and greatly respected governor of Massachusetts in the eighties. John Murray Forbes of Boston, president of the Michigan Central Railroad before the Civil War, became president of the Chicago, Burlington and Quincy in the seventies. Ralph Waldo Emerson summarized his character in the following words: "Never was such force, good meaning, good sense, good actions, combined with such domestic lovely behavior, such modesty and persistent preference for others. Wherever he moved, he was the benefactor." Members of Boston's Perkins, Hunnewell, Paine, Thayer and Endicott families all were able executives in the Burlington system before it was sold to Morgan in 1901. Thomas Nickerson and E. P. Ripley were presidents of the Atchison, Topeka and Santa Fe, and Howard Elliott of the Northern Pacific. Charles Francis Adams served with great distinction in the presidency of the Union Pacific Railroad, pulling together its financing and improving its service at a time of crisis in the eighties. In mining, Boston's Quincy A. Shaw organized such Lake Superior companies as Calumet and Hecla, of which Alexander Agassiz was superintendent. The latter's profits went into the founding of Harvard's Agassiz Museum.

Boston's Victorians produced one of Massachusetts' most brilliant periods in the extension of education. Not content with being the nation's champion of public primary education in the seventeenth century, and the principal pioneer in secondary schools, normal schools, and the first colleges for women in the first half of the nineteenth century, Massachusetts now launched a campaign for the founding of technical schools and colleges to which the modern United States pays tribute by sending students from every state in the Union. In this field the poor immigrant, the Back Bay aristocrat, and the old Yankees of the country towns were in complete agreement: children deserved to have a better education than their parents. This theme runs like a refrain through the entire history of Massachusetts.

Already at the close of the Civil War, Tufts College, Boston College, Holy Cross at Worcester, the New England Conservatory of Music, Harvard's Lawrence Scientific School, and the Massachusetts Institute of Technology had been founded. The following founding dates are a sample of what followed: 1867, Massachusetts Agricultural College at Amherst (the progenitor of the University of Massachusetts); 1869, Boston University; 1875, Wellesley College, Smith College at Northampton, and Boston's Normal Art School; 1876, Radcliffe College; 1887, Worcester's Clark University; 1893, Simmons College, and Tufts Medical School; 1896, Northeastern University, and the Lowell Institute School for Industrial Foremen at M.I.T.; 1897, Lowell Textile Institute, and 1899, Tufts Dental School.

Such a list is only the bare bones of an intellectual revival into which hundreds of men in Massachusetts poured such driving energy and zealous enthusiasm that nothing could stop them. The imaginative leadership of Charles W. Eliot and his famous modernizers of the Harvard curriculum were matched in zeal by a whole host of lesser crusaders who fought their battles in trustees' meetings and boards of education and in the classroom. Elizabeth Peabody's first kindergarten in the United States, Colonel Francis Parker's revitalization of the Quincy schools by the slogan: "Learn to do by doing," and the brilliant lectures on education for teachers in Boston by G. Stanley Hall and William T. Harris were examples of the trend. Massachusetts continued to lead the way through her astonishing pioneering in the education of women in new Bay State colleges like Wellesley, Smith, Radcliffe, and Boston University. Alice Freeman Palmer and John D. Philbrick brought new vitality into the State Board of Education. Eminent college professors like William James, Nathaniel Shaler, Louis and Alexander Agassiz, Charles Sargent and Josiah Royce established completely new horizons and goals in teaching.

The public high schools adopted rapidly expanding facilities for technical and scientific training. Geography, drawing, manual training and domestic science entered the curriculum, together with such basic sciences as physics, chemistry and biology. The foundation was thus laid for rapid establishment of schools in the applied sciences in agriculture and the industrial and domestic arts. Boston's Mechanic Arts High School, of 1893, and the Cambridge Rindge Manual Training School for Boys, 1888, are examples. Similarly new textile schools were set up in New Bedford and Fall River, and these were followed by more than a hundred state-aided vocational schools in all the large cities of the commonwealth in subsequent years. Private endowments have supplemented these with such schools as Wentworth Institute, Franklin Union, and many business and secretarial schools.

All this seething activity in the world of education was, in one sense, merely the response of the people to one of the most exciting periods in world history. Invention after invention was emerging from the laboratories: the transatlantic cable in 1866; transcontinental railways in 1869; the first telephone in 1876; the first submarine in 1877; the earliest electric lights in 1878; the electric streetcar in 1880; linotype printing in 1884; and the internal-combustion engine in 1885. New techniques in grinding machine tools, in chemistry, and in electricity were transforming the sources of power and the machines of industry with breathless speed. Overnight Massachusetts was embarked on a new General Electric Company at Lynn, a new rubber industry in Watertown. People returned home from the Philadelphia Exposition and the Chicago World's Fair fairly bursting with admiration for scientific progress. A new America was being born, and all could feel the driving enthusiasm of the scientists. Typewriters, automobiles, airplanes, motion pictures and phonographs were on the drawing boards. Boston was building the world's first subway. The creative inventors who were building the new machines were not pompous aristocrats but scholarly frontiersmen, charged with hope and enthusiasm. Men like Charles Sargent, who founded the Arnold Arboretum, Reginald Fitz, the discoverer of appendicitis, Henry I. Bowditch, founder of the Boston Medical Library and of Massachusetts' State Board of Health, first in the nation, were men with a mission, men with a gleam in the eye. The Boston Museum of Fine Arts, the Boston Public Library, the Isabella Stewart Gardner Museum, and Thomas Wentworth Higginson's Boston Symphony Orchestra were all in process of birth, led by enthusiasts who would not relent from their driving sense of urgency. Better legislative arguments were hammering out a State Board of Arbitration, 1882, and the Employers' Liability Law of 1887, pioneer solutions of fundamental problems in labor relations. Massachusetts was alive with new projects, new ideas, new civic organizations. No more fertile period of social readjustment, scientific progress, educational reform, and liberalization of public institutions ever occurred in Massachusetts than this often-maligned Gilded Age, with all its Back Bay aristocrats, its horse and buggy quaintness, and its money-mad materialism. So fertile was it that state after state sent delegations to study and copy its libraries, its colleges and schools, its factories, its laws, and its multitude of pioneering projects that became models to be imitated elsewhere. It was pompous and self-righteous, but it was competent.

Massachusetts thus continued to respond to the difficult problems within her society with the same resourcefulness that she had in revolution, and in the young Republic. Surely the Gilded Age was pompous, and was dominated by aristocrats who were intolerant enough to give the Back Bay and the Proper Bostonian labels a faintly sarcastic quality in the eyes of the nation. Indeed there was social snobbishness that made of unfortunate immigrants a hornets' nest of second-class citizens. Surely it is true that American railroads headed by Boston merchant princes were built by the exploited and underpaid muscles of those same immigrants. Massachusetts' industry for many years was certainly sustained and enlarged by similar exploitation of cheap labor working long hours for small wages. Yet work was thus found to keep these originally helpless, skill-less people alive, and to provide time for the process of teaching them skills and of educating their children

(still far better than Europe)

to better careers. And always in Massachusetts there were enough earnest people, alongside the industrial tycoons, with civic conscience enough to insist on establishing the employers' liability laws, the arbitration mechanisms, the civil service and health department reforms, the public libraries and industrial schools to accomplish this difficult Americanization of the swarming immigrants. Massachusetts did digest the undigestible, and showed the country how to do it. Meantime its pursuit of its traditional intellectual curiosity never slackened. Its colleges, its museums, its great libraries, constantly added to the country's store of learning, in science, medicine, music and the fine arts. No other state in the Union has a public library in every town. Few have comparable museums of art and science, symphony orchestras, research laboratories, trade schools, graduate schools, teaching hospitals, art schools, and above all, colleges. Alumni of all these institutions migrated to all parts of the nation to become leaders and founders of similar institutions elsewhere. Massachusetts in this way pointed the direction by which the Republic could remain a land of opportunity. Wherever there was the will to make the melting pot work, Massachusetts had a method for carrying it out. That peculiar old civic conscience of the Yankee, which was a little laughable in its self-righteousness, nevertheless again carried into the national character an intellectual integrity and a social morality which was badly needed throughout the United States to counter the materialism and the immigrant pressures of the turn of the century. This was Massachusetts' contribution to the flamboyant era of the Gilded Age.

CHAPTER NINETEEN

The Horse and Buggy Age

Charles W. Eliot is said to have remarked that it takes seventeen years to educate the public to a new idea. As applied to Massachusetts, so provocative a statement might easily initiate a whole evening of debate over its psychologic implications, but basically it was an observation that was especially true of Eliot's own generation. The rapid changes that were occurring in the Bay State's immigration, industrial techniques, scientific invention, education and public institutions, were coming so fast that few outside Boston could keep up with them. These changes necessarily produced some physical and social monstrosities, slums, châteaux, and ornate practices and devices that even Boston people learned to regret at leisure. Meanwhile a fundamentally conservative Yankee populace in the towns went its own way for a considerable period, little influenced by the "city slicker" pretensions that characterized the Gilded Age in Boston. Not just for seventeen years, but for nearly two generations life went on in Massachusetts' small towns without much alteration from its usual simple village ways. There was a lag in adopting new ideas. Whether one looks upon this conservatism as ignorant resistance to needed liberalism or as a wise tendency to go slow in abandoning proven elements of the good life depends on one's viewpoint. The vast majority of Massachusetts people, those in the small towns, certainly clung to the "go slow" course and produced a tradition of resistance to change that made of Yankee towns a legendary symbol of conservatism, often referred to as the "horse and buggy age." The two contrasting tendencies, on the one hand, of Boston's intellectual revolt and, on the other, of the unspoiled simplicity of village life, both contributed to shape the national character at the turn of the twentieth century.

Since the language of symbolism has singled out the horse as the *bête noire* of the period, it should be of some interest to record here some of the near-forgotten folklore that made that animal attain such recognition. Despite the incursions of early automobiles, the year 1909 is believed to have been the climax of horse travel in the United States, for in that year no less than 26 million horses and mules were used on American highways, traveling 13 billion miles, or about 500 per animal each year. According to the National Safety Council, 3,850 persons were killed in accidents involving horses or horse-drawn vehicles in 1909, or above thirty fatalities for each hundred million horse-travel miles. Inasmuch as recent motor vehicle fatality rates have run about seven deaths per hundred million automobile-travel miles, one must conclude that horse and buggy travel was more than four times as dangerous as modern travel by automobile.

Lest such figures seem to overemphasize the significance of the horse in the early twentieth century, a brief digression into the uses of the horse around 1909 will serve to document the matter. For until 1910 almost all business in Massachusetts towns moved on horse-drawn wheels or runners and large industries existed to furnish the needs of the animal, and to manufacture and service the great variety of conveyances which he hauled. Every town had its blacksmiths, its livery stables, its carriage makers, its dealers in hay and grain, its harness makers, wheelwrights, saddlers, veterinarians, and carriage painters. In coastal Massachusetts towns gaily colored coaches and barge lines provided regular commuter and travel service to railroad stations and steamboat docks, and farther inland they furnished a network of long-distance transportation as comprehensive as buses do today. Throughout the state horse-drawn barges daily carried the children to school. Greengrocers, bakers, butchers, tinsmiths, ice men, dealers in coal and wood, knife and scissor sharpeners, newsdealers, and itinerant peddlers of many kinds everywhere drove horses hauling hundreds of picturesque vehicles, announcing by shrill cries the wares they hawked all day at the housewife's door. Farmers used horses in hayrakes, tipcarts, hayracks, manure carts, mowing machines, delivery wagons, buckboards, democrat wagons, sleighs and pungs. Horses turned windlasses for cider presses and for hauling out ships, moved houses on rollers, and pulled the saws that cut the ice in the ice ponds. Coachmen and hostlers serviced the doctors' horses, chaises and buggy and managed the great private stables of the wealthy, with their broughams, carryalls, sulkies, victorias, phaetons, surreys, dogcarts, their racing and show horses, and the children's ponies. In every town miles of fences surrounded hundreds of acres of pastures and hayfields, and the mark of prosperity was a barn twice as big as the house. In every town square stood a watering trough, and every country road had a turnout "watering place" wherever a brook ran under the road. Horses hauled the fire engines, the road sprinklers, the early streetcars, the hearses, the hurdy-gurdies, hackney carriages and gypsy caravans. They filled the language with such idioms as "hold your horses" and "horse of another color." Horse trading was as vehement and as speculative as a used-car lot is today. Young men scraped and saved to buy a horse and buggy for courting, and then

soon found it necessary to replace these with a democrat wagon and a plow horse.

Enumeration of the objects themselves cannot alone revive the picture of the horse era. Only with an effort can young people today visualize a mode of living without automobiles and electric refrigerators, and without tin cans, plastic bags, supermarkets and frozen foods. In reversing history to imagine the horse and buggy period, one has to eliminate these everyday modern conveniences and then improvise with what is left in order to reconstruct the past. The resulting reconstruction promptly brings the labor of horse and man closer to the kitchen. It evokes a situation where Mom is dependent on the local farmer for fresh meat and vegetables and on the local iceman to keep the icebox cold until they are cooked. Since there is now no family car to do the shopping in, no artificial ice, no tractor or truck for the farmer, and no sterile containers except Mason jars, the problems begin to appear in high relief.

The solution began to be effected last winter. The iceman, during that prolonged cold snap, chopped a hole in the ice pond, found seven inches of ice and took a mare to the blacksmith, who applied sharp-shod shoes to her hoofs, so that she could now go out on the ice without slipping, and haul behind her the saw that cut a canal from the icehouse ramp out into the pond. By judicious use of the horse-drawn saw and hand saws, the resulting blocks of ice were freed and hauled up the ramp into the double-walled icehouse and bedded down in insulating sawdust for the summer trade. So today Mom can put a colored signal card in the front window, and the iceman will stop his horse, swing a proper-sized cake of ice with tongs onto the creaking scales at the back of his canvas-roofed ice wagon, chip it down to size, carry it on his back to the kitchen door, and deposit it in the family icebox.

Similarly a local truck farmer, who has grown his own lettuce, corn, tomatoes and squash, and the local butcher, who has slaughtered an animal that morning, drive their respective horse-drawn wagons to the back door, and so the larder is replenished. Fresh milk and butter are driven in every day from the local dairy. For molasses, vinegar, sugar, kerosene, flour, oatmeal and potatoes, Mom sends you to the store in the family wagon usually with your own containers, for these bulk products have to be dispensed from the barrel; there is no packaging, unless you buy a barrel, or a whole burlap bagful. You also have to haul bags of grain and oats for your horse, and every summer you get in the hay and pile it in the haymow in the barn, to be stuffed down the chutes into the horse stalls all winter to keep your transportation alive. This is your "gasoline station." Instead of a car wash, you have a currycomb. You also make your own periodic visits to the blacksmith shop, the harness maker, and the carriage painter. If perchance you also have a newfangled automobile, it sits up on blocks all winter in the barn while you use the horse and sleigh, because the roads are not plowed, and snow tires and chains have not yet been invented.

If all this seems toilsome and grim, it is not unrelieved by enjoyment. Even in the deep snow of the Massachusetts winter there are hay rides of an evening in a big hayrack half filled with straw and put on runners like a pung, where everybody snuggles up and sings like mad at the moon. In other seasons there are barn dances, church socials, Hallowe'en parties, harvest festivals, and that big event, the county fair, with its horse races, side shows, farm exhibits and a midway. At Topsfield, Worcester, Brockton, Marshfield, Barnstable, and Springfield, these fairs have been annually held for generations. Many towns now have a choral society and a band, and if you want to be a useful community man you can take your pick of the Odd Fellows, the Knights of Columbus, or the Masons. There are stereopticon lectures at the school, and the Men's Club and Women's Club are combining to produce a play in the Parish House. There is even talk of getting a quartet of players from the Boston Symphony to give a chamber music concert in the Town Hall. And up around the Common, a group of people have formed a Literary Society which plans to have professors from various colleges come to speak at meetings every month, like a Chautauqua.

The pace is leisurely. Men have time to sit on cracker barrels in the village store and talk politics or hear the news from upstate, highly colored by the traveling salesman's version of events, replete with lurid anecdotes. Women's talk is nourished by quilting parties, sewing circles, and the Ladies' Aid Society. Waiting for the mail to be sorted at the post office, or for the newspapers at the news store, or for the arrival of the evening trains, are social events, where one passes the time in neighborly conversation, with one's horse and team tied to the row of hitching posts, a feed bag dangling from the horse's nose. No one has ever heard of a time clock, a radio, or a television set. Information spreads slowly, by word of mouth or through the newspaper. House painting, barn raising, woodcutting and harvesting are often neighborhood projects, participated in by groups of families working together to satisfy a mutual need. As a result there is a good deal of payment by barter, and bills are paid in cordwood, hay, green corn, or personal services. A large proportion of people keep hens, a truck garden, a family cow, a pig or two, and a wood lot, and the maintenance of these, and the horse and carriage in the barn, consumes several hours of daily chores in addition to the regular day's employment. In outlying houses there are still kerosene lamps to trim and fill, water to pump from the well, and kindling to split for the fires. Every house has coal fires to tend, ashes to sift, wood baskets to be filled, and the weekly duties at the washboard and clothesline. A house without a cellar and a shed is unheard of. A "cold cellar" room contains a cabinet loaded with jams, jellies, and preserved vegetables and fruits in Mason jars, a pile of sand filled with root vegetables for winter consumption, a stack of winter squashes, and a row of earthenware crocks in which eggs are preserved in "water glass." The heated cellar stores the winter's fireplace wood, a coalbin, ash barrels and the ash sifter. No game room has yet been invented. The shed is filled with tools and a workbench, a chopping block, and a pile of pine kindling. Here also are the storm windows or screens, and whatever unfinished carpentry or cabinetmaking projects currently occupy the spare time of the head of the house.

The big Massachusetts barn is higher than the house and is covered by a decorative cupola which serves the twin purposes of ventilation and support of a weather vane or a lightning rod. The top floor is the haymow, completely filled with loose or baled hay in which the young fry love to jump and make tunnels. Its rafters provide storage for old flagpoles, apple pickers, and ladders. Its second-story door opens beneath a hoisting beam with which baled hay is loaded by block and tackle from wagons in the haying season. The ground floor is divided into a carriage shed and the stable stalls. The carriage shed is often equipped with a washstand and drain for hosing down the family carriage, or a horse, and there is a horse trough for watering the animal. The rest of the space is storage, for whatever buggies, sleighs, or farm wagons the owner maintains. Sometimes overhead space is used by suspending a sulky or a sleigh from the ceiling in the off season. The stable area contains whatever stalls are needed for the owner's horses and cows. These have wrought-iron feeding baskets in a corner below the hay chutes, and are bedded with clean straw for warmth in the winter. A back door leads to a barnyard for manure disposal. In the working area of the stable there are harness lockers, grain bins, pitchforks, and equipment for grooming the animals. Often a dairy room and a garden-tool shed complete the equipment. Behind the barn there are often hen houses, cold frames for starting early plantings, possibly a greenhouse, the family vegetable garden, accumulations of plows, hay rakes, and rabbit hutches, and often an animal graveyard for cherished horses and dogs.

Such a recital of ordinary home equipment common in every Massachusetts village little more than a generation ago seems almost uncalled for to those who grew up in such a community. Yet all this is rapidly becoming a part of history. Acres of housing developments are constantly removing the physical manifestations of the horse and buggy era from the Massachusetts landscape. To older readers, all this is becoming a subject for nostalgia. But there is a generation growing up who have no direct knowledge of the horse civilization. For them this brief record of Grandfather's way of life needs to be set down. The conservative village life did not last forever. Eventually the scientific achievements of the Victorian age, vastly supplemented by twentieth-century additions, were bound to displace the hand labor and the leisurely pace of the old country life. The migration of people out of cities that characterizes the middle years of the twentieth century is a tribute to the nostalgia created by the horse and buggy period, but it is not a reproduction of it. It shares with it the love of the outdoors and of nature which our grandfathers enjoyed despite their grueling labor of maintenance, but it has eliminated most of that labor. Even the lawn mower now has gasoline power. The machine has removed not only the horse but the barn, the chickens, the cellar, the wood lot and the hayfield. The automobile has maddened the pace, and the refrigerator and the supermarket have eliminated much of the neighborliness, the understanding of the value of work, and of the close relationship of man to the earth. These are losses that will never be wholly regained. To match these, life has become cosmopolitan and less ignorant, far less burdensome, especially to women, and the horizons of ordinary life have been extended to the far corners of the world instead of into the next county. The home, which used to be a self-sustaining household in a village, has come to be a kind of ranch house in outer space.

The steps by which these changes in Massachusetts village life came about were gradual and unsuspected. At first they had little to do with the automobile, for the early versions of that horseless carriage were not calculated to inspire either confidence or a desire to travel far. Nor were the rutted dirt turnpikes of that period any inducement to travel beyond the county line. The first subtle steps in these changes were rather of an administrative character within the forms of town government. The first assaults were on the prerogatives of the town fathers. Most Massachusetts small towns had for years been governed by boards of selectmen who held the office for many years and administered numerous town departments in their own individualistic manner and with a high hand. Often one member of the board served also as superintendent of schools, another as highway surveyor, and a third as fire chief and police chief rolled into one. The whole board also acted as overseers of the poor, which meant they supervised the town Poor Farm, and served as a Board of Health, and as assessors, or fixers of every houseowners real estate tax. In the performance of these manifold functions they were traditionally high-minded and public-spirited men, who received only token salaries for their part-time civic duties, but nonetheless sometimes were less than expert in their fields and inclined to rule with vehemence rather than with the informed wisdom of trained civil servants. They were regarded with considerable affection by the voters, who returned them to office year after year. Yet by business standards they lacked many of the qualifications of governing in the special fields which modern engineering and social sciences were developing so rapidly in the universities.

The reform movement which in the late nineteenth century was already producing changes in administration of the commonwealth's departments in the Boston State House, began to reach down and set standards for administration in the towns. State-wide civil service and accounting improvements more and more called for properly budgeted reports and standardized accounting procedures from the towns. While the pressure at first was in the form of permissive legislation recommending forms of by-laws for the towns which must be adopted by town meetings to be effective on them, and the towns often resisted these reforms by repeated rejections of the new proposals, nevertheless the trend could not long be denied. By 1910 most Massachusetts towns were abandoning horse and buggy government by setting up town Finance Committees, and also trained town accountants who had passed civil service examinations in order to qualify for their posts. As the needs for state roads, state-supervised sanitation facilities, state subsidization of welfare rolls and schools, and state-co-ordinated police activities grew, the town fathers gradually lost their character of being experts in every field of knowledge and found themselves supervising a departmental team, whose detailed reports were audited by standards over which they could no longer exert any control.

These new reforms in municipal administration paved the

way for the end of the horse and buggy age. Under these new systems networks of modern roads were built; motorized fire departments appeared; local electric light companies merged to form extensive regulated public utility corporations; the old Poor Farm was torn down and a trained social worker and a visiting nurse were installed. Then all the mechanism of the modern community began to roll. The village lost some of its identity as a self-sustaining unit, but was now ready for machines to take over communications, engineering projects, and heating, lighting, feeding, housing and transporting the populace. Down came the livery stable; up went a garage. In the retired harness maker's shop, a boy just out of trade school set himself up as an electrician. The blacksmith turned to repairing machines and building wrought-iron railings. The coachman became a chauffeur, or drove a taxi. Tipcarts became trucks, barges buses, and the buggy a model T. Main Street was now a county road, macadamized with tarvia. Everybody gawked at the Fire Department's new ladder truck and pumper. The local grocer was fighting a losing battle against the chain store.

The horse just disappeared. In Massachusetts the junk man and the hurdy-gurdy man, the itinerant peddler and the scissor sharpener still drove horses, for a while. Wealthy dowagers still took afternoon rides under their black parasols, on the back roads where noisy automobiles would not scare the horse. And once a year the high steppers and pacers were paraded out for the horse show, where nostalgia could reign supreme. But commercially, or for everyday travel, the automobile took over. Hitching posts and carriage sheds began to go, along with the watering troughs and the barns. The horse and buggy age was gone, and with it a whole civilization. The roar of the tractor plow woke the town on snowy mornings instead of the sleigh bells. World War I, soon to revise the way of life of every village in Christendom, would turn even the cavalry into a tank corps. After that there would be no more one-horse towns. Even cowboys would be preserved only in the village movie theater.

CHAPTER TWENTY

Changing Patterns in Science and Industry

The retreat of the horse and buggy age was symptomatic of profound changes that were occurring throughout the Massachusetts economy. These changes involved prodigious shifts in the concentration of population as well as in the character of industry. A commonwealth that in 1790 had consisted of only 378,000 people scattered in villages rarely larger than 5,000 had grown by 1900 to 2.5 million, 30 per cent of them foreign born, and 438,000 of them employed in 11,000 factories in crowded urban centers. In the cities the industrial population steadily grew until the 1920's, but in the towns the number of industrial workers began to decline. Just as in the instance of the Douglas axe industry, towns like Hanover, Wareham, Hingham, Bridgewater, Stoneham, Peabody and Melrose lost ground industrially after the 1880's. Their factories gradually became incorporated into the gigantic textile and shoe combines of Fall River, Brockton, New Bedford, Lawrence and Lynn. Unlimited steam power, the immigration surplus, better transportation facilities, and mass production techniques not only killed off the craft industries of the towns but inevitably, through larger overhead costs, made their smaller mechanized mills noncompetitive with those of the huge urban centers. In a few towns, like Walpole, Milton, Waltham, Athol and North Adams, the development of specialized industrial techniques enabled industries to survive into the 1920's or beyond. But the relentless urbanization of the general population continued, changing the character of Massachusetts life as profoundly as had the earlier decline of the days of sail. In this period the cultural and emotional gap between the laborer and the employer widened steadily, producing in many cities problems similar to those previously described in Boston and Holyoke. Aggressive new labor unions quite justifiably fought the millowners for improvements in pay and working conditions. Their strikes often embittered community life, however, and sometimes destroyed the capacity of marginal industries to survive in a competitive world. Many communities helplessly watched an industry which was their main livelihood disappear in the course of recurrent labor disputes for which there seemed to be no solution. Town after town slipped from prosperity into depression as its mills went bankrupt or moved to the cities. The deserted millpond and the vacant mill became a tragic legend in hundreds of Massachusetts villages, while the cities spawned acres of millworker tenements and miles of clattering factories. In retrospect these changes seem to have been an unavoidable part of the over-all economic adjustments in a shifting national pattern, but they were no less painful to the participants.

Meanwhile the fierce competition hammered out, among the surviving companies, certain brilliant success stories of firms whose very names have become century-old landmarks in their fields. Whether these triumphs were primarily the result of intelligent management, co-operative labor, or enlightened community leadership, such businesses maintained in the nation a respect for Massachusetts' continuing industrial capacity. Bird and Son, Tileston and Hollingsworth, Crompton and Knowles, Plymouth Cordage, Revere Copper and Brass, Reed and Barton, Norton Company, Draper Corpora-

tion, Carter's Ink, Whitin Machine—such Massachusetts names are regarded with the same admiration for their substantial integrity in manufacturing in mid-twentieth century as they were in 1890 or before, and are so recognized in New York or San Francisco as readily as in Boston. That other equally distinguished names like Wamsutta, American Woolen, George E. Keith Shoe, Glenwood Stove, Carver Cotton Gin, Taunton Locomotive, Ames Shovel, and Durfee Cottons have fallen on evil days casts no discredit on their loss of the magic of success. Theirs was the misfortune of being period pieces in a changing world, like the Hingham bucket, the Braintree thick boot, Willard clocks, and the Douglas axe.

Yet this new age was in turn producing its own period pieces. Out of the welter of research and scientific invention were emerging totally new activities which eventually would produce bright new stars in the gleaming constellation of Massachusetts industries. Godfrey Cabot's researches in German gliders in 1894 were responsible for the founding of the Boston Aeronautical Club the following year. By 1906 Samuel Cabot was taking off in gliders from Cape Cod sand dunes. Lincoln Beachey and Roy Knabenshue were flying small dirigibles from Boston Common and at the Brockton Fair. Squantum, in Quincy, attained early recogntion as an airfield in 1909 when Claude Grahame-White flew his airplane to Boston Light and took up Eleanora Sears as his first woman passenger. There also in 1911 the Harvard University Flying Club held the nation's first air meet. In 1913 Captain Harry M. Jones flew a plane from Saugus race track to a landing on Boston Common's ball field, and then carried to New York the first air parcel post package, propelled at the amazing speed of 45 miles per hour. At Marblehead seaplanes began to appear, built and flown by yacht-designer Starling Burgess. Godfrey Cabot even picked up burdens from Salem harbor on the fly,

Glenn Curtiss stunted over the Brockton Fair, John F. Fitzgerald, grandfather of John F. Kennedy, used the airplane to advertise his campaign for the Boston mayoralty. Thus the stage was set for the exploits of Boston's Norman Prince in the Lafayette Escadrille in World War I, soon followed by the barnstorming "jennies," regular air-mail flights, and the pioneering air services of Colonial Airways, the Boston and Maine Airway, Crocker Show, Amelia Earhart, and Richard E. Byrd. Soon the aerodynamics schools at Harvard and the Massachusetts Institute of Technology were offering wind tunnel experiments and the country's first courses in aeronautical engineering. While Massachusetts never became as prominent as other states in the manufacture of aircraft, its early stimulus to experimental flying and study of the technical problems involved in flight led to airfield development whose modern monuments are Logan International Airport and the military airports at Hanscom Field, Bedford, Westover Field, Chicopee, and Otis Air Force Base on Cape Cod. That the Massachusetts Port Authority can enter the jet age with a field like Logan Airport, handling 2.5 million air passengers each year, is in large measure due to the imaginative and far-sighted pioneering of the Bay State's early enthusiasts in flying, who were determined to make of Boston an overseas air terminus as great as its sea frontier had been in the days of sail. That this has come to pass is illustrated by the commonplace experience of a thousand transatlantic passengers on a dozen huge planes being set down safely at Logan in a single night when all other airports from Providence to Washington, D. C., are closed in by fog. In an age when more people cross the Atlantic by air than on the sea this is an impressive achievement for Massachusetts, whose eastward thrust toward Europe is its major geographic advantage.

Massachusetts has also, however, some geographic disadvantages which were never previously cast in as villainous roles as they have played in the twentieth century. So long as thousands of sailing ships were the principal links of Boston's port with the markets of the nation and the world Massachusetts prospered in both industry and commerce. But when overland transportation developed to a point where it carried the main bulk of raw materials and manufactured goods to population centers steadily migrating westward across the continent the northeast corner of the nation became progressively more isolated from the great trading routes of the United States. In the marketing of many New England goods the high costs of transportation became a differential that would unavoidably price them out of national markets when similar goods could be produced as well elsewhere.

The economic history of New England in the first half of the twentieth century has been an agonizing adjustment to this fact. Massachusetts has fought for two generations a delaying action, a Dunkirk, a battling withdrawal, in the attempt to find substitutes for production of cotton textiles and manufacture of shoes, the two industries in which she held preeminent leadership in the nineteenth century, both of which have been reluctantly moving south and west. Cotton and hides once came by sea, and Massachusetts cloth and shoes were shipped by sea. When rail replaced shipping, and markets moved west, the attrition began. No tariff could protect any industry from the free competition of the other states of the Republic. The result, with bulk products like cotton and hides, was certain. As soon as adequate labor could be found to man factories nearer the centers of population, these New England industries were gradually forced out of their markets. For a while Yankee ingenuity, more efficient production techniques, and a pool of trained labor could stem the tide, and did. But when the flow of overseas immigration slowed down in the 1920's, when westward migrants, no longer needed on mechanized farms, turned to factory employment, and when enterprising midwestern and southern investors acquired sufficient capital, electric power, and efficient management to build the plants, the process of competition operated inexorably to reduce the Yankee supremacy.

The situation with regard to rail traffic did nothing to help Massachusetts in this developing economic crisis. Massachusetts, still being a maritime economy during the early years of rail development, had never been aggressive in encouraging this sort of transport. This turned out to be a serious error. Between 1900 and 1913 financial interests outside of New England tried to seize control of all the New England railroads, almost wrecking them in the process. By 1900 consolidations of the many small lines had produced the present triumvirate of the New Haven, the Boston and Albany, and the Boston and Maine. The following thirteen years were characterized by a vicious battle on the part of the New Haven managers to attain dominance over all the other New England transportation services, by fair means or foul. Profligate expenditure of stockholders' funds, poor railroad service, and the justified anger of the public resulted in indictment, trial, and finally acquittal of nationally prominent men. The federal Department of Justice then insisted, after a housecleaning, that the New Haven relinquish its control of the Boston and Maine. The New Haven had meanwhile been seriously crippled by acquisition of unprofitable little trolley and coastal steamship lines, and small branch railroads. In this condition it struggled through World War I, but reorganization of its financial structure after the war was thus made even more difficult. The Boston and Albany also had suffered as a result of absentee management by the New York Central, and this was corrected only when the Massachusetts legislature in

1908 threatened to cancel the Central's lease and assume state ownership.

In the boom years of the 1920's there was a respite. But then came the depression of the 1930's. By that time the increasing competition of automobiles, trucks and buses caused large curtailments of service, with abandonment of many branch lines. Again World War II provided a temporary stimulus through government operation of all railroads. But after that war public interest in transportation had so far shifted toward automobiles and airplanes that tax subsidization of express highways and of airlines doubled the competitive problems of the railroads. Only a minority of commuters seemed interested in railroad passenger service. In serious straits, with bankruptcy threatening, whole divisions of Massachusetts rail services continue to abandon activity.

The coincidence of this degenerative process in railroads with the decline in bulk freight shipments by the old, failing textile industry intensifies the problems of both. New England railroads were scarcely in a position to lower freight rates in order to help equalize textile competition between Massachusetts factories and their southern competitors. Nor were the textile companies in a position to help the rails by promising them freight business if ambitious trucking concerns could supply service cheaper. So the problem of the fighting retreat continued. Massachusetts textile companies frequently met the problem head on, by building their own southern factories and conducting a gradual, orderly withdrawal as fast as new industries could be found to occupy abandoned Massachusetts plants, but often, of course, before that happy substitution could be effected. The effect of this is more readily understood if one considers a few specific examples. Between 1919 and 1935 the production of New Bedford fell to one-fourth of its previous volume, half its workers lost their jobs, and many of its 68 textile mills, with 55,000 looms and 3.5 million spindles, closed down. Taunton lost 94 industrial plants in the same period. Fall River lost half its payroll and three quarters of its spindles. With a full quarter of its population on public welfare rolls in 1932, the city was forced to default on its bonds. Lowell and Lawrence went through similar experiences.

Painfully the textile cities have learned how to pull themselves out of the awful depression of the 1930's. It was noticed that in the very years when the textiles were at their lowest ebb certain Massachusetts industries were growing, despite general world-wide economic depression. Electrical machinery production, some metal fabrication, and apparel manufacture were thriving. Unlike the textile business, these growing industries had two important characteristics. They required more highly skilled workers and their products, when ready for shipment, had a far higher value per pound than cheap cotton cloth. If Massachusetts labor were put into the production of goods whose value was about ten times that of the raw materials imported to fabricate them, then the differential in freight charges became a smaller proportion of total cost and could be made up by superior production techniques, laborsaving devices, and good management. In such industries Massachusetts could compete with the whole world. One more lesson also was learned: that of diversification. Never again should a Massachusetts city build itself into a huge single factory complex in a single industry, vulnerable, like a one-crop farm, to violent swings in the economic cycle.

The validity of these principles has been proven by the subsequent experience of the textile cities. In Fall River 140 new companies moved in before 1940 to occupy space in the closed cotton mills. Some of these mills now employ more people than they did in textile days, and they now make clothing, optical goods, curtains, bathrobes, overalls, felt hats, paper boxes, mattresses, iron castings, thread, ice-cream cones, hosiery, trunks, towels, brushes, shoe laces, smokers' supplies, and raincoats. In New Bedford' the Industrial Development Legion, under Frank J. Leary and T. A. Haish, organized an unremitting campaign to sell the city and its vacant factory space to new industries. They succeeded so well that they produced total weekly payrolls comparable to those in the best of the textile era, and this time in a stable, well-balanced industrial pattern that ensures steady employment even if one type of product is temporarily depressed. Only 30 per cent of the resulting New Bedford economy is in cotton goods; in the 1930's it was 90 per cent. By 1947 a hundred new firms were operating in sixteen abandoned cotton mills. Nineteen thousand wage earners were at work, earning $46 million, in manufactures other than cotton textiles. Nonferrous metals, electrical and electronic apparatus, machinery products, bread, liquors, molded rubber, foods, artificial leather and cordage served to diversify New Bedford's industrial pattern and along with these came a shift to synthetic fibers not as vulnerable as cotton to the swings of overproduction and fickle demand. Similar readjustments have improved the industrial climate of the Merrimack cities of Lowell, Haverhill and Lawrence. In the million square feet of factory space at the vacant six-story Everett Mills building in Lawrence, Russell W. Knight, through prodigious effort, succeeded by 1940 in placing 60 new companies, employing 4,000 workers, 2,500 more than cotton textiles had previously employed. Much of the great Wood Mill of the American Woolen Company has been torn down, but some of it is now firmly occupied by Raytheon. Brockton has undergone analogous diversification maneuvers in a more gradual reaction to loss of some of its shoe factories. While Massachusetts as a whole has not compensated fully

for all its losses from the migration of its earlier industria
giants, it has come through its most difficult period in a healthy
and aggressive mood, and with certain assets for growth that
promise continued improvement. In chemicals, apparel, electrical and nonelectrical machinery, instruments, and a variety
of manufactures growing out of new research, the economy
is growing steadily.

The influence of research and invention has always been
limitless in its effects on Massachusetts productivity. The introduction of the beam trawler in 1904 transformed Gloucester's fishing industry almost overnight, eliminating promptly
the hazards of hand-line fishing in open dories. Filleting and
quick-freezing of fish, introduced respectively by the Dana
Ward and Birdseye companies, immensely broadened the
domestic market for fish products. Packaging machines and
automatic weighers introduced by Quincy's Pneumatic Scale
Company profoundly altered the marketing of hundreds of
consumer products. Research-minded firms, like Polaroid,
Monsanto, Sylvania, Raytheon, American Optical, Dennison,
Gillette, Sprague Electric, U.S. Envelope, Crompton and
Knowles, and Draper, have contributed thousands of new
products to the nation's industrial spectrum. Nor should it be
forgotten that the original telephone research on which all
the telephone industry depends was performed in Massachusetts by that first "long wire" conversation of Alexander
Graham Bell with Thomas Watson in the Walworth Company
in 1876. The original unit of the General Electric Company
at Lynn is still Massachusetts' largest employer, still fertile in
its contributions to jet aircraft engines and innumerable items
of electrical hardware.

Since World War II a particularly concentrated group of
Massachusetts research facilities has grown up in what is
generally known as "Research Row," a loosely co-ordinated

cluster of laboratories combining the advantages of pure research in endowed university facilities with those achieved by commercial analytical companies in Cambridge. Here the many-sided talents of the faculties of the Massachusetts Institute of Technology and Harvard work in close liaison with such inventors of whole new industries as Arthur D. Little and Company to explore the possible applications of new discoveries in nuclear physics, colloid chemistry, computers, high-voltage x-ray, cyclotrons, spectrophometers, solar heating, radar, stroboscopic photography, differential analyzers, and hundreds of other highly technical devices and machines. To this awesome assemblage of human and electronic brains there flows daily an increasing procession of consultants from all branches of government and every conceivable industry and business throughout the free world, seeking the solutions to problems of human error, distribution, new products, new weapons, the determination of potential markets, new alloys, new testing methods, new uses of nuclear energy, and the elimination of gremlins from production lines. Time after time the consultants go home with the correct answers. Hundreds of successful new corporations emerge from these meetings. Research Row has become, quite seriously, Massachusetts' most valuable asset. Through the desire for easy access to this magnificent consultation service a whole ring of industrial plants has been constructed in the suburban area around Boston, which itself draws to its laboratories a rising young generation of engineers eager to participate in the expanding fortunes of the many as yet small but promising growth industries shepherded by this awesome scientific center. This whole phenomenon of Research Row and its satellite industries along Route 128 and in adjacent towns carries probably the most explosive portent for the future of Massachusetts' economy that has occurred since Salem's *Grand*

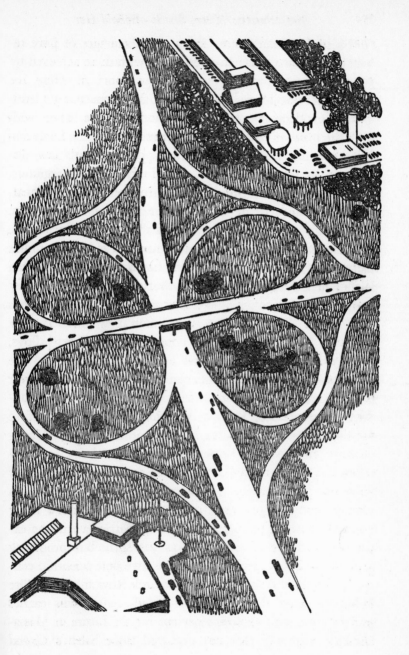

Turk returned from Canton laden with China goods. Rivaled perhaps only by a similarly awesome aggregation of university scientists in California, Research Row contains within its brain cluster possibilities of drawing to Massachusetts a center of modern electronic and nuclear industry that may well make the losses in textile and leather manufacture seem eventually a minor incident. The federal government's Lincoln Laboratories are a recognition of the trend. Taken together with many already existing achievements of the Boston area in other sciences, particularly in medicine, the phenomenon of Research Row is to be considered a historic landmark for Massachusetts whose consequences no one as yet can adequately evaluate. As a sequel to the horse and buggy age this development is a triumph for the scholarly aspects of Boston's intellectualism.

CHAPTER TWENTY-ONE

A Yankee Appraisal

In mid-twentieth century Massachusetts finds herself with her horse and buggy age gone and with the "battling withdrawal" from the supremacy of her textile industry largely accomplished, but with a host of new social and economic problems which throughout the United States have followed the impact of science and invention on the modern world. The quality of these problems does not differ in the Bay State from that experienced in other regions, but in certain respects Massachusetts and New England generally do differ in the type of community organization which has to digest these changes. It has already been made clear in this book that the development of distinctive self-governing towns is the hallmark of Yankee culture and that citizen participation in town affairs is a basic and unique heritage of the Yankee. This is true in government, in schools, in politics, and in all the voluntary civic institutions, the social clubs, philanthropic societies, and intellectual associations that so typically enrich community life in Massachusetts. In order to understand the impact of the automobile, of suburban migration, rapid transit, radio and television on Massachusetts, it is important to keep in mind the jealous, almost parochial loyalty which three centuries of small-town life have built up in the older Yankee communities. Theirs has always been a small-town culture.

The town is still administered by a board of three or five elected selectmen, exercising general supervision over all town departments except the schools. Welfare boards and boards of assessors likewise are chosen at annual town elections. Under Massachusetts laws the public schools are independently administered by a local school committee, whose complete control over the school budget is so absolute that no other town officials, and no state or county officials, can veto it. The management of education is thereby kept jealously independent of any outside politics. All these town agencies publish reports of their stewardship in a printed annual "Town Report" volume which the voters read assiduously before attending the annual March town meeting. At this open assembly all appropriations and budgets are discussed and voted on, item by item, in open meeting under the chairmanship of an elected nonpartisan town moderator. Every citizen has an equal right to speak his mind, and many do so. So effective has this process been over the centuries that it is still carried on in essentially unmodified form in all the smaller towns. Larger towns, like Brookline and Wellesley, have had to adopt the representative town meeting system for lack of a large enough auditorium to house all the voters, but the principle and the procedure are the same. In the history of the world there is no more striking example of the durability of actual democracy in local government.

The hidden strengths in Massachusetts' culture stem also from those associations of men and women volunteers, organized to accomplish, in their spare time, nonpolitical objectives above and beyond the call of duty. A community's vitality is best measured by the number and effectiveness of these voluntary groups. Dramatic Clubs, Civic Symphonies and Choral Societies, Community Centers, Improvement Associations, Historical and Literary Societies, Visiting Nursing Associations, School Survey Committees, Service Clubs, Sportsmen's Clubs, Hospital Associations, and philanthropic societies of countless variety fill the Bay State towns. No one would claim that these are characteristic exclusively of Massachusetts, but they are as typical and extensive in the commonwealth as were the old philosophical societies and literary groups of the nineteenth century. Men and women trained in such vigorous community activities as these are more often than not the human material from which state leadership emerges into the national life. Many instances could be cited of people from these Bay State towns who have climbed the ladder to national prominence. Henry Cabot Lodge, David I. Walsh, Calvin Coolidge, Charles Francis Adams, Leverett Saltonstall, Felix Frankfurter, Christian Herter, Cabot Lodge and John F. Kennedy are a few recent examples of such Bay State-trained leaders on the national scene. In towns where this kind of active citizen participation exists society cannot become reactionary, nor can tyranny or corruption long go unpunished. The old civic religion stays sharp and keen, and continues to produce strong leadership.

Thus the Bay Colony that migrated out of a rebellious segment of England in whole towns or parishes has maintained its traditional forms of citizenship, first expressed in republican churches, but eventually in republican towns. Concern for the common weal, for what the Romans called the *res publica*, has been an outstanding feature of this society from the beginning, and still is. The same community impulse that produced the Revolutionary Committees of Correspondence and the free public schools still builds community centers and runs scholarship funds. Out of these pools of human endeavor in the towns, constantly replenished by the support and interest of new citizen participants, have come the men and women who have built and still maintain the great museums, colleges, libraries and symphony orchestras. The gospel of good works that filled the nineteenth-century churches and towns with social projects has repeatedly emerged from the towns into the state and nation, commandeering people of good will in all faiths to join in civic enterprises. But the emphasis has always been on the town as the originating unit.

Across the lines of community loyalty, which all this feverish public service has built, has fallen in the twentieth century a shadow—the disintegrating influence of the automobile, radio, television and suburbanization. Fringe communities around all the larger cities have become lodgings for commuters whose attachment to their bedroom towns is often only casual. The cities themselves have lost to suburban towns many leaders who once lived in city mansions. As a result the cities find themselves dependent for civic leadership on absentee owners whose interest is divided or on men of lesser ability who still live within city limits. Suburban residents often refuse to participate in the correction of the city's ills, preferring the splendid isolation of suburban life (with vacations at the seashore or in the mountains) and letting the old-timers run public affairs as best they can. Machinery has made parasites of a certain proportion of the population who no longer belong to any community, but move about in the commuter flow without any bases save those of shifting rented homes and office spaces. Meanwhile the fine old residential areas in the cities degenerate into slums. These are problems in modern Yankee society for which only a larger regional loyalty can find answers. Unfortunately the old parochial loyalty to the individual township, so ingrained in the Yankee character and tradition and so built into the town government system, is often acting as a deterrent to progress in development of the regional metropolitan thinking and planning that must come if the cities are to be saved from economic stagnation. A horizon-of-citizenship larger than that of the individual town is badly needed. A new county system with metropolitan implications needs to be set up around each of Massachusetts' great cities to unify planning among co-operating communities for the betterment of all as a group. This is particularly true of the Boston metropolitan area, where co-operative studies by such agencies as the Civic Foundation, comprising the Greater Boston Chamber of Commerce, Greater Boston Economic Study Committee, Retail Trade and Real Estate Boards, the Municipal Research Bureau and the Civic Progress Committee are already in formative stages. But whether the traditional small-town attitude of the competing communities within each metropolitan area can be broken down sufficiently to serve regional goals is still an unanswerable question. As this book is written, the competitive jealousies of the suburban and fringe towns are still a serious obstacle to concerted planning for the over-all improvement of Massachusetts' metropolitan centers.

Such problems are well exemplified by current struggles over suburban transportation systems. The placid independence of fringe towns like Lynnfield, Andover, Wellesley, Norwood, Randolph and Hanover, and of proud suburban cities like Salem, Cambridge, Newton and Quincy, has been rudely shaken by the construction across their territories of teeming concrete expressways along which pour thousands of commuting automobiles, ebbing and flowing in and out of Boston every day. These have already largely displaced the commuting railroad services and are rapidly destroying the economic base of Boston's rapid transit system. The resulting peripheral migration of commuter population is explosive, throwing on outlying towns vastly heavier burdens of services for schools, water and sewer utilities, fire protection and police service, and changing the character of these towns by too-rapid additions of huge housing developments for people who possess little understanding of the traditions of small-town life. Meanwhile Boston's streets are choked with traffic, some of her public schools stand half empty, and her residential tax base has become so restricted as to threaten solvency. The social revolution thus produced, with its accompanying economic problems, has rather suddenly become a unified dilemma for a continuous populated region extending all the way around from Plymouth to Brockton, to Framingham, to Concord, to Woburn, to Gloucester. For practical purposes this huge crescent of a hundred towns and cities, containing three million inhabitants, finds itself drawn inexorably into the new vortex of Greater Boston, to which each community steadily relinquishes item after item of independence as the years go on. No one of these towns can any longer claim mastery of its rate of growth, its traffic patterns, or the speed of its school building program. Each is worried about zoning restrictions, shopping centers, parking problems, industrial sites, and the over-all problem of attempting to stem its rising real estate tax. No one of them can exert as much control over its own destiny as it did a generation ago. Each fights a separate rear-guard action against population pressure and attempts, vainly, to keep its separate identity as a lovely New England village, reluctant to surrender the peaceful pace of a generation gone. Yet each looks every year more like a suburban establishment, with its open woods and ponds and streams closed in and made smaller by steadily encroaching housing, stores and highways.

Inevitably, against this suburbanization of the towns, the ancient Yankee character of village life is losing ground. While Greater Boston presents the most dramatic instance, the same process surrounds Worcester, Springfield, the Merrimack cities and Buzzards Bay. The south shore of Cape Cod is rapidly becoming a continuous commercial area. Population migrates outward at an accelerating pace, limited only by the time it takes to build superhighways, transplant industries to the suburbs, and construct housing. The eastern half of Massachusetts is headed for an eventual confluent suburbanism that will extend from New Hampshire to Rhode Island and from Cape Cod to the Connecticut valley.

So much of prophecy seems justified by contemporary history. The total implications would better be left to the imagination or to a later historian. But already the changing patterns are placing upon state government many decisions that would normally have been jealously retained by the towns a generation or two ago. A larger and larger segment of financial responsibility formerly vested in the individual towns and cities has already passed to the commonwealth. Road-building, school construction, welfare administration, law enforcement, harbor maintenance, sanitation, labor-management regulation, recreation areas, and industrial promotion are among the activities that are subsidized or standardized for the towns by agencies at the state or county level. Local option in the towns is shrinking. The mechanisms of matching grants, bureau supervision, commission government, and standardization of procedures have steadily whittled away the prerogatives of cities and towns in the determination of their own future. The picture at mid-twentieth century seems to portend inevitable regionalization of the traditions of local government in Massachusetts. A new era begins, in which fragmentation must gradually diminish as the needs of integration grow. Regional trade schools, regional health offices, regional civil defense agencies are already in operation. This is the current trend of American history, nationwide.

The resources of Massachusetts, out of which urban redevelopment and metropolitan reconstruction must be financed, are still huge. Industry is the driving force, and only the brains and hands and capital of industry can provide the real wealth necessary to create the needed changes. In Massachusetts 44 per cent of nongovernment workers are employed in industry. The national average is 26 per cent. Massachusetts is also strong in insurance, mutual funds, a growing recreation and vacation industry, and in education. It is not by accident that Boston's finest new buildings are devoted to colleges and insurance offices, nor that large private construction elsewhere pivots on new manufacturing plants. The state's industrial base has been shrinking since World War II, because the commonwealth is a high-cost state in which to do business. Massachusetts has the highest state debt and one of the heaviest corporate tax burdens in the nation. It pays the penalty of pioneering in employers' liability laws by having higher workmen's compensation rates than any other state, and its unemployment compensation program is the most liberal in the nation. It also suffers from the highest per capita property taxes in the nation. For a state with few natural resources and high costs of transportation these financial burdens place a considerable deterrent on the acquisition of new enterprises, and even on the retention of those currently operating.

These burdens on business can only be balanced by sedulous nourishing of Massachusetts' distinctive advantages, which are those of an unexcelled pool of skilled labor, a highly organized machinery for technical research and training, and a standard of community life which consistently attracts people of substance. From this viewpoint the fine schools, universities and libraries, the attractive historical shrines, the recreational facilities of beaches, mountains, parks and reservations, and the facilities for travel, vacations, conventions and summer camps represent a financial factor of vast importance.

Curiously enough, the maintenance of these intangibles, the human attractions which appeal to research and development personnel, are probably the real key to Massachusetts' industrial future. Since the state has been throughout its history a specialist in these particular fields of education, culture, scientific research and community projects encouraging the good life, it continues to reproduce the basic skills and to attract the outstanding researchers who are needed to maintain the economy.

An obvious corollary of this reasoning is that in the process of suburbanization that is sweeping over much of the state the maintenance of good schools, outdoor recreation facilities, community associations, fine residence areas, hotels, motels, and truly hospitable historical centers is of the utmost importance to healthy economic progress. These are in a very special way the real natural resources of the state, and to the extent that jealous conservation of these resources is a goal of local pride, the parochialism and provincialism of the towns serves the purposes of every one. But state-wide conservation planning for the purposes of holding inviolate large remaining areas of forest, beach, mountain and lake areas is essential.

Massachusetts has become the third most densely populated state in the Union. Yet vacation travel is considered to be its third largest industry. The peculiar configuration of its geography provides it with almost two thousand miles of ocean shore line; yet in its Berkshire Hills it has hundreds of lovely mountain villages. The same glaciation which robbed it of huge fertile areas for agriculture endowed it with innumerable ponds and lakes and running streams that make of the state a paradise for campers, hunters and fisherman. Striped bass and tuna, raccoon and red fox and deer, pickerel and lake bass, lobsters and scallops and sea clams, black duck and coot and mallards are regularly taken within forty miles of the golden dome of Boston's State House.

Bay State yachtsmen and skiers, mountain climbers,

skaters and trainers of fox hounds win laurels in national competition. Massachusetts teams thrive in basketball, hockey, baseball, football, track, golf and swimming. Thousands of ponds and coves are filled with boats all summer. Almost every one among the population has access in vacation months to some camp or cottage, some beach or lake or country farmhouse, some favorite mountain or harbor or string of sand dunes where the rehabilitation achieved by sunshine, sport and peaceful fun can trim down the tensions of the working year. Many state parks provide camping areas, and for children there are hundreds of supervised summer camps, sometimes built around such special activities as theater, sailing, swimming, tutoring, scouting, medical rehabilitation, and the modern dance. Innumerable clubs and associations put on weekend field trips in geology, botany, rock climbing, archaeological excavation, white-water canoeing, drag hunts, bird study, trailmaking, sports-car rallies, skin diving, fishing derbies, and photography contests. There is no end to the recreational opportunities.

The terrain and the climate of Massachusetts are so varied that the spectrum of activities is limitless. From snowshoeing and iceboating to fly fishing and gardening, to swimming and summer cruising, to autumn hunting for grouse and deer, the year's wheel turns, and Massachusetts Yankees try them all and choose their favorites. They are outdoor people, and they are often Jacks-of-all-trades during a lifetime. All these activities, and more, make the good life which the challenge of the climate and their own ingenuity afford them. The landscape provides the tools. Their heritage of restless curiosity and serious improvisation is sufficient motivation. Thus a habit of avocations and hobbies continuously enriches their leisure hours.

These are the aspects of Massachusetts life that attract

not only the vacationing tourist but the visiting student and, subsequently, often the resourceful engineer or teacher or technician who decides that this is the state he will choose to live and work in. These make a not-inconsiderable contribution to the assemblage in the commonwealth of talented and imaginative people from other states, who settle down in Research Row or add their abilities to the growing research industries that ring the Bay State cities. This reimmigration into Massachusetts of skilled people, nourished often by the memories of student days in her great universities, constantly replenishes her business talent and strengthens her economy. This is a striking and hopeful manifestation of vitality in the old commonwealth. It is a phenomenon which may completely heal the wounds suffered as a result of emigrating textile mills. With proper attention to the conservation of all the resources of the good life with which Massachusetts abounds, the central cities, the suburbs, and the small towns may yet see in the nuclear age a brilliant revival of industry. The solid resourcefulness with which the commonwealth solved problems in the Andros rebellion, in the Revolution, in the fading of maritime supremacy, and in the crises of immigration and industrial competition may well repeat its demonstration of vitality all over again. But in order to do this the towns will have to learn to work together with suburbs and central cities, in wise and intelligent planning based on the good of the greatest number. Similarly the cities and the suburbs will have to learn to make concessions to the local pride and autonomy of the towns in matters that should remain within their individual guidance as traditional little republics. Only by mutual respect and tolerance of the special problems of each can metropolitan vigor be maintained. If this can be accomplished by co-operative leadership, the proud old statement of Daniel Webster will need no change: "I shall enter on no encomium upon Massachusetts; she needs none. There she is. Behold her, and judge for yourselves. There is her history; the world knows it by heart. The past, at least, is secure. There is Boston and Concord and Lexington and Bunker Hill; and there they will remain forever. The bones of her sons, falling in the great struggle for Independence, now lie mingled with the soil of every State from New England to Georgia; and there they will lie forever. And, Sir, where American Liberty raised its first voice, and where its youth was nurtured and sustained, there it still lives, in the strength of its manhood and full of its original spirit."

BIBLIOGRAPHY

Chapter One

GRAY, EDWARD F. *Leif Eriksson, Discoverer of America, A.D. 1003.*
New York: Oxford University Press, 1930.

JOHNSON, FREDERICK. *The Boylston Street Fishweir.* Andover, Mass.:
Robert S. Peabody Foundation for Archaeology, 1942.

WILLOUGHBY, CHARLES C. *Antiquities of the New England Indians.*
Cambridge: Harvard University Press, 1935.

Chapter Two

ROWSE, A. L. *The Elizabethans and America.* New York: Harper &
Brothers, 1959.

Chapter Three

BOLTON, CHARLES KNOWLES. *The Real Founders of New England—
Stories of Their Life along the Coast, 1602–1628.* Boston: F. W.
Faxon Co., 1929.

HOWE, HENRY F. *Prologue to New England.* New York: Rinehart &
Co., 1943.

Chapter Four

ADAMS, CHARLES Francis. *Three Episodes of Massachusetts History*
(2 vols.) Boston: Houghton Mifflin Co., 1896.

ADAMS, JAMES TRUSLOW. *The Founding of New England.* Boston:
Little, Brown & Co., 1927.

American Iron & Steel Institute. *Steel's Old Homestead.* New York:
American Iron and Steel Institute, 1950.

BRADFORD, WILLIAM. *History of Plymouth Plantation.* Boston: Little,
Brown & Co., 1856.

HOWE, DANIEL WAIT. *The Puritan Republic of Massachusetts Bay in
New England.* Indianapolis: Bowen-Merrill Co., 1899.

ROSE-TROUP, FRANCES. *John White, the Patriarch of Dorchester (Dor-
set) and the Founder of Massachusetts 1575–1648 with an Account*

of the Early Settlements in Massachusetts 1620–30. New York: G. P. Putnam's Sons, 1930.

SHIPTON, CLIFFORD K. *Roger Conant, a Founder of Massachusetts.* Cambridge, Mass.: Harvard University Press, 1944.

WILLISON, GEORGE F. *Saints and Strangers.* New York: Reynal & Hitchcock, 1945.

WOOD, WILLIAM. *New England's Prospect, a true and experimental description of that part of America commonly called New England, etc.* London, 1634; reprinted 1898 with introduction by Eben M. Boynton.

Chapter Five

ANDREWS, CHARLES M. *The Fathers of New England, a Chronicle of the Puritan Commonwealths.* New Haven: Yale University Press, 1920.

BOWEN, RICHARD LeBARON. *Early Rehoboth.* Privately printed, 1948.

COOK, SHERWIN LAWRENCE. *Governmental Crisis (1664–1686)* (In Vol. I, "Commonwealth History of Massachusetts.") New York: States History Co., 1927.

DICKINSON, JOHN. *The Massachusetts Charter and the Bay Colony (1628–1660).* (In Vol. I, "Commonwealth History of Massachusetts.") New York: States History Co., 1927.

MORISON, SAMUEL ELIOT. *Builders of the Bay Colony.* Boston: Houghton Mifflin Co., 1930.

Chapter Six

CURTIS, JOHN GOULD. *Expansion and King Philip's War (1630–1689).* (In Vol. I, "Commonwealth History of Massachusetts.") New York: States History Co., 1927.

ELLIS, GEORGE W., and MORRIS, JOHN E. *King Philip's War.* New York: The Grafton Press, 1906.

LEACH, DOUGLAS EDWARD. *Flintlock and Tomahawk—New England in King Philip's War.* New York: Macmillan Co., 1958.

Chapter Seven

ANDREWS, CHARLES M. *Colonial Folkways, a Chronicle of American Life in the Reign of the Georges.* New Haven: Yale University Press, 1920.

FORBES, ALLYN BAILEY. *Social Life in Town and Country—1689–1763.* (In Vol. II "Commonwealth History of Massachusetts.") New York: States History Co., 1928.

GIPSON, LAWRENCE HENRY. *The Great War for the Empire;* Vols. vii & viii: *The Victories Years* and *The Culmination.* New York: A. A. Knopf, 1949–1953.

SLY, JOHN F. *Geographical Expansion and Town System.* (In Vol. II, "Commonwealth History of Massachusetts.") New York: States History Co., 1928.

TARBELL, IDA M. *In the Footsteps of the Lincolns.* New York: Harper & Brothers, 1924.

WRONG, GEORGE M. *The Conquest of New France, A Chronicle of the Colonial Wars.* New Haven: Yale University Press, 1920.

Chapter Eight

ADAMS, JAMES TRUSLOW. *Revolutionary New England—1691–1776.* Boston: Little, Brown & Co., 1922.

BARNES, VIOLA F. *Massachusetts in Ferment (1766–1773).* (In Vol. II, "Commonwealth History of Massachusetts.") New York: States History Co., 1928.

MILLER, JOHN C. *Origins of the American Revolution.* Boston: Little, Brown & Co., 1943.

Chapter Nine

FRENCH, ALLEN. *The Nineteenth of April, 1775.* (In Vol. II, "Commonwealth History of Massachusetts.") New York: States History Co., 1928.

FROTHINGHAM, THOMAS G. *Bunker Hill and the Siege of Boston.* (In Vol. III, "Commonwealth History of Massachusetts.") New York: States History Co., 1929.

Chapter Ten

ALLEN, GARDNER W. *A Naval History of the American Revolution.* Boston: Houghton Mifflin Co., 1913.

HOWE, OCTAVIUS T. *Massachusetts on the Seas in the War of the Revolution.* (In Vol. III, "Commonwealth History of Massachusetts.") New York: States History Co., 1929.

Chapter Eleven

ADAMS, JAMES TRUSLOW. *New England in the Republic 1776–1850.* Boston: Little, Brown & Co., 1926.

BELKNAP, HENRY SYCKOFF. *Artists and Craftsmen of Essex County, Mass.* Salem, Mass.: The Essex Institute, 1927.

BEVERLY HISTORICAL SOCIETY. *Cotton Mill Papers.* Beverly, Mass.: 1949.

PEABODY, ROBERT E. *Merchant Ventures of Old Salem, A History of the Commercial Voyages of a New England Family to the Indies and Elsewhere in the XVIII Century.* Boston: Houghton Mifflin Co., 1912.

RILEY, STEPHEN T. *Dr. William Whiting and Shays' Rebellion.* Worcester: American Antiquarian Society, 1957.

Chapter Twelve

ALLEN, GARDNER W. *Massachusetts in the War of 1812.* (In Vol. III, "Commonwealth History of Massachusetts.") New York: States History Co., 1929.

WHITEHILL, WALTER MUIR (ed.). *New England Blockaded in 1814, the Journal of Henry Edward Napier, Lieutenant in HMS Nymphe.* Salem: Peabody Museum, 1939.

Chapter Thirteen

BROOKS, VAN WYCK, *The Flowering of New England, 1815–1865.* New York: E. P. Dutton & Co., 1936.

MUMFORD, LEWIS. *The Golden Day.* New York: Boni & Liveright, 1926.

PARRINGTON, VERNON L. *The Romantic Revolution in America.* New York: Harcourt, Brace & Co., 1927.

Chapter Fourteen

BIGELOW, E. VICTOR. *Narrative History of the Town of Cohasset.* Committee on Town History, 1898.

BRIGGS, L. VERNON. *History of Shipbuilding on North River-1640–1872.* Boston: Coburn Bros., 1889.

COLLIER, EDMUND POMEROY. "Cohasset's Deep Sea Captains," in *Cohasset Genealogies and Town History.* Committee on Town History, 1909.

CURTIS, JOHN GOULD. *Industry and Transportation.* (In Vol. IV, "Commonwealth History of Massachusetts.") New York: States History Co., 1930.

KITTREDGE, HENRY C. *Shipmasters of Cape Cod.* Boston: Houghton Mifflin Co., 1935.

LEONARD, ELISHA CLARKE. *Reminiscences of the Ancient Iron Works and Leonard Mansions of Taunton.* Taunton, Mass.: Collections of the Old Colony Historical Society, 1889.

LONG, E. WALDO (ed.). *The Story of Duxbury, 1637–1937.* Duxbury Tercentenary Committee, 1937.

MORISON, SAMUEL ELIOT. *The Clipper Ships.* (In Vol. IV, "Commonwealth History of Massachusetts.") New York: States History Co., 1930.

———. *The Maritime History of Massachuetts, 1783–1860.* Boston: Houghton Mifflin Co., 1921.

Chapter Fifteen

COPELAND, ALFRED M. *Our Country and its People, a History of Hampden County.* Boston, 1902.

CORBETT, SCOTT. *We Chose Cape Cod.* New York: Thomas Y. Crowell Co., 1953.

CRANE, ELLERY B. *History of Worcester County.* New York, 1924.

CRAWFORD, NITA M. "Salt Industry on the Cape," in *Pictorial Tales of Cape Cod.* Hyannis, 1956.

DWIGHT, TIMOTHY. *Travels in New England and New York* (4 vols.) New Haven: T. Dwight, 1821–22.

HARD, WALTER R. *The Connecticut.* (In Rivers of America Series.) New York: Rinehart & Co., 1947.

HOLLAND, JOSIAH GILBERT. *History of Western Massachusetts, the Counties of Hampden, Hampshire, Franklin and Berkshire* (2 vols.). Springfield: Samuel Bowles & Co., 1855.

LOCKWOOD, JOHN. *Western Massachusetts, a History, 1636–1925.* New York, 1926.

PIERSON, GEORGE WILSON. *Tocqueville in America.* New York: Doubleday & Co., 1959.

SMITH, CHARD POWERS. *The Housatonic, Puritan River.* (In Rivers of America Series.) New York: Rinehart & Co., 1947.

SYLVESTER, N. B., *et al. History of the Connecticut Valley in Massachusetts.* Philadelphia: L. H. Everts, 1829.

Chapter Sixteen

BRUCE, DAVID K. E. *Revolution to Reconstruction.* New York: Doubleday, Doran & Co., 1939.

FUESS, CLAUDE M. *Daniel Webster, Statesman (1782–1852)* (In Vol. IV, "Commonwealth History of Massachusetts.") New York: States History Co., 1930.

GARRISON, WILLIAM LLOYD. *The Liberator.* Boston: Old South Assoc. (reprint), no date.

SWIFT, LINDSAY. *William Lloyd Garrison.* Philadelphia: G. W. Jacobs, 1911.

VILLARD, OSWALD GARRISON. *The Antislavery Crisis in Massachusetts.* (In Vol. IV, "Commonwealth History of Massachusetts.") New York: States History Co., 1930.

Chapter Seventeen

CARR, CHARLES C. *Alcoa, An American Enterprise.* New York: Rinehart & Co., 1952.

COMAN, KATHERINE. *Industrial History of the United States.* New York: The Macmillan Co., 1921.

EMERSON, WILLIAM A. *History of the Town of Douglas, Massachusetts.* Boston: Frank W. Bird, 1879.

HAYES, STEPHEN P. Jr. "The Forests of Cape Cod," in *Pictorial Tales of Cape Cod.* Hyannis, 1956.

ROZMAN, D., and SHERBURNE, R. *Historical Trend in Massachusetts Industries 1837–1933.* Amherst, Mass.: Agricultural Experiment Station, Bulletin No. 340, 1938.

State Street Trust Co. *Some Industries of New England.* Boston: State Street Trust Co., 1923.

———. *Other Industries of New England.* Boston: State Street Trust Co., 1924.

STONE, ORRA L. *History of Massachusetts Industries.* Boston-Chicago: S. J. Clarke Publishing Co., 1930.

Chapter Eighteen

AMORY, CLEVELAND. *The Proper Bostonians.* New York: E. P. Dutton & Co., 1947.

BROOKS, VAN WYCK. *New England Indian Summer, 1865–1915.* New York: E. P. Dutton & Co., 1940.

CHAMBERLAIN, JOHN. *Farewell to Reform, Being a History of the Rise, Life and Decay of the Progressive Mind in America.* New York: Liveright, 1932.

DRAKE, SAMUEL A. *History of Middlesex County.* Boston, 1880.

HACKER, LOUIS M. and KENDRICK, BENJAMIN B. *The United States Since 1865.* New York: F. S. Crofts & Co., 1936.

HANDLIN, OSCAR. *Boston's Immigrants, 1790–1865, A Study in Acculturation.* Cambridge: Harvard University Press, 1959.

HANSEN, MARCUS LEE. *The Immigrant in American History.* Cambridge: Harvard University Press, 1940.

Hart, Albert Bushnell. *Charles William Eliot, Educator of the Community*. (In Vol. V, "Commonwealth History of Massachusetts.") New York: States History Co., 1930.

King, Moses. *King's Handbook of Boston*. Cambridge: Moses King, 1879.

Tyler, H. W. *Education and Science in Massachusetts*. (In Vol. V, "Commonwealth History of Massachusetts.") New York: States History Co., 1930.

Winship, Albert E. *Education (1820–1890)*. (In Vol. IV, "Commonwealth History of Massachusetts.") New York: States History Co., 1930.

Chapter Nineteen

Barck, Oscar Theodore Jr., and Blake, Nelson Manfred. *Since 1900, a History of the United States in Our Times*. New York: The Macmillan Co., 1947.

Parkes, Henry Bamford. *Recent America, A History of the United States Since 1900*. New York: Thomas Y. Crowell Co., 1941.

Pratt, Burtram J. *A Narrative History of the Town of Cohasset, Massachusetts* (Vol. II). Cohasset: Committee on Town History, 1956.

Chapter Twenty

Cunningham, William J., *Transportation in Massachusetts (1890–1930)*. (In Vol. V, "Commonwealth History of Massachusetts.") New York: States History Co., 1930.

Dame, Lawrence, *New England Comes Back*. New York: Random House, 1940.

Hammond, John W. L. *Twentieth Century Manufactures*. (In Vol. V, "Commonwealth History of Massachusetts.") New York: States History Co., 1930.

Mount Holyoke College, *Massachusetts in a Defense Economy*. South Hadley, Mass.: Studies in Economics and Sociology No. 3, 1941.

Hoyt, Homer, Assoc. *The Economic Base of the Brockton, Massachusetts, Area*. Brockton: Committee for Economic Development, 1949.

Chapter Twenty-one

Angell, Roger. "The Effete East," in *Holiday*, March, 1958.

Bowles, Chester. "New England Is More than a Museum," in *New York Times Magazine*, Mar. 19, 1950.

Editors of Fortune. *The Exploding Metropolis,* 1958. New York: Doubleday & Co.

ERICKSON, JOSEPH A. *Growth Trends in the New England Economy.* Boston: The New England Council, 1950.

Federal Reserve Bank of Boston. *The Present Position and Prospects of New England Manufacturers.* Boston: Research and Statistics Dept., Federal Reserve Bank of Boston, 1949.

————. *Employment and Earnings of Workers in Thirteen Areas in Massachusetts.* Boston: Dept. of Labor and Industries (Division of Statistics), 1950.

————. *Statistics of Manufactures in Massachusetts 1920–1938.* Boston: Dept. of Labor and Industries, Public Document No. 36, 1940.

————. *New England Economic Almanac,* 1957.

McCRACKEN, RICHARD A. "Travail of Suburbia," in *Magazine of Wall Street,* July 4, 1959.

MARTIN, HAROLD H. "Our Urban Revolution," in *Saturday Evening Post,* Jan. 2–9, 1960.

Massachusetts, Commonwealth of. *Employment and Earnings of Production Workers in Manufacturing in August 1950.* Boston: Dept. of Labor and Industries (Division of Statistics), 1950.

RUBENSTEIN, ALBERT H. *Problems of Financing and Managing New Research-based Enterprises in New England.* Federal Reserve Bank of Boston, 1958.

STRASMA, JOHN D. *State and Local Taxation of Industry, Some Comparisons.* Federal Reserve Bank of Boston, 1959.

WAKEMAN, SAMUEL. *Address,* May, 1959.

WEBSTER, DANIEL. *The Works of Daniel Webster.* Boston: Little, Brown & Co., 1853.

GENERAL

BEARD, CHARLES A., and MARY K. *A Basic History of the United States.* New York: Doubleday & Co., 1946.

DRAKE, SAMUEL ADAMS. *A Book of New England Legends and Folklore, in Prose and Poetry.* Boston: Little, Brown & Co., 1901.

GARRETT, EDMUND H. *Romance and Reality of the Puritan Coast.* Boston: Little, Brown & Co., 1897.

HOWE, HENRY F. *Salt Rivers of the Massachusetts Shore* (In Rivers of America Series). New York: Rinehart & Co., 1951.

TOURTELLOT, ARTHUR BERNON. *The Charles.* New York: Rinehart & Co., 1941.

WPA, Federal Writers' Project. *Massachusetts, a Guide to its Places and People*, Boston: Houghton Mifflin Co., 1937.

BIOGRAPHICAL

ADAMS, JAMES TRUSLOW. *The Adams Family*. Boston: Little, Brown & Co., 1930.

BOWEN, CATHERINE DRINKER. *John Adams and the American Revolution*. Boston: Little, Brown & Co., 1950.

CHINARD, GILBERT. *Honest John Adams*. Boston: Little, Brown & Co., 1933.

FUESS, CLAUDE M. *Daniel Webster*. Boston: Little, Brown & Co., 1930.

GREENSLET, FERRIS. *The Lowells and Their Seven Worlds*. Boston: Houghton Mifflin Co., 1946.

INDEX

ABOUT THE AUTHOR

Henry Forbush Howe is a physician whose hobby is writing New England history. Author of *Prologue to New England* and *Salt Rivers of the Massachusetts Shore*, he has served on the Council of the Massachusetts Historical Society. He lives and practices medicine in the house in Cohasset, Massachusetts, where he was born and where his father, also a physician-historian, practiced for fifty years before him. Dr. Howe has been Orator of the Massachusetts Medical Society, and is a member of the House of Delegates of the American Medical Association. Actively participating in community organizations—Rotary Club, summer theater and medical associations—he has an intimate knowledge of how Yankee towns function. He is familiar with seagoing from small boat cruising and from service as a transport surgeon in the Atlantic in World War II. As a part-time industrial physician he has a special interest in New England manufacturing. A graduate of Yale, his writing stems from the famous daily themes course of the late Professor John Berdan. He has edited a volume of Cohasset history and has published several monographs on Massachusetts history. *Massachusetts: There She Is—Behold Her* represents a culmination of twenty-five years of historical study.